About the author

With over 15 years of experience in the HIV/AIDS field – and working in London, Cambridgeshire, Norfolk – Patriic is an accomplished gay men's health worker and HIV trainer. He has also written health columns for several publications including *ff magazine and Oi! His humour, irreverence and common-sense approach to gay men's health is the hallmark of this work. In 1993, he co-founded Rubberstuffers, a condom pack distribution service for gay men living in London. Two years later, he wrote the Hand Book for Gay Men, which explains some of the technicalities of sex practice. In 1996, Patriic devised The House Party campaign, which provided health information through an interactive game with prizes. Launched by Sir Elton John, it is considered to be the first campaign in the UK to encourage gay men to look at health and lifestyle issues holistically. The following year, The House Party 2 collaborated with national HIV agencies, culminating in the campaign's launch in six major UK cities. Patriic lives in London, and is working on his next book.

About the illustrator

Crofty moved from Bologna, Italy, to the UK in 1999. Combining a formal education with work experience, she has studied interior decoration, illustration and cinematic visual effects. More recently she has been studying costume design and is currently enrolled at the London College of Fashion. She has developed her passion for illustrating over ten years, and has illustrated several children's books. Her extensive portfolio includes a storyboard for Bzzz, a vegetarian mosquito, as well as a gang of street cats inspired by London's youth scene culture and a day in the life of a hostess in a Soho peep show. Crofty is currently working on several projects, including stage set illustration and interior design.

Together

First published 2001 by Gay Times Books
an imprint of Millivres Prowler Group
116 - 134 Bayham Street, London NW1 OBA
Copyright © Patriic Gayle 2001
Illustrations Copyright © Crofty 2001
Primal Elements "Boy Boy" soap © Pacific Innovations 2001

A catalogue record for this book is available from the British Library.

ISBN 1-902852-22-2

together
Patriic Gayle

illustrations by Crofty

Together is dedicated to
Philip, Kenny, Will and Mark
James and Charles
Nettle

contents

acknowledgments

My gratitude to my peers and friends who have made comments, suggestions and reviewed text.

Kate Baker for your hugs and encouragement. Will Devlin for being so utterly right. Mark Platt for your support and for arguing with me. Kenny Hermansen for taking a different stance. Mike Taylor for your passion when I had none. Dr Christopher Whitely for your patience while I butchered and re-butchered text. Steve Worrall and Anthony Worth who were on hand to answer my quickie questions… yeah, right! Dr Mike Youle for your usual panache and expertise.

Gay Men's Health Project, Wiltshire; Lesbian and Gay Employment Rights (LAGER); Release; Money Advice; The Libra Project; The Hand Book for Gay Men and The House Party 1 and 2 (HIV Prevention Campaigns), Rainbow Icon Archive for permission to use and adapt text. Craig Nelson for an extract from his book Find True Love in a Man-Eat World. Pacific Innovations for their kind permission to use Primal Elements "Boy Boy" soap on the cover. The Oppenheim-John Downes Memorial Trust for their support.

Darren Brady, Ian Dancy, Simon Ellis, Phil Greasley, Matt Horler, Gary Jefferson, Glyn Mcintosh, Jackie Palmer, Rez, Ian Robinson, Sarah Schenker, Ronnie Seery, Jack Summerside, Grainne Whalley, and Karen Young. Neil Kittle and Lucy Ashby. Alex and Helen. Geoff (things can only get better). Gary (17/03/01, 1.54 - 2.58am). James – wishing you a full recovery in your own time. Rob for being so attentive. Mick and Debs and the kids for giving me a family to go home to and the lovely Nettle for patching me up when I got hurt.

Special thanks to Richard Collier, and to Nick Hilton, my publishing editor at Gay Times Books, for their creativity, encouragement and generous support.

starthere

Together is intended to be a comprehensive guide to life, love and lube for gay men.

Introductions to books are usually very dull, so you're not going to get one. Together is fun, informative and should help you get the best out of life and being gay. Getting the best out of this book is the same as getting the best out of life: you have to do it your way. You might read Together cover-to-cover in one go, but you're more likely to just dip into the chapters that interest you. You'll find a selection of useful contacts and further information at the end of each chapter and there is a local contacts and group listings at the end of the book.

comingout

The UK has a population of around 61 million. If you accept the one-in-ten rule, that means there are about three million gay men – including you and me – getting on with our lives. Now, that should give Baroness Young a few sleepless nights! What many of us have in common is that we've 'come out' and acknowledged our sexuality. In simple terms, being gay means that you are sexually attracted to members of your own sex and that you identify with other gay people or the larger gay community. Sexuality is a term used to describe a whole range of feelings, desires and actions relating to sex. We may have been attracted to guys for many years before making this connection or have only recently begun to question our sexuality as a result of a crush on a friend or a glance on the street that we can't get out of our mind. This doesn't mean that everyone who questions their sexuality in this way is actually gay; some men explore same-sex relationships (or the idea of them) and then decide that they are in fact straight.

Why am I gay?

Nobody knows for sure why some of us are gay and some of us are not. Lots of theories have been put forward ranging from genetic differences to overbearing parents. Evidence so far suggests that random genetic factors play a part in determining our sexuality in the same way they play a part in determining, for example, left-handedness.

One thing we do know is that no one chooses their sexuality. Some gay people knew they were different, if not gay, from as young as five or six. It is said that, for most of us, our sexuality is determined by the age of 12 or 13 and probably 16 at the latest. By and large, society tends to assume that everyone is, or wants to be, heterosexual. This is known as heterosexism. Some people continue to believe that it is a choice and that we can be persuaded into heterosexuality. By assuming heterosexuality, society gives rise to the dilemma, for those of us who know we are gay, of whether to hide our sexuality or to come out – with all that this involves.

There have been noticeable changes in the way British society views homosexuality, but there is a long way to go before it will accept us in the same way as it does people who are, say, left-handed. This has more to do with society's hang-ups around sex and sexuality than with individual gay people. More often than not, once people know someone who is gay, their prejudices and fears about homosexuality disappear altogether.

Growing up gay

For many young gay or bisexual people, adolescence can be a time of particular anxiety and fear. Many lesbians and gay men look back on this part of their lives with sadness and regret. There are very few positive gay role models and a lot of hostility towards openly gay people. Gay teenagers can become painfully aware that they are not like other people and many become withdrawn and lonely, convinced that only they are feeling this way. They learn to hide their true feelings or act as others want them to, for fear of being ostracised, ridiculed or rejected by loved ones and friends.

Above all, there can be a sense that we are somehow different, that we are abnormal and that we are going to disappoint people. Some people believe that if they get married their gay feelings will disappear. It is unusual for this to happen. Most store up a great deal of stress and anxiety for their later years. Coming out as a gay parent has particular challenges. Breaking out of a clearly defined role, or even attempting to shift the definition of it, involves tremendous courage and strength. The conflict between the relationship with a spouse and family and the need to be true to oneself can be enormous.

Coming out

There are several stages in the process of coming out. It's your life so take your time – do things for yourself and only when you are ready.

Coming out to yourself

Acknowledging that you are gay can take many years. Some of us probably hoped these feelings were 'just a phase'. In time, we realise that these feelings are not going to go away and we have to find a way of accepting them and dealing with the fact that we are sexually attracted to members of our own sex. This realisation is the first stage of coming out. There is no hard and fast rule when this point is reached. For some it happens in their teens, for others it may happen much later in life. Some people describe this time of accepting their sexuality as being like riding an emotional roller-coaster. One day they felt happy and confident and ready to tell everyone; the next they felt confused, scared and relieved that they hadn't. You may want to talk to someone who understands what this is like. It's a nerve racking time – the fear of rejection is likely to be immense. Bear in mind that there are many ways to tell someone that you are gay.

Coming out of the closet

The next stage involves going public in some way, of coming out of the closet. Who you tell next is really up to you. You may decide to tell your best friend or a member of your family. Remember, once you have told someone about your sexuality it can become known to others within a short period. This is human nature and there is very little you can do to prevent it. Be prepared to deal with any negativity that this disclosure may bring.

Why do I want to come out?

This is the most important question to ask yourself. If you answer something like 'Because I'm proud of who I am or 'It is impossible to become a fully happy human being if my sexuality remains suppressed' or 'I want to meet other gay people' then these are good reasons. If you're doing it principally to shock or hurt people, think again. Often the person who gets hurt will be you.

Who should I tell?

Many gay people describe how important it is to tell someone outside the family first. Make sure it's someone you trust and whom you believe to be open minded and supportive. Be careful if you decide to confide in a teacher at school – they may be obliged to tell someone else what you have told them. Find out the school policy on confidentiality before you go ahead. If you have decided to tell your family it may be easier to talk to one parent before the other. You could then ask them for help in approaching the other. Sometimes brothers and sisters are a good starting point as they are likely to understand more about homosexuality or bisexuality. Make sure you understand why you are going to tell them. One of the best reasons to come out to your family is to become closer to them. There are a number of typical responses that parents, particularly, are known to say:

- 'How can you be sure?'
- 'I went through a phase like this at your age.'
- 'You'll grow out of it.'
- 'You haven't tried hard enough with the opposite sex.'
- 'How can you know at your age?'

It's definitely worth thinking about how you respond to these questions before you tell anyone. You might find it helpful to discuss these questions first with a trusted friend or a lesbian and gay helpline or switchboard. There may also be a local gay youth group in your area.

Support for your family

This can be a traumatic time for some members of your family. You may feel unable to answer all their questions or to deal with all of the issues that come up for them. They, in turn, may not feel comfortable talking about homosexuality or bisexuality with you. Information for parents is available and there are several organisations that offer support to parents who are coming to terms with their sons' and daughters' sexuality. Details can be found at the end of this chapter. This can be a difficult time if your happiness is dependent to some degree on your family's reaction. If this is the case for you, we would advise that you talk it over with someone who has been through it already – perhaps a gay switchboard or helpline.

How should I tell them?

There is no rule that says you have to sit down and talk to others about this; there are other ways. You might like to write to people first and give them time to react in their own way. This is probably a better approach if, for example, you live a long way from your family or friends. Remember that you have probably taken a long time to get used to the idea yourself and others might need the same amount of time. Writing a letter allows you to take your time and to compose your thoughts carefully and clearly. It can also give the person you are writing to space to react and consider the news before discussing it with you. This could be a useful approach if you are expecting a very hostile or negative reaction. If you decide to talk face to face, remember not to rush it or to do it when one of you is in a hurry or distracted. It probably won't help to memorise a script either – you can guarantee that some people do not respond in a predictable manner. If you are worried about their reaction, tell them of your fears and that you don't want to hurt them but need to be honest with them. Remember to listen to what they have to say – it should be along the lines of a chat, not a speech or a performance, unless you've rehearsed!

When shall I tell them?

As with everything in life, timing is everything. Choose the moment carefully – do it when you (and they) have lots of time – not last thing at night when you are likely to be more tired and emotional. Think about the way you are feeling, allowing for nerves, which are perfectly natural under the circumstances. Don't do it if you are feeling angry or emotionally sensitive – this will affect what you say and how you say it. For obvious reasons don't do it when you are drunk (even if you think you need a drink to steady your nerves). And remember – only when you are good and ready. A friend once said that he knew he was ready to tell his family only when he realised that, if he had to, he could live without their support. Fortunately for him (and his family) this didn't happen.

Consequences

So you've told someone. You are either balancing on the edge of an erupting volcano or dancing with joy on the moon – or both! Some people describe a huge weight being lifted from their shoulders, of feeling euphoric and giggly and childlike again. Don't feel guilty about it – go on and enjoy yourself, you deserve it. The thrill of revealing something long kept hidden can give a tremendous sense of relief. Use this new found energy wisely and remember that close friends and family may be worried that you have changed out of all recognition. Reassure them that nothing has really changed, only their perception of you, in fact after a while they may even realise that the 'new' is better than the 'old' you. Most people will experience many positive reactions. For example, 'We're so pleased you could tell us' or 'Well we had already guessed and were just waiting for you to say something'. Some gay people have also met with the response, 'So am I'. Equally, if it hasn't gone too well – don't lose heart. Time is a great healer and things will get better. If you are experiencing rejection from close friends, ask yourself whether they were really so close if they couldn't support you through this important part of your life? If your family is reacting badly, this is inormal. They may be experiencing a whole range of emotions including shock, grief, guilt, blame, disappointment and lots of pain.

Remember how long it took for you to come to terms with being gay. Many parents will feel a loss in some way – perhaps of future grandchildren or weddings and other family gatherings. This can blur their happiness and their love for you. Here are a few examples of how parents and family can react negatively:

- 'My parents refused to talk about it. They dismissed it and said they didn't want the subject brought up again. I decided that I was going to continue to live my life as a gay man. I stopped going home as often as I used to and attending family occasions. It is only now, three years later, that they have begun to broach the subject with me.'
- 'My family say that they accept that I am gay but they don't want to see me being affectionate with another man. They say that they won't be able to cope with it.'
- I was at a wedding recently and everyone was there with their partners. I was upset that I couldn't bring mine. Everyone asked the usual embarrassing questions about girlfriends and I just had to smile and make excuses. I didn't want to row with my family about it but it's just not fair.'

At the end of the day, your parents are still your parents and, in time, few reject their children because they are gay. If they go quiet on you, give them time to react and think about what you have told them. If they ask lots of questions, it's a good sign. It may help to think of it as though it is in your interests to respond to them – they are likely to be the same ones that you have asked yourself many times along the way. If things are so bad that you feel like giving up with the whole process of coming out, it's important to talk to someone about your fears and concerns. It's probably better to persevere and keep going, after all, you have come this far and in many ways it would be difficult or impossible to go back now. The next person you talk to will probably give you a huge hug and say that they were relieved that you had found the courage to tell them and that they had suspected that something may have been on your mind for a long time. However – and perhaps it could only happen in the USA – one account of coming out was recalled like this: 'It wasn't easy telling my family that I'm gay. I made a carefully worded announcement at Thanksgiving... I said, "Mom would you please pass the gravy to a homosexual?" She passed it to my father. A terrible scene followed.'

Coming out at work

Some of us prefer not to discuss our personal lives at work – it's got nothing to do with why we're there and it's as straightforward as that. However, human nature being what it is, colleagues often guess or find out particularly if you don't talk about 'her' or get involved in the 'who shagged who on Saturday night' office gossip. For other guys, feeling able to be themselves and chat about what they did at the weekend – perhaps with a boyfriend – is an important part of who they are. While it may be possible to gauge the kind of response you'll get, the only way to find out for certain is to come out again – but, in this instance, to the people you work with. Furthermore, there are some circumstances where coming out can seriously affect your job security and promotion prospects. The bottom line is being careful and seeking advice first.

The armed forces

In January 2000, the Secretary of State for Defence formally announced the end of the policy banning gay personnel from serving in the Armed Forces. A new guide, Code of Social Conduct, was also announced. The code also covers relations amongst serving members of the armed forces, be they gay or straight. If you work for the Armed Forces and you wish to seek the latest information, or need to talk to someone about your sexuality, contact a confidential service. You are strongly advised to do this before declaring your sexuality to anyone:

- **Rank Outsiders** 0870 740 7755 / www.rank-outsiders.org.uk / BCM Box 8431, London WC1N 3XX
- **Stonewall** 020 7881 9440 / www.stonewall.org.uk / 46-48 Grosvenor Gardens, London SW1W 0EB

Your doctor

A good GP is hard to find, but is a vital part of maintaining your health. Unfortunately, the response by GPs varies enormously and while it shouldn't matter – indeed they should be willing to support you – there is a wealth of anecdotal evidence to the contrary. If you're looking for a GP, consider phoning up the prospective practice anonymously to ask whether its 'gay friendly' and gauge the response. This may seem absurd but disclosing your sexuality to your GP may mean that it is recorded on your medical notes. Medical records can be accessed by a range of organisations including life insurers, which can raise the whole question of HIV and testing. You'll probably get the 'all the doctors are professional' response but go with your gut feeling and don't be afraid to ask questions. You never know when you might need your GP, and having to handle all the homophobic crap during a home visit (when he meets your boyfriend) can make matters worse.

If you don't have one, register now! Simply phone NHS Direct on 0845 4647 who will be able to provide you details of GP practices in your area. Open 24hrs, NHS Direct is a confidential nurse led service providing health care advice and information. You can also reach it on www.nhs.co.uk. (For your sexual health, you are strongly advised to register with a sexual health/ clinic. The National AIDS Helpline on 0800 567123 can provide details of clinics in your area).

Meeting other gay men

There comes a time to stop talking and to get on with living your (new) life exactly how you want to. It's time to meet other gay and bisexual people and to explore your sexuality safely and confidently. A common reaction to this statement, especially in rural areas is 'Fine – but where do I start?' Remember that being gay is about expressing yourself in the way you want to. Despite the stereotypes, there is no single way of being gay. We are all as different as any other group of people. Going out with friends and meeting new ones at clubs or parties can be great. But the scene isn't for everybody and it's not everything there is to being gay. Most towns and cities have gay social groups and gay men's health projects. These can be excellent places to meet new people and to find out what there is to do locally and most will arrange to meet first-time visitors beforehand. As with any group of people, there will be some you get on with and some you won't. If you feel that you have little in common with the gay people you have met so far, you could try different ways of contacting more gay men, for example as pen pals, or through the many special-interest gay groups (like gay men's choirs or gay football supporters' networks).

Homophobia

Most lesbians and gay men understand what it is like to be discriminated against because of their sexuality. We grow up in a world where heterosexuality is the assumed norm and anything different is considered unnatural or perverted. Even when friends and families give us love and support, we are usually aware of others who don't or won't. Homophobia is the deliberate targeting of lesbians and gay men based on ignorance, prejudice and fear. Gay men experience this in many forms, including:

- Laws which forbid intimacy in public places.
- Lack of understanding of gay relationships.
- A virtual invisibility of positive role models and stereotyping on TV and in film.
- Negative reporting and abuse in the media.
- Sex education in schools based on reproduction.
- Laws preventing same-sex marriage.
- Discrimination or dismissal from work on the grounds of sexuality.

Homophobia is made worse by stereotypical images of what lesbians and gay men are, and often takes the form of verbal abuse, physical violence, or attacks in the media. Even today, homophobia is rife and creates an environment in which we can feel less valued and more vulnerable than our straight counterparts. Moreover, the law provides little protection and, in some cases, actively discriminates against us. For example, Section 28 of the Local Government Act 1988 states that no local authority shall 'promote the acceptability of homosexuality as a pretended family relationship'. While it has few teeth, its mere existence has fuelled discrimination and hampered effective HIV prevention. For some organisations (often funded to carry out work targeting gay men) Section 28 has legitimised homophobia and given them grounds to downgrade work or take it off health agendas all together.

Currently, law in the UK perpetuates the notion that lesbians and gay men are second-class citizens and legitimises situations where there is no easy redress for discrimination on the grounds of sexual orientation. As part of the Local Government Bill, the current government has tried to repeal Section 28 but was defeated in the House of Lords in July 2000. The government has now dropped the repeal of Section 28 so that other parts of the bill are passed.

Age of consent

In 1967, the Sexual Offences Act decriminalised sex between two consenting males – as long as those involved were aged 21 or over. This remained in place until the Criminal Justice and Public Order Act 1994, which lowered the age to 18, although for straight men and women it was 16. In May 1996 the European Court of Human Rights heard a case challenging the unequal age of consent and ruled that the unequal age of consent was unlawful. Between 1998 and 2000, the House of Commons and House of Lords played ping pong voting for and against an age of consent of 16. Finally, in November 2000, the Parliament Act was invoked and the Sexual Offences (Amendment) Bill was passed for Royal Assent, bringing the age of consent for gay men in line with everyone else – 16.

What's next?

While society is becoming more understanding of lesbians and gay men this is mainly confined to urban areas and larger cities. But don't think for one moment that the battle for equality is over or that the removal of homophobia is in sight. It's easy to feel safe, cocooned by a large city or ghetto. Fundamental changes to the law, in education and a concerted effort by government will be essential if we are to eliminate discrimination and achieve the equality so easily squandered by our heterosexual counterparts. If you can support any of organisations listed below – do so. Many of them have fought for gay rights for many years and are often neglected by the majority of gay men who seem to think that changes in the law just happen.

Gay symbols

Over the years, gay and lesbian communities around the world have used symbols to identify who we are. Often worn as badges and displayed as flags, some of the better known symbols include the rainbow flag, the pink triangle, the lambda and gender symbols. Probably the most recognisable symbol today is the rainbow flag, but other symbols have been an integral part of our history in the fight for recognition and equality. While the red ribbon is not a symbol of being gay, many gay men wear them, which is why it is interpreted by some as an indication that the wearer is gay; this is not necessarily so.

Rainbow flag

Use of the rainbow flag by the gay community began in 1978 when San Francisco artist Gilbert Baker designed the rainbow flag in response to the need for a symbol that could be used year after year. The flags had eight stripes, each colour representing a component of the community: hot pink for sex, red for life, orange for healing, yellow for sun, green for nature, turquoise for art, indigo for harmony and violet for spirit. Due to production difficulties (hot pink was not commercially available), pink and turquoise were removed from the design, and royal blue replaced indigo. This six-colour version spread from San Francisco to other cities, and soon became the widely known symbol of gay pride and diversity that it is today. If you're looking for a gay venue, a flag above the door is a welcome signpost.

Pink triangle

The history of the pink triangle begins before WWII, during Hitler's rise to power. Paragraph 175, a clause in German law, prohibited homosexual relationships. Convicted offenders were sent to prison, and then later to concentration camps. Their punishment was to be sterilized, and this was most often accomplished by castration. In 1942, punishment for homosexuality was extended to death. Concentration camp prisoners each wore a coloured inverted triangle to designate the reason for their incarceration. Criminals wore a green triangle, political prisoners a red triangle, Jewish prisoners two yellow triangles overlapping (to form a Star of David) and the pink triangle was for homosexuals. Stories of the camps reveal that homosexual prisoners were given the worst tasks and were the focus of attacks by the guards and other inmates. Although homosexuals were only one of the many groups targeted for extermination by the Nazi regime, it is, unfortunately, our group that history often excludes. Estimates of the number of gay men killed during the Nazi regime range from 50,000 to twice that figure. In the1970s, gay liberation groups resurrected the pink triangle as a symbol for the gay rights movement. Not only is the symbol easily recognized, but it also draws attention to oppression and persecution – then and now. In the 1980s, ACT-UP (AIDS Coalition To Unleash Power) began using the pink triangle for their cause. They inverted the symbol, making it point up, to signify an active fight-back rather than a passive resignation to fate. Today, for many, the pink triangle represents pride, solidarity, and a promise to never allow another Holocaust to happen again.

The lambda

The lambda symbol seems to be one of the most controversial of symbols, as regards its meaning. However, most sources agree on a few things: The lambda was first chosen as a gay symbol when it was adopted in 1970 by the New York Gay Activists Alliance. It became the symbol of their growing movement for gay liberation. In 1974, the lambda was adopted by the International Gay Rights Congress held in Edinburgh, Scotland. As their symbol for lesbian and gay rights, the lambda became internationally popular. However, no one seems to have a definitive answer as to why the lambda was originally chosen as a gay symbol. Some suggest that it is the Greek lower-case letter for 'liberation', others cite its use in physics to denote energy, eg: the energy we have when we work in concert. It's also thought to mean a 'wavelength', eg: gays and lesbians on a different wavelength. Lambda may also denote the synergy of the gay movement, the idea that the whole is greater than the sum of its parts. The lambda may also represent scales and balance, and the constant force that keeps opposing sides from overcoming each other. The ancient Greek Spartans regarded the lambda as meaning unity, while the Romans considered it "the light of knowledge shed into the darkness of ignorance". Reportedly, Ancient Greeks placed the lambda on the shields of Spartan warriors, who were often paired off with younger men in battle. (There was a theory that warriors would fight more fiercely knowing that their lovers were both watching and fighting alongside them).

Gender symbols

Gender symbols are common astrological signs handed down from ancient Roman times. Gay men have used double interlocking male symbols since the 1970s. Double interlocking female symbols have often been used to denote lesbianism, but some feminists have instead used the double female symbols to represent the sisterhood of women. In the 1970s, gay liberation movements used the male and female symbols superimposed to represent the common goals of lesbians and gay men.

The red ribbon

The red ribbon is a symbol of solidarity and of the commitment to the fight against HIV and AIDS. The Ribbon Project was conceived in 1991 by Visual AIDS, a New York-based charity group of art professionals that aims to recognize and honour friends and colleagues who have died or are dying of AIDS. The ribbon made its public debut at the 1991 Tony Awards, but since then – in some circles – has become a popular and politically correct fashion statement for celebrities at other awards ceremonies. Because of this popularity, some activists have rightly worried that the ribbon is simply paying lip service to AIDS causes. Nevertheless, it is a powerful symbol for all of us around the world, and a unifying symbol on World AIDS Day (1 December). Today, the red ribbon is an international symbol and, for many, stands for care, concern, hope and support.

Further contacts and information

- **London Lesbian and Gay Switchboard** which also has details of regional Switchboards
  020 7837 73 / www.gayswitchboard.org.uk
- **National Friend** UK network of helplines in local lesbian gay and bisexual communities
  0121 684 1261/ www.friend.dircon.co.uk /216 The Custard Factory, Gibb St., Birmingham B9 4AA
- **FFLAG** offers support to parents whose sons and daughters are gay, lesbian or bisexual
  01454 852418 / FFLAG, PO Box 153 Manchester M60 1LP / www.fflag.org.uk
- **Gay Men's Health Project, Wiltshire (GMHP)** which has an excellent website
  www.gmhp.demon.co.uk
- **Stonewall** Campaigning group for lesbian and gay equality
  020 7881 944 / www.stonewall.org.uk / 46-48 Grosvenor Gardens, London, SW1W 0EB
- **LAGER** Help with all legal and employment related issues for lesbians and gay men
  020 7704 6066 (11am-5pm Mon-Fri) / Unit 1G, Leroy House, 436 Essex Road, London N1 3QP
- **The Internet** Check out ww.bgiok.org.uk, www.gayyouthuk.co.uk, www.queercompany.co.uk, www.gay.com, www.gaydar.co.uk, www.rainbownetwork.co.uk
- **Student unions** often have contacts or groups.
- **The Samaritans** 0345 90 90 90

And finally, don't forget your local gay groups (gay socs if you're at college or university), gay switchboards and the regional gay press, all of which carry useful and interesting information.

gettingtogether

Barely 40 years ago one of the few places you could meet other gay men was in a public toilet. Not only was it frightening and dangerous, but police arrest and the subsequent court appearance would almost certainly cost you your job, family and home. Any friends you had would vanish, if only to protect themselves. Coming out to your family was unheard of, health advice and support for gay men were virtually non-existent and access to the small homosexual scene was only for those in the know.

If you're in your 70s you'll remember this all too well. If you're in your 60s you'll have witnessed the fight for recognition and the law that legalised sex between men. If you're in your 50s you'll have visited the new pubs and clubs. If you're in your 40s you'll have experienced the emergence of the AIDS epidemic. And, if you're in your 20s or 30s and screaming your tits off under the illusion that you invented gay life – get real! Ever since the 60s, when the SK (Gay Social) Group was formed, gay men and women looking for a little bit more than a backstreet bar or cottage, have set to and baked, knitted and organised their own communities, and today we enjoy their legacy. If you were around in the early 70s, you had little option but to make your own 'amusement' hence the existence of the Gay Liberation Front, the Campaign for Homosexual Equality or a local befriending group. Thirty years ago, they were playgrounds in the same way that Mardi Gras is today. We would do well to spare a thought for the small group of flamboyant people prepared to give us all a bad name by taking to the streets and laying the foundations of the major festivals and events which exist today. Gay men and lesbians also laid the foundations for the effective responses that our community had in spreading the message about AIDS when it came along. Gay men became – and often still are – the backbone of many AIDS organisations and self-help groups who took that ethos of self-help and went on to apply it to all people with HIV. Still in our thousands we volunteer or give money, or provide other support, to our communities and groups. Volunteers get involved for as many reasons as there are people, giving a few hours a week to a lifetime of commitment. And forget the woolly socks goody two shoes image, along the way we find lovers, get skills we never dreamed of and meet people we would never normally talk to in a million years. It's a great way to find out more about yourself and what you can do. One thing that's true is that not only do you get back what you put in, but you can end up with a whole lot more beside – community, friends, respect and a more rounded understanding of who we are, pride in the fact that you didn't wait for the plague wagon to carry your friends off, pride that you got accepted because of who you are not in spite of it, pride in the fact that when someone is in the same difficult spot as you once were, you can be there for them.

Cafés, bars, pubs and clubs

While the gay scene grew steadily from the early seventies, in the last decade that it has changed dramatically. The boarded-up windows and alleyway entrances of the 'twilight world of the homosexual' have evolved into a thriving industry of trendy bars, restaurants, cafés and shops filled with the latest fashion, lifestyle accessories and sexual accoutrements. A new generation of gyms and saunas have exploded on to the scene while myriad pubs and clubs continue to serve up a wide range of music, theme nights and sex venues. Pride, Mardi Gras, and other festivals and exhibitions have helped to revolutionise our image. Even the smallest town can usually boast a gay pub, and new venues spring up every year. Nevertheless, access to the 'playground' is often dependent on living near a town or city with a scene of some kind, and having sufficient cash and the confidence to go out and play. Many gay men still live in desperate isolation, survive on nominal wages and have yet to find the confidence and opportunity to travel the yellow brick road.

Cruising the bars

Pubs, clubs and bars are an obvious place to meet friends, and are still among the easiest places to find other gay men. While the growth of the gay scene provides an increasing range of alternatives in which to meet and socialise, bars are still very popular and are central to many local communities. The skills we use for cruising, meeting and chatting-up are pretty universal and can be adapted for use just about anywhere. Above all, be realistic about your expectations: if you go out thinking you're going to find 'him' you are likely to be disappointed. The air of desperation is easily recognised and drives many men away. Go with the flow, relax and enjoy yourself. You'll be a much better mood, you'll communicate better and if you don't pick up it'll be a case of 'so what... there's always tomorrow' rather than beating yourself up over 'failure'.

- As you walk in, it does no harm to say hello to the security person. You never know when you might need them.
- A lot of bar etiquette is macho stuff inherited from traditional pub culture where you can only 'be a man' if you look tough and drink a man's drin,k and it's against this you're sometimes measured. You should drink exactly what you want but bear in mind that certain combinations may make you suddenly less attractive to others. When was the last time you saw a skinhead with a pina colada, or a screaming queen holding a pint of Guinness?
- If you smoke, make sure your pack is to hand and you're not wrestling with a drink, lighter, and a pack of cigarettes. Better still, give up the smoking and you'll have better health and only have your drink to worry about!
- Find a place that gives you a decent view of what's going on, but, if it's busy, avoid the main thoroughfares to and from the bar, coat-check, toilets, dance floor and loudspeakers.
- A busy venue is not necessarily a great place to cruise. If the venue's packed with punters moving around like herds of cattle it can be difficult both to see and be seen.
- Guys are likely to look at you so, even if you're shy, try to acknowledge them with a friendly look or smile rather than looking as if you've lost a contact lens at the bottom of your glass.
- Difficult though this might be to believe, you can't cruise everyone so identify a few guys and concentrate on them.
- By all means move around, but not so much as to appear desperate or nervous. Someone could be looking for you, and staying in a couple of regular spots improves his chances.

Sex venues

- If you're going to a sex venue, check out the busier night, as some midweek events can be poorly attended. Also check the dress codes; some venues will refuse entry if you're wearing the wrong gear.
- Depending on what you choose to wear (and whether you're travelling in public) consider taking your gear with you and changing at the venue.
- Don't forget to take, condoms, lube, chewing gum and a pack of tissues as required.
- If you've not been there before, it's well worth checking out where everything is before you get down to business.
- If you're going with a friend agree a check-in time and place to meet.
- If you've had some great sex, think about leaving rather than being greedy, as than can often lead to disappointment.

- While there is tendency to have sex and move on to the next, don't be afraid to talk to a guy if you think they're maybe something more going on.

Cruising the streets

Meeting guys on the street happens all the time, but while the theory is simple, the practice requires a little more balls and timing. So, if you see a guy you like, here are a few handy tips.

- First things first, check your 'gaydar' (that exclusive sixth sense only known to gay men). Looks can be deceptive, and many straight men dress gay for fashion.
- Depending on the distance between you, you may need to change your angle of approach to ensure you pass by. Be casual, and if you're unfamiliar with the art of subtlety it's possibly best not to try. As you near each other look straight into his eyes in friendly non-threatening manner. If he does the same – and any longer than is usual between strangers – continue to look at him as you pass him.
- Now this is the hard part. At what point do you look over your shoulder to see if he's doing the same? When you're doing it he might only be thinking about it or he could be doing it while you're making up you're mind! Hopefully, five or ten paces on you'll both do it at the same time. If not, you'll never know what you missed, quite literally.
- If he's doing the same, you'll both pretend not to cruise when in fact you both know what you're both doing. Your heart pounds as you work out who's going to make the next move. A friendly smile, a casual remark or a straight forward 'Hi!' can break the ice but it does help if one of you has the courage to speak. His body language, his voice and facial expression should all tell you whether he's interested or not.
- If, after talking to him, you change your mind, you should make a clean polite getaway. 'Nice to meet you' or 'see you around' and a friendly smile will usually do it, but say it as you're leaving so as to make it clear that the encounter is over.

Chatting up

The key to chatting up a guy is patience but, since we're usually thinking with our dicks and driven by an uncontrollable urge to shift our load by morning, we can move very fast. Unfortunately, this can be at the expense of some common sense stuff that can help a first meeting get off to a flying start. On some of the larger scenes we can also compromise our chances: if one guy doesn't fit the bill within a nanosecond, we move on to the next. This sort of behaviour can become habitual and you'll miss out on some great men. It can often be attributed to the 'me, me, me scene queen' who tends to lose out in the end through his impatience and selfishness. Unless you're carving notches on the bed post, it's the quality not the quantity that counts. How we connect with other men varies enormously but if you like someone let him know. If you don't he'll never know what he's missing. The looks… the glances… the 'ballet' to find better vantage points (from which to see or be seen) or to engineer a close encounter are all part of the ritual to reduce the possibility of rejection. We often aim to find a balance between showing interest, casually ignoring him and making our intentions clear. Eventually though, you should do something about it, if only to spare yourself the nagging doubt as you go home alone. Many of us have developed our own individual styles of chatting to and picking up men and so the following suggestions may seem contrived. But, if you go through the following points, you'll probably pick at least one thing you could do better (apart from him).

- Everyone has an opening line and it's not as if we haven't heard them all before – particularly the crap ones. Even if it's terrible, you've plucked up to courage to say 'Hi!' and that's more than he's done if he's just standing there waiting for you to make the first move. However, just for the record, here are a few chat-up lines that didn't quite work out as intended:

  'Is that a gun in your pocket or are you pleased to see me?' 'It's a gun.'
  'What would it take to get a kiss from you?' 'Chloroform.'
  'My friends have told me about you…' 'What friends?'
  'What's your idea of a perfect date?' 'The one I was having before you came over.'
  'Got a light?' 'Yes.'

- In the first instance, conversation should be easy-going and relaxed and any questions should be relatively straightforward. If you start with something clever or devastatingly witty you may catch him off guard or put him on the spot. He may then feel he needs to match you and if he's shy or out of practice then you've immediately put him at a disadvantage. On the other hand, some guys do it to sort out the men from the boys, so if it works for you do it – but you know the risks.

- Your voice should be friendly confident and relaxed – not pushy, smarmy or over-eager.

- Find out his name, **remember it**, use it every now and then and **don't forget it**.

- Keep the eye contact going.

- Get him to talk about himself but don't turn it into an interrogation or forget that you're part of this too.

- If you don't want to talk to him be polite, firm and honest.

- Consider your body language and observe his. Unless he's been explicit about what he wants, don't get too close in the first instance. Believe it or not we all need some time to get accustomed to being in each other's space. Instinct and practice will let you know when it's time to get closer, particularly if his hand wanders on to your arse or crotch. Mirroring each other's body language can also help relax you both. For example, taking a drink when he drinks, lighting up when he has a cigarette, and re-positioning yourself when he does generates a comfortable rhythm between you. Mind you, it needs to be casual – not a comedy routine.

You're the weakest link, goodbye!

Indications that you're not onto a winner usually include minimal eye contact and/or his eyes scanning men other than you, one word replies, the tone of his voice, an unwillingness to initiate or respond to conversation. If he turns you down, don't neccessarily think that it's you; it could be for a number of reasons:

- He's already got plans.
- He's drunk.
- He's got a boyfriend.
- He's just broken up.
- He's just had sex.
- He's nervous or shy.
- He's not in the mood.
- He's off on his drugs.
- He's not good enough for you.
- He's got an STI.
- Maybe you just don't turn him on.

Types

Anyone who says they don't have a type of some description, is lying. There's always something that pushes our buttons. If he likes hair and you don't have any, or if you go to the gym and he likes skinny guys, or if you're shorter than him and he likes taller guys – then it's just not going to work out. It's not your fault and it's not his fault, it's a fact of life and there's nothing you can do about it. Of course we're going to take it personally – we're human and no one likes to be told 'no', 'won't', 'can't' or 'fuck off'. This said, skulking around like a wounded animal isn't attractive to anyone. Nevertheless, some of us set ourselves up for failure, perhaps with an overbearing manner (and frightening the 'prey' witless), coming on too strong, or badgering some poor sod who has made it very clear that he's not interested. You need to look at what you're doing and this chapter should give you some clues as to what you maybe are doing wrong and suggest where you could improve. The more we cruise the more experienced we become... and the more likely we are to be successful. It can sometimes help just to talk to people and while you may go home alone you will not have not been alone for the evening. If you have been knocked back, there is always tomorrow.

How to make 'No!' nice

If you're not interested in a guy who's obviously got you in his sights it goes a long way to be polite when saying 'No'. OK, you may want tell the guy to stop bothering you or fuck off but imagine if the shoe was on the other foot, how would you feel? You should always aim to make a polite getaway. Speak firmly to make it clear that the conversation is over but – if you can – smile genuinely. This way no one is made to feel uncomfortable or embarrassed. We've all been there so don't do it to others. If he won't go away and you've shown him every reasonable courtesy, then tell him to fuck off!

Contact / personal advertisements

Whether you're looking for friendship, a relationship or sex, contact or personal advertisements can deliver just about anything that appears in print. You'll find them in a wide range of magazines and papers although the gay press includes more explicit ads. It can be an exciting way to meet men and, in some cases, dispense with the niceties of cruising. For some, it provides opportunities to meet men who prefer not to use the scene or who don't have easy access to pubs and clubs. Answering ads is relatively simple and most papers and magazines operate a similar process:

- Find an ad you like and reply in writing. Advertisers often want a photograph and preferably not from a photo-booth at 9am on a Monday morning when you're hungover.
- Put the letter in an envelope with its box/reference number clearly marked on the outside.
- Post it to the advertiser care of the publication including a first class stamp (for each reply).
- Wait and hope.

If you're placing an ad, check out the costs and the terms and conditions first. Advertisements are usually charged by the word which is why they're short and why a dictionary of abbreviations has evolved:

ALA – All letters answered.	NSm – Non smoker.
ALAWP – All letters answered with photo.	NTW – No time wasters.
BND – Boy next door.	SA – Straight acting.
CS – Clean shaven.	SL – Straight looking.
CT/A – Can travel/accommodate.	VGL – Very good looking.
GL – Good looking.	VWE – Very well endowed.
GSOH – Good sense of humour.	WLTM – Would like to meet.
NSc – Non scene.	

Sexual practices are usually abbreviated similarly: corporal punishment – CP, sadomasochism – SM etc. or defined by hanky codes. If a guy is explicit about what he's looking for sexually then it's reasonable to assume he's being honest. Some ads are prone to gross exaggeration and dick size can often stray into fantasy world. By all means have the fantasy but you may be disappointed. When it comes to writing your own ad, phrases like 'genuine', 'seeks similar' and 'for good times, maybe more' are fine but just scan through the ads and they appear with unerring regularity. While phrases like 'would like to meet a guy who's DNA hasn't fallen off the back of a lorry' and 'you've tried the best… now I'm the rest' may not be your cup of tea – your eye does at least stop on the page. Think about what you're going to say and try to be original.

Phone sex

Both newspapers and some telephone chat lines offer voice-mail alongside other contact services. First things first, check out the charges! Costs, terms and conditions of use are often hidden in millimetre high text and explicit language is often a no-no. Usually, you record a short description of what you're into or want in around 30 seconds. Remember that callers are going to hear your voice, so make a note of what you want to say in advance, try not to sound monosyllabic and avoid using the word 'Umm…' For newspaper or magazine ads, they will then make up an edited version of your recording which is printed. After reading it, interested guys phone a central number where you punch in the appropriate reference to hear your recorded ad in full. Some systems have a text-messaging feature that alerts you that someone has answered your ad. You then follow the menu on your handset to retrieve the message. With the telephone services it's even easier – you can either leave your number in the advert or, if you want to be mysterious, you can choose to have a box and pin number to retrieve any messages left for you at a later point.

Gay Press

Ways to meet gay men extend far beyond the pub, club and street scene and the gay press is a good place to start. Many publications provide news, views and information together with listings and contact details of social, sports, special interest groups, voluntary, self-help support groups and organisations, and details of regional events, festivals and campaigns. Published weekly or monthly, most of the publications are free, although some carry a small charge.

+ve Monthly Magazine for people living with HIV **01895 637878**

Attitude Monthly glossy fashion/lifestyle magazine **020 7308 5090**

Boyz Weekly newspaper magazine **020 7296 6000**

DNA Magazine Monthly-ish irreverent and funny magazine **020 7682 0832**

Gay Times Monthly long running lifestyle and news magazine **020 7482 2576**

Gay to Z UK Listing of gay/gay friendly businesses **020 7793 7450**

North of Watford (NOW) Monthly glossy magazine for life out outside London **08701 255 577**

Pink Paper Monthly news magazine **020 7296 6110**

Positive Nation Monthly HIV/AIDS magazine and related issues **020 7564 2121**

QX Magazine Weekly London scene guide **020 7379 7887**

Scotsgay Monthly magazine for the Scottish gay scene **0131 539 0666**

The internet

The internet provides numerous opportunities to meet other gay men and find out just about anything gay. You can visit websites, chat rooms and access directories and bulletin boards packed with information. You can send and receive pictures, set up meetings and wank each other off on line – albeit through cameras. The Internet is particularly of use to guys who have a special interest, or who live in rural or more isolated areas, or who are just shy. That's not to say that everyone has access to a computer but increasingly – through internet cafés, libraries and other public access sites – we are communicating in ways unheard of a few years a go.

Top tips

- When on line (eg: using chat rooms) you may wish to adopt a false name.
- Think carefully before giving out your credit/debit card details over the internet. A key symbol usually shows up in the bottom of the screen to say that the site is secure.
- Think carefully before signing up to sites, paying subscription/membership fees – they can mount up.
- Be careful as to what picture files you download – some may be illegal.
- Think carefully before giving out your email/home address and telephone number.
- Be sure that you can trust the person sending you files or pictures as it is an easy way to pick-up a computer virus. Better still, install an up-to-date virus protection programme.
- If you're using someone else's computer you may wish to delete any 'incriminating' evidence, including emptying the re-cycle bin and history file.
- What guys say they are on the internet is not necessarily what they are in reality!
- Pictures of yourself are often required when chatting with guys.

Personal safety

When you are out and about, it's easy to forget personal safety and that assaults on gay men still happen. If you're on the street or on your local cruising ground, remember:

Out and about

- Keep your wits about you. Try to avoid being on your own in an unfamiliar area, especially if you are drunk or have taken recreational drugs. Be vigilant when leaving gay venues.
- Always walk with a purpose, head up, and as if you know where you're going. Be alert. Know who or what is behind you at all times. If you think you're being followed, cross the road to check. If possible keep to well lit and peopled streets.
- If you feel threatened, try to attract attention or go into a shop, a pub, even knock on a door using the premise that you're looking for someone who you thought lived at the address.
- If you think there is going to be trouble – get out. Think about how you might defend yourself if you had to – screaming, shouting, and/or running. (If available, self-defence courses are excellent for teaching you disabling tactics.)
- If you can, carry a whistle or attack alarm and use it. Scream for help, bang on doors or flag down passing cars. But try not to look totally mad or they're likely to ignore you.
- If you see someone being attacked, trying to help without putting yourself in danger. If you can't help yourself – get help.
- Always use a registered taxi firm that you can trust. Be wary of unregistered cabs and taxi touts. Agree the fare before you get in. Also be cautious about travelling in a taxi alone. Consider sharing.
- In an emergency always call 999.
- If you feel threatened on public transport, stand near the exit, change carriage or seek the company of others.

Cruising grounds

- Cruising grounds can be dangerous places: know your exits. Tell a friend where you are going. If you know someone else there, make contact, you can look out for each other.
- Personal stereos make you less aware of danger or attack.
- Try not to carry valuables.
- If you've met some one for the first time you may be tempted to take them home or go home with

them. Beware of the risks. Get their phone number and suggest meeting another night.

- Sexy though they may appear to be – stay clear of groups of straight men, particularly if they're loud or drunk.
- Be wary of accepting lifts from strangers. If you are with a group of friends but do not know the driver, you should be cautious about being the last person to be dropped off. Hitchhiking can be dangerous. Try not to hitch alone although this may make getting lifts more difficult.

Reporting violence

- If you've been attacked or assaulted, call the Police and ask for the Gay and Lesbian Liaison or Community Officer. If you draw a blank, don't hesitate to phone GALOP which has a 'Shout Line' on (020) 7704 2040 offering assistance to lesbians, gay and bisexual men who have experienced violence, abuse or harassment (and this includes by other gay men).
- Call a trusted and reliable friend for support.

Meeting guys: a safety check

When meeting a guy for the first time:

- Tell a friend what you're doing and where you're going.
- Arrange to meet in a public place.
- Consider asking a friend to phone you on your mobile after 20 minutes (just in case you need to make an escape).
- If you have any serious doubts: make an excuse and leave.
- Don't give out your address until you're sure you want to continue seeing him.

Further information and contacts

- **Black Lesbian and Gay Centre** Advice, information, health, social and cultural events
  020 7620 3885 / 5 Westminster Bridge Road, London, SE1 7AX
- **Brothers and Sisters Club for Lesbian and Gay People who are Deaf**
  109 Kessock Close, Ferry Lane Estate, London, N17 9PW
- **Deaf and Hearing Lesbian Group (DAHLING)** 54-56 Phoenix Road, London, NW1
- **Deaf Lesbian and Gay Groups DLAGGS** minicom / evenings only 020 8660 2208
- **Gay and Disabled Computer Bulletin Board** 01638 743 655
- **Gay Times** Gay Times is the only talking newspaper in the UK 01273 729663
- **Jewish Gay and Lesbian Group** 020 8905 3531 / email 106257.3510@compuserve.com
- **London Bisexual Group** 020 7569 7500 Tue-Wed, 7.30pm-9.30pm
- **Long Yang Club** Social club for gay Orientals and Western friends
  SAE to BCM/Wisdom, London, WC1N 3XX
- **Regard** Group for disabled lesbian and gay men 020 7738 8097 / BM Regard, London WC1 3XX
- **Visually Impaired Gay Group (VIGOUR)** 01705 524739
- **London Lesbian and Gay Switchboard** with details of Regional Switchboards
  020 7837 7324 / www.gayswitchboard.org.uk
- **Friend Counselling, helplines and support groups for lesbians and gay men**
  BM National Friend, London, WC1N 3XX.
- **PACE** Counselling, advice, advocacy and workshops
  020 7700 1323 / 34 Hartham Road, London N7 9JL
- **Survivors** Advice, information and support for men who have been sexually assaulted
  020 7833 3737 (7-10pm / Mon-Tue) / P.O.Box 2470, London SW9 9ZT

mates

Friends

For most of us, a day won't go by without calling or seeing a friend whether it's to catch up on the latest gossip, make plans or do something together. When our world seems to fall apart or we just need cheering up we often turn to our friends. While friendships can sometimes take a back seat when a man walks into our life, they're there to help you pick up the pieces after the little sod has moved on (despite the fact you deserted them while you were holed up in your flat fucking Mr Right across the kitchen floor). Friends often become the 'family' that not only protects us against loneliness and isolation, but also provides a space where we are loved, supported and valued. Many friendships endure against all odds – many gay men's experience of HIV and AIDS bears testimony to that. Consequently, friends should be chosen with care, protected, and should never be taken for granted. Underlying the magic which brings friends together is time, mutual give and take and respect if friendships are to remain happy and healthy.

Do...

- Make time and keep in regular contact.
- Do different stuff together.
- Be honest.
- Be constructive in your criticism.
- Admit to your mistakes and be willing to apologise when you fuck up.
- Remember birthdays and learn first and second names and addresses.
- Listen before opening your mouth.
- Accept weaknesses and praise strengths.
- Support him when he's down.
- Be polite to his boyfriend and friends.

Don't...

- Always wait for him to phone first.
- Put off or cancel arrangements.
- Lie or steal from him.
- Sleep with his boyfriend or recent ex or family.
- Throw a queeny fit if he criticizes you.
- Pretend to listen when you're really cruising.
- Be malicious or intentionally put him down in front of people.
- Leave him if he's on drugs.
- Borrow money unless you intend to pay it back.
- Be rude about his boyfriend and friends even if you think they're wankers.

Casual sex and one night stands

Not everyone feels the need for a relationship. There are times in our lives when we're ready to settle down, other times when we prefer to play the field or be alone. Gay men may not have invented the one-night stand, but we have certainly turned it into an art form and, for many of us, it's how many friendships or relationships start. The unique sexual experience which comes with each new encounter also gives us an opportunity to develop our techniques and experiment with new practices. Casual sex is not restricted to bedrooms or clubs. It any happen just about anywhere and sometimes when you're not expecting it. It can also involve more than person. Casual sex should be about taking your sex drive out for a spin and having fun – without feeling guilty or feeling as if you're settling for second best. It's important to see casual sex for what it is. It should not be a substitute for that ever elusive relationship, although it's understandable that finding a boyfriend can mean having sex with several – perhaps many – men.

While multiple partners can mean more experience, more confidence and more sexual satisfaction – it can also mean the reverse. Occasionally, a string of disappointing one-night stands can lead to a decrease in confidence and, over weeks or months, it can feel as if you're never going to find anyone again. All of us experience this and it's perfectly natural to have peaks and troughs. However, if you start to feel lonely or desperate or if you find yourself pining at two o'clock in the morning, its time to take a fresh look at your plan to get a man. Casual sex can be a response to a fear of closeness or loss, anxiety about rejection, or some other difficulty. It may help just to talk about it with your friends, but if that's not possible (or may be uncomfortable) this chapter has a few suggestions that may be of help.

Etiquette

Over the years, unspoken rules of etiquette have evolved to help make sure we get the best of the encounter – even if there's no plan or arrangement to see each other again.

- Guys may have different interests to you, and if you're into one thing sexually, make this clear beforehand. Deciding ahead of time what you are going to do sexually can seem tacky (or be a turn-on) but it's nothing compared to the disappointment you may both feel when you discover you're not sexually compatible.
- If you're taking a guy back there's usually an assumption on his part that it's okay to stay the night. If he can't stay the night – tell him in advance. If you're going back but can't stay, sort this out before you get into the taxi. Also, make sure that you can get home. Always have cab money, and refuse invitations to the middle of nowhere.
- If you later discover that you don't click or the sex doesn't seem to be working out, or if you start to feel uncomfortable, make your excuses and leave. At this point you may regret having told him that you can stay over, but there's no point in being over-polite if it's quite clear that you'd rather be some where else. Sometimes casual encounters work – sometimes they don't. Conversely, if you ask some body to leave, it's not essential but it's certainly a considerate gesture to make a contribution towards his fare home.
- Once you've got down to business, don't roll over and fall asleep until you have both had an opportunity to cum unless one of you has said that he's not going to.
- When you've done your stuff, it's usual to go your separate ways. Do not feel obliged to exchange phone numbers. You've (hopefully) both got what you want and the 'contract' is finished. But does that stop us? No. More often than not we play that fucking ridiculous telephone numbers game!

Telephone numbers

If you don't want to see him again, don't hang around. Get dressed, say something casual like 'see you around' and leave before the ritual of exchanging phone numbers can start. The tone of your voice can be friendly but be just that. You should only offer him your number because you want to see him again and *not* because you're trying to be polite and/or let him down gently. If he offers you his number and you're not going to use it – be polite, but decline. Remember: it's a casual encounter… you're not married… there are no obligations. If you want to see someone again and you have a partner – be honest and tell him the score.

The bottom line is that many numbers are scrawled down in haste and never used again. It's just what we do to tie up the end of an intimate sexual encounter with the harsh reality that you've both done the business and are now getting on with your lives. Learning and understanding this stuff can be both slow and painful particularly when you think you've met some really special who then never calls. The pit opens up and you start wondering if you should… If you shagged on Saturday and it's now Monday, do you call on Tuesday, Wednesday or Thursday? How long do you give him, two, three or four days? You feel wretched and vow never to feel like this again. Maybe he didn't call you because he's gone home to the boyfriend he didn't tell you about, he's met someone else, he's afraid of getting too close or he 's just an arsehole. Maybe he likes you but not enough.

Fuck buddies

Fuck buddies are guys with whom we have sex on a regular basis without the complexities of a relationship. You might have met through the scene, the internet or a personal ad but the pleasure you get is a sexual quid pro quo *and* an explicit understanding that you can stop seeing each other without anyone getting hurt. Fuck buddies only work if you are both clear and honest about this arrangement. You can phone each other up, meet when it's convenient but know intuitively that you will not become boyfriends. You can experiment, swap roles, practice technique or just fuck your brains out because you both just love it – not each other. If this presents a problem, then it's possible you're actually looking for a boyfriend. Sometimes it happens, but if you develop feelings – let him know. He may not be interested, or he may be thinking the same, but the arrangement has changed and you owe it to each other to be honest.

Relationships

Relationships are as individual as you and your partner and it's up to you to find type of relationship that meets both your needs. There is often a magic which is undecipherable but which intuitively draws two guys together. It's the heady stuff which makes us feel so alive when we fall in love and can also help to keep the relationship fresh and alive years later. Underpinning the emotional stuff are practical things we can do to give the relationship the best climate in which to grow. All relationships are risky, there is no guarantee they will work but this should never stop you trying.

I say potato, you say potarto...

You should have interests that are similar or complement each other, and accept that there will be differences between you. Trying to change someone into what you would like them to be will drive you apart, so acceptance of who he is is a pre-requisite. Fortunately, differences are often part of the attraction and so trying to smooth off the rough edges can dull the magic which brought you together. For example: gym bunnies and couch potatoes, opera queens and disco divas, vegans and carnivores are not necessarily going to work out but – stranger things have been known to happen. Sex is often an important (but not obligatory) factor in a healthy relationship but, all too often, it is the instrument against which we measure compatibility. It's been said that sex is 90% of a bad relationship and 10% of a good relationship. Think carefully before dismissing out of hand a man who has everything except a truncheon knob; equally, beware of starting a relationship with someone's dick (it might be all he is).

Honesty

You only have to read problem pages (gay or straight) to see that many relationship problems hinge on an inability to communicate honestly. Misunderstanding, conflict and mistrust are the staple diet of many a soap opera and invariably stem from partners not being open about their feelings. A relationship where partners are honest with each other makes it much easier to face up to problems and find solutions and, as an added bonus, you will learn to understand each other better. This can sometimes be difficult where someone close to you is concerned – but it will be a testament to your abilities that he won't feel threatened, betrayed or hurt. Love and respect between two people cannot exist if niggles, gripes, tensions, frustration and resentment are allowed to fester. In short, if you can't be honest: you're screwed.

Support and sharing

When a guy gives a damn about you, life's little arsewipes become that bit easier to manage. Equally, when you succeed in life, having your man there to share it with you is a big part of why guys get together in the first place. If you've been there already you'll understand, if not: it comes highly recommended. Successful relationships are based on mutual support and sharing. He's there for you and you're there for him. You're sick and he cares, he's sick and you care. He's sad and you hold him. You cry and he *doesn't* go clubbing. Bless. However, If you make all the effort in the relationship, he may soak it up like a sponge and in a short space of time you'll be drained, angry and resentful or vice-versa. He'll wonder what the fuss is about while you're making his thousandth cup of tea… he'll tell you not to be so stupid… and he'll say he loves you… Tears and big dramas will follow.

Flexible friends

Like everything in life, relationships change. Be grateful: it would be a sorry world if Westlife were still in the charts ten years from now or flared jeans were permanently fashionable. The first year or so of a relationship is usually very special: you still want him all the time, you're fucking like rabbits, and you're both very happy. Over time this changes and usually not for the worse. You will still want him but it's okay that he's not attached to your hip, the sheets are changed less often but the sex has got better through trust, experimentation and familiarity, and the happiness has found a home inside you. As the relationship grows you will need to be willing to accept change, be flexible in your approach and in some cases, take the initiative before you get stuck in a rut. As you and he grow as individuals it's likely that expectations and priorities will also change. Your lives together may become predictable, safe and dull and – while this may be okay for some – there is ample room for resentment, disappointment and missed opportunities.

Being your own man

Being in a relationship should not mean that you give up who you are. You are both individuals with your own personality, friends, and interests – some of the very attributes that attracted him to you in the first place. The differences between you should be appreciated and save you from becoming two archetypal clones with matching clothes and whiny lovey-dovey voices. Get the picture? We all need that 20th century cliché 'space' where we can be by ourselves and enjoy some privacy. It's perfectly natural and gives us an opportunity to chill out and relax. Relationships can be fantastic but are also hard work. Time alone is essential to re-charge the batteries. It may mean a night apart or an evening set aside to see respective friends. Whatever you decide remember that you'll be doing this because you care for each other not because you don't.

If you can't leave your partner alone, it's a sign that you are feeling insecure and/or jealous. You may have good reason but that's no reason to behave like this. It's a real killer and a sure fire way to drive him away. You need to look at why you're doing this and take it from there. If, on the other hand, you feel trapped, suffocated or resentful then you also need to examine the root cause. You need to sit down and talk things through before you get angry and upset. If not, you'll get on each other's nerves: one will feel that the other doesn't love him while the other one runs away from his 'clingy' boyfriend.

Couch relationship?

Relationships run the risk of becoming too comfortable, easy and predictable. You start to take each other for granted, make assumptions and become lazy. All relationships need a work-out occasionally. It doesn't have to be anything major but it does need to blow away the cobwebs away and get your hearts beating again. Surprise him with a weekend break or a holiday (then both panic when you can't find the passport). Tell him how you've longed to be strapped to the showerhead. If you're used to cinemas – go to a theatre. If you go to theatre – go to a gallery. If you always go to one club – choose another. Do stuff on the spur of the moment. If you're used to lying in bed on a Sunday, why not visit a market or jump on a train and while you're there – suck him off.

Open relationships

When we start a relationship it is often with an expectation that we will only have sex with each other. One-to-one or monogamous relationships can provide security and be particularly helpful in getting to know each other without distractions. This works well for some, but for others living up to this ideal can be difficult as time goes by. As the immediate intensity, horniness and passion of a new relationship settles, we may feel the need for something different. While it's natural for sexual needs, desires and fantasies to change over time, a partner may not be necessarily able (or willing) to adapt to meet them. Additionally, scene culture endorses and promotes sex with multiple partners, and,for some of us it can be a difficult to break the habit even if we've met the man of our dreams.

It can be hard to stop ourselves from making comparisons, believing – often mistakenly – that the grass is greener on the other side of the bar. If you care enough about your partner you won't slip off behind his back for an illicit shag. If you don't care enough you probably will and – in time – you will reap what you sow. (No sympathy there then.)

Contrary to popular myth, successful open relationships don't just happen, and if one appears out of the blue then one of you is probably trying to rationalise or conceal an indiscretion. Open relationships are consensual agreements, negotiated jointly – which should allow you and your partner to have sex with other men. This should not threaten your commitment to each other and you should both sort this stuff out before you start shagging around. Just because the sex has become less exclusive doesn't mean that the relationship is any less devoted and committed. When talking stuff through, key ingredients should include honesty, being upfront about fears and concerns, and respecting each other's viewpoints. For example, you should talk about the difference between sex and love: meeting another guy should be about getting your rocks off, not about falling for him. You also need to manage and overcome feelings of jealousy. Take your time: don't feel as if a cast-iron agreement has to be signed sealed and delivered in a single session. It could take a period of weeks or even months; this is a very big step for both of you.

Suggested rules for open relationships

- Sex with other men is restricted to once-only shags, or times when one of you is away
  or threesomes (which doesn't mean one of you is shagging while the other is asleep).
- If you don't use condoms within the relationship – use them every time you have sex with someone else.
- If you go out together, you return home together.
- You talk openly about who you've been with, or don't talk about it at all.
- If you go back with someone you don't stay overnight.
- Sexual partners are never brought back home, or always introduced when they are.
- Express any fears, concerns or worries as soon as they occur.
- Agree times when you intend to be together.
- Revisit the agreement every now and then to ensure you are both comfortable with it.

Open relationships are unlikely to work if:

- Either of you breaks the agreement.
- Either of you is jealous or possessive.
- Either of you fears losing your partner to someone else.
- Either of you has doubts about the existing relationship.
- Either of you conceals any fears or worries.
- Sex is the main or only thing keeping you together.
- The true motive of the open relationship is to hunt for new partners.

For some couples, it's helpful to write out the agreement. Most important though is that you both stick to what you have agreed and are prepared to discuss any issues promptly should they arise. One of the more obvious problems is falling for one of the guys you've met. Talking it through with your partner first is essential but, if you can't do that, chat to a trusted friend and ask yourself the following questions:

- Why can't I talk to my partner?
- What has the new guy got that my current partner hasn't?
- How might these feelings for this guy be a response to something else in my current relationship?

Relationship difficulties

We wouldn't be human if our relationships didn't have difficulties and problems and many of them are simply part and parcel of being together. The secret is to tackle them early before they fester and resentment builds up. However, some behaviour – by either of you – can indicate deeper and more serious problems. While the list is virtually endless, here are some typical examples:

- Bad moods, disagreements and rows.
- Being argumentative or deliberately contradicting each other.
- Monosyllabic conversations or the silent treatment.
- Sniping and backstabbing when out with friends.
- Being demanding and bossy.
- Interrupting privacy and space.
- Long work hours at the expense of the relationship.
- Resistance to touch, cuddles and hugs.

- Noticeably less sex, or hurried, emotionless sex.
- Abuse of drugs and alcohol.
- Refusal to return calls or take messages.
- Failure to keep appointments and agreements, eg regarding open relationships.
- Moving out!

Being in love can skew your judgement, and while the shit has been hitting the fan on a regular basis we can be oblivious to the fact that something is wrong. In the end, if you don't work it out for yourself nothing gets sorted out. We tend to be optimistic and reluctant to admit shortcomings, eager to rationalise or forgive inappropriate and destructive behaviour. Before long, we can't see the wood for the trees. Even if we do recognise there is a problem our ability to act can be hindered by a fear of losing him, being lonely (again) and throwing away everything we've built up together. One of the most difficult things to do is to get him into a frame of mind where he will tell you what's wrong, so that you can work towards a solution together. If you're the one being the arsehole then you've got to get through the anger and resentment before you can start making things better.

Rescuing relationships

- Deal with the difficulty or problem as soon as it arises – don't let it fester.
- When you're ready to talk avoid airports, football matches or pubs. Choose a place that provides privacy, quiet and gives you space. A neutral location is often best.
- Stay calm and adopt non-threatening body language.
- Tell him what you think the difficulty is without being accusing. It's the things people do that are the problem and not the people themselves.
- Avoid embarrassment or humiliation.
- Be honest, straightforward but tactful and remember that you're here to save the relationship – not to get your own back.
- Listen… listen… listen.
- Acknowledge his perspective even though you may not agree with his point of view.
- Reassure him that you want the relationship to work.
- Give him time to talk and listen to what he has to say.
- Be prepared for him to be critical of you and recognise that the difficulty may also lie with you.
- Sometimes these talks don't find solutions in one go and accept there may be limitations to what you can achieve initially. Be clear that you both need to continue the discussion at a later date.

- If you are able to find a solution, make sure you both understand what it entails and agree to it.
- If you love him, say so. If you can be affectionate ,be so.
- Afterwards you may be physically and emotionally drained. If you need to take a day off work, do it.
- Remember that solutions can take time and may raise other problems. Take it a step at a time.
- Don't just jump back into bed as a quick fix solution and at the expense of resolving problems fully.

Violence and abuse

Some partners can become abusive or violent. If you are in an abusive relationship or know someone who is, the following may be of help:

- Domestic violence and abuse does exist between gay men.
- Domestic violence cuts across all groups regardless of race, age, class, religion, lifestyles or disability.
- Domestic violence is about control of one person by another.
- Alcohol, drugs, stress, etc. are not an excuse for violence.
- There is no provocation or justification for domestic violence – the batterer is responsible for their behaviour.

If you keep going from one violent or abusive relationship to another then you should examine why, how, and when it happens. This should be a useful start when seeking further help, advice and, perhaps, counselling.

Violence and abuse can happen in many different ways and settings. Violence is not always physical, but can also be emotional, mental ,verbal and sexual. Violence or abuse can be considered as an intrusion into your life that does not involve your consent or agreement. It is a very personal thing and what one person feels is abusive another person might not. If it feels abusive to you, try and do something about it. If you feel unable to confront the abusive person – seek advice and help as a matter of urgency. You might be able to get someone to help or act on your behalf. If you are in a abusive relationship you may:

- Feel that you are to blame.
- Make excuses for your partner's behaviour, 'he can't help himself, it's his work... his family... his debts... it's me... it's just the way he is...'
- Find yourself forever anticipating your partner's next mood swing.
- Feel trapped and believe there is no way out of the relationship.
- Go on loving your partner even though you know what's happening is wrong.

- Feel confused, depressed, angry, alone, and frightened.
- Do things to make you forget – drink more, smoke more, take drugs, harm yourself.
- Feel that no one else will love you or take care of you.
- Think it will stop soon.

If you are on the receiving end of violence, it is important to get out as soon as possible and get help. Do not feel guilty that this has happened to you and that, in some way, it's your fault. It is also important that you do not feel embarrassed about your reactions after the event – you have been through a traumatic and stressful situation. You do not deserve to be on the receiving end of any form of violence or abuse. The abuse or violence only gets worse and can lead to permanent damage or death. If it wasn't you, it would somebody else.

If you are being abusive or violent towards you partner – there is something you can do to stop. There are a number of groups and organisations that will work with you to help you understand why you are doing this and how to stop. They are there to help you… not to judge you.

What can you do?

- If violence is happening on a regular basis, find out what help is available to prevent this happening to you. It is also important to record what is happening in case it needs to be used as evidence.
- Tell someone what is happening! Speak to a gay organisation/helpline, or tell someone you can trust. Have someone you can call anytime.
- Go to a safe place or plan ahead so that you can get to a safe place quickly if you are abused again or are scared.
- Use a helpline or call an organisation for lesbians and gay men who are victims of violence or who can help in dealing with the police. You can call just for emotional support, for referrals to support groups or for practical help about possible police/legal remedies.
- The police have specially-trained officers, some of whom are gay or lesbian themselves. When you phone police ask if a gay liaison officer is available.
- In an emergency always call 999.

Breaking up

If all efforts to solve relationship difficulties fail, you will need to decide whether you wish to finish it. Take your time, perhaps talk to a friend – preferably one who doesn't hate his guts and won't just agree with you. In the final analysis you will need to ask yourself: will I be happier with him in or out of my life? If you decide to finish the relationship:

- Tell him face-to-face, difficult though this may be for both of you.
- Try and stay calm and adopt non-threatening body language.
- Tell him that you want the relationship to end and explain the reasons.
- Avoid embarrassment, humiliation or blame.
- Be honest, straightforward but tactful.
- Give him time to talk and listen to what he has to say.
- Remember: he might try to persuade you to stay, so you need to be clear that you have reached the best decision you can before talking to him. If you start wavering, you could be open to accusations of emotional blackmail or 'crying wolf'.
- Own what you say and the decisions you take.

Some relationships work, others don't, many reach a natural conclusion. It's best that we recognise it and move on rather than being swallowed up by unhappiness, boredom and resentment. Some relationships are short but have been bursting with life while others simply rumble on interminably – a marriage of convenience devoid of warmth and love. So before you throw your hands up in despair try and recognise that it is the quality of a relationship that matters most, not necessarily its length. Eventually though, it's often changes in our emotional, physical, and spiritual needs – combined with other interests and lifestyles – which outgrow relationships however hard we have tried.

Gay men have a remarkable capacity to remain close friends with their ex-partners and if there is a possibility of bringing a relationship to a civil close, do so. However, don't feel you have to. Discuss your feelings, remember the good times, reflect on the not-so-good times. Tie up any practical matters, eg property, furniture, personal possessions, and legal/money matters. Recognise that breaking up is hard and can be very emotional but ending a relationship on an even note makes its much easier to let go and move on. It will be at times like these that your friends are all-important. Good friends are a selfless bunch and you'll be able to be wistful, whinge and cry your little heart out. Mind you, some won't miss the opportunity to say something like '…what you need is a man' or '…you'll get over it.' Just slap them and cross them off your Christmas card list.

When the relationship is over

- If it hurts: let it hurt – it's okay to miss him but you will get by.
- What's done is done and you can't change the past.
- It's okay to miss him but you will get by.
- Recognise that he is not your responsibility any more. Make a clean break and don't allow him to creep in through the back door.
- You may want to take some time off the scene. If not, recognise that you may be vulnerable.
- Sometimes, it can be many months before you feel able to even consider another commitment. There's nothing wrong with that.
- You have gained valuable experience: use it positively. If mistakes were made, learn from them.
- Don't mope about at home – get out and about, have a meal with friends, go on holiday.
- Exercise and sports are a great way of burning off the calories and the angst.
- Don't look for blame or blame yourself.
- Hold on to the good times and the positive aspects of the relationship.

He's a bastard!

Putting aside the caring and sharing stuff for the moment… he could just have been a complete bastard. Sometimes the anger, hurt and resentment we feel towards an ex-boyfriend can be overwhelming, particularly if he has really fucked you over and there's nothing you can do about it. It can be months sometimes years before it seems to matter less and then an unexpected reminder can bring it flooding back. However right it feels to be angry, these feelings will have an impact on new relationships and will use up emotional energy that could be better used making yourself a happier and healthier life without him. Sometimes the sweetest victory is using a painful experience to rebuild your life and – if you see him again – let him know it… with a smile. Lastly, if you seem to end up with all the bastards, you should examine why. Talk it through with a trusted friend, contact a helpline or consider seeking professional help.

Barriers to love

We probably have at least one friend or acquaintance who seems to be genuinely happy being alone and another who seems to fall in and out of relationships quicker than you can say 'I'll call you…'. We probably know some guys who synonymise relationships with dramas and others who have been together so long we're secretly envious. We also know guys who can pick up every night of the week but whom we suspect are lonely and those who seem to have an unerring capacity to be vicious, self-centred and hell-bent on destroying the men they says they love. We should also recognise that it is unlikely that we will be in back-to-back relationships all our lives. Finding the right man can take time and just because he's not by your side now doesn't make you a bad, unreasonable or inadequate lover. Despite everything you can do, there's a surprising amount of chance involved and you shouldn't feel guilty or angry if you've been unlucky today, this week or this year… If, however, you feel that there is a barrier between you and a relationship then this section should help.

Healthy on the inside

It's one thing to find a man – it's a bonus to discover that he wants to spend time with you. It's miraculous that the sex is just what you both want but are you ready? We buy the right clothes, cut our hair, exercise, shave and tan ourselves into oblivion, immerse our skin in creams and lotions and decorate our homes… even the cat leaves the bedroom at the appropriate signal. But while we spend time, effort and money to look our best it can often be at the expense of preparing ourselves from the inside. If you're not happy by yourself – in yourself – then you're not going to feel much better with someone else. In fact you'll be trading one set of problems for another and dragging someone else into the crap. The axiom that you can't love others until you love yourself is very true, but equally you can't receive love unless you feel at one with yourself.

Particularly on the scene, we're constantly comparing ourselves with other gay men and that's where all self-esteem and self-worth stuff gets in the way. It keeps us from seeing ourselves as whole people preferring instead something better, younger, more handsome, better built and more together – not forgetting that extra inch or two. Consequently, our self-esteem plummets, we fill the space with self doubt and question our ability to become involved with other men. You will probably recognise some of the things we do to avoid giving and receiving tenderness, affection and love:

- **Iain** focuses on his weaknesses instead of his strengths, his bad points rather than his good ones. He thinks that he doesn't deserve to be happy and when he finds a man convinces himself that it's all going to go pear-shaped. The negativity can be so strong and his sense of self worth so low that he undermines whatever good things he's got going for him.
- **Tim** is lonely but gets himself a man – and is happy. But, as things start to get serious he finds excuses as to why his boyfriend isn't right. When hunting, he's upfront with other men but can also turn cruel to test his lover's devotion. You can never show him enough love and he's always finding new hurdles for you clamber over. Typically, you'll say 'I love you' and he'll say 'who are you trying to kid.'

- **Carl** thinks he's inadequate as a friend and boyfriend, and doesn't deserve love, intimacy or companionship. He keeps his distance, never letting anyone get too close. This makes him feel very lonely. He tries to make things better with anonymous backroom sex but complains that's all that gay men want. You'd think that Carl had it all going for him but as he sleeps his way across town he's constantly looking to others to confirm that he's good, worthwhile, attractive and lovable.

- **Andreas** is charming, funny, intelligent and would make someone a great boyfriend, but all of this just goes out the window when he's out clubbing. All he sees are beautiful men with washboard stomachs and buns to die for; all he can think of is that he's fat and unattractive. In reality he could lose some weight but he gets so depressed by this one issue he can't bring himself to diet or exercise. Consequently, he feels increasingly isolated each time he goes out.

- **Matthew** always seems to know what you need and insists on getting it for you… a cup of tea, tickets to that film you've been meaning to see, or weekend drugs. Nothing is too much trouble but he gives so much that he ignores his own needs. He doesn't think well enough of himself to enjoy sex but will do anything to please you. He's nervous about being touched, moves away after you've cum and tends to play the martyr.

- **Massimo** doesn't think anything he has to say is important. If he does tell you how he feels, he's frightened that you won't like him for him – a lovely guy who just doesn't know it. This fear of rejection is 'protecting' him from getting close to anyone, but while he doesn't have to show his true feelings he's thoroughly miserable by himself.

- **Brian** knows what makes you feel bad about yourself and never lets you forget it. He's the first to embarrass you in front of friends and broadcast your failed sexual exploits. This brittle screaming queen can only feel good about himself at the expense of others. Consequently, he has a never-ending stream of fair-weather friends who stay just long enough to be mauled by his malicious sense of humour. Hemlock pales beside this bitch and he'd rather take it than admit that he is unhappy and intensely lonely.

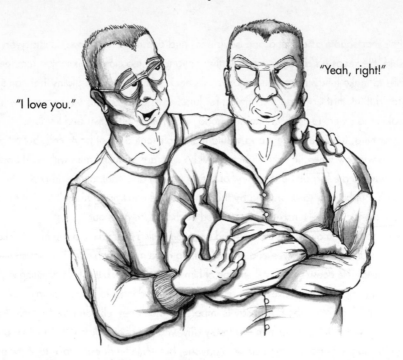

No matter how often someone tells you that he finds you attractive or that he cares, you cannot quite believe it. In fact, the more honest and genuine the compliment the more painful it can be to accept. This is not to say that you can't love or don't love, but getting yourself into mental and emotional shape helps raise your self esteem and replaces self doubt with positive thoughts and feelings.

What to do

- Surround yourself with good friends and dump the ones who put you down or use you as a punch- bag. Being with the wrong people who don't love you for who you are can damage your self-image and do more harm than practically anything else.
- Sit down and write out what makes you a good guy and what points you would like to change or improve. Aim to tackle them in turn and set yourself realistic goals to achieve them.
- If you can relate to one or more of the characterisations above, talk it through with a trusted friend, counsellor or therapist. There is nothing shameful or embarrassing about doing this. You've recognised a potential problem and are prepared to deal with it. This a strength, not a weakness.

- If you have family, childhood or (ex) boyfriend stuff which makes you unhappy or depressed, talk it through with a counsellor or therapist or maybe a trusted friend. Again, these are healthy and positive steps to take.
- Get enough sleep, manage your stress effectively and learn to relax.
- Take regular exercise and eat sensibly.

Being assertive

Assertiveness should be about feeling, understanding and believing that *you* matter in your friendships, relationships, at work and at play. For some gay men claiming the same rights as everyone else can be hard. It's also about breaking patterns of behaviour and can take time.

We aren't always treated equally by the law or society in general, though things are getting better. Despite these improvements, a background of discrimination might make you feel you have no rights at all – even within our own community. Wrong! You do have rights – though sometimes the way gay people treat each other you'd be forgiven for thinking otherwise. Wouldn't it be great if we were treated with respect by other people and, in turn, felt able to respect them. This is the part of what assertiveness is about. It's also about building your own self-respect and dealing with your own feelings. Would you like to:

- Increase your self-confidence?
- Be clear and direct?
- Be properly understood?
- Feel better because you've expressed your feelings?
- Stand a better chance of getting what you want?
- Have fewer situations that are unresolved?
- Be treated as an equal?

This is what being assertive can achieve. It's not achieved by being aggressive, we don't need to act like steam rollers. Being passive will not help us get what we want either. When we are passive in situations, we don't express our feelings. This builds up anger and frustration inside us until finally we blow up over a tiny thing. We often feel bad after this outburst and revert to being passive again. Being assertive can help you break out of this circle of passive to aggressive behaviour. Being assertive can use up a lot of energy. You don't have to keep it up 24 hours a day. Go slow. Take it easy and choose your moment. The decision is yours.

'I'll tell you what I want, what I really, really want.'

There are no magic words or set phrases for being assertive. However, there are several vital ingredients in becoming more assertive:

1 **Listen** – even when the person is expressing strong feelings or being aggressive.
2 **Demonstrate understanding** – not by using the stock phrase 'I understand how you feel' but by referring to what you have heard. For example: 'you seem angry and disappointed.'
3 **Say what you think and feel how the situation is affecting you** – take responsibility for your feelings. Be clear about what has given rise to your feelings and attribute them to the event or the behaviour – not the person. For example: 'I feel upset and hurt that you left me at the club when you said you would give me a lift home.'
4 **Say specifically what you want to happen** – this minimises the chances of being misunderstood and increases the possibility of getting it. It doesn't guarantee you will get what you want. Listen to the response you get and be prepared for the person to have a different point of view.
5 If you need to negotiate, **consider the consequences** for you and others of any joint solutions where both of you are satisfied, rather than make a compromise where neither of you get what you want. Don't give in to passive or aggressive behaviour at this point – you're nearly there.

Right, now here's the hard bit. Think about whether you're happy with your lot. What about...

- Having friends and relationships around you that matter.
- A job you enjoy and puts some money in your pocket.
- A home where you're happy and where you can relax.
- Getting the medical and health services you want or need.
- Getting he sex you want.
- Disclosing your HIV status.
- Dealing with the gay scene.

Try writing down real situations where you would like to be more assertive. Use a variety of situations that aren't frightening but which you'd still like to deal with better. Build up to more difficult situations that you encounter or are avoiding. Then, working through the five points listed above note down possible assertive approaches to these problems and, if you need to initiate the conversation, start from point 3. Practise saying them in your head before you try it out for real. Remember that words on their own do not convey an assertive message. Communication researchers have found that only 7% of a message is based around the words you say, 38% of the message comes from the tone of your voice, and 55% comes from your appearance or body language. Your words, voice tone and body language should all say 'I'm confident and your equal, I expect to be treated with respect..'

Further information and contacts

- **London Lesbian and Gay Switchboard** with details of Regional Switchboards 020 7837 7324
- **PACE** Counselling, advice, advocacy and workshops 020 7700 1323 / 34 Hartham Road, London N7 9JL
- **Survivors** Advice, information and support for men who have been sexually assaulted 020 7833 3737 (7-10pm).
- **Face2Face Sex Advice** One-to-one sex and relationships advice for gay and bisexual men.
  This service is free and by appointment only. 020 7816 4566 / www.tht.org.uk

gettingolder

Contrary to popular myth, gay men get older too! Unless you're flattened by a bus, most people live until 85 although a few of us thrive for more than 100 years. Several factors seem to make us grow old:

- Every time a cell divides (to replace those which have died) the blueprint for making them gets a little fuzzier introducing less precise copies. Consequently, more faulty cells are made.
- The body is gradually poisoned by a build-up of waste and toxins that it cannot process.
- There is a progressive decline in the immune system's ability to detect and destroy micro-organisms and developing tumours.
- Diet, exercise and hereditary traits.

Put like this ageing doesn't sound so great – it might even sound a little grim – but, eventually, that's what bodies are designed to do. Nevertheless, with more of us living longer, more of us will still be here. Getting older is a fact of life and worrying about aging just wastes time we could be living. Hopefully, older means wiser, calmer and clearer about what's important to us. As an added bonus, friends we made when we were younger may still be our friends decades later. Obviously there are exceptions, but from about 35-40 years plus – older gay men tend to have:

- A more rounded sense of who they are.
- Greater emotional stability.
- Grown increasingly comfortable with their sexual identity.
- A more considered approach to life.
- More confidence and are usually wiser.
- Built up strong networks of friends.

- Genuine interests … other than alcohol, shopping and drugs!
- An established home and financial security.
- More sexual experience and a better understanding of what they like.
- The potential for the security of a long-term, mutually supportive, relationship.

As we get older, the body's ability to have sex changes – we may need more time to get turned on, get a hard-on and to cum. Erections may not be as stiff, you may prefer sex in the mornings when you're rested and erections can occur spontaneously. Having said that, the quality of sex tends to matter more over the numbers of shags we get, we are more likely to know what stimulates us, and we tend to be more considerate bed partners. Gay men in their 40s and above tend to put sex into perspective, prioritising life differently and developing other interests. This is perfectly normal. Sex is still great in later life but it doesn't occupy every waking moment. Mind you, while there is no reason why you cannot have sex until your 100th birthday, if you insist on fucking like a rabbit every night, you might resent your body if it sometimes refuses to co-operate.

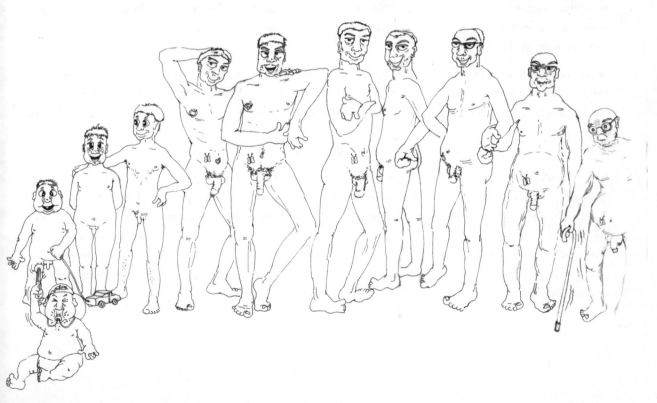

Age and the gay scene

There is no doubt that the gay scene and gay media play a role in making older gay men feel unwelcome. Many younger gay men (particularly in their teens, 20s and 30s) have a distorted view of what it means to be older, often equating it with becoming less attractive, an inability to get or have sex, and leading a sad and sorry life. Younger gay men also assume that because older gay men are not like them – or don't look like them – they cannot be happy. Some men resent older gay men on the scene and scorn their efforts when they try to make conversation. Of course there will always be a few older gay men who just want one thing! But, as a rule, younger gay men make arrogant and simplistic assumptions about what older gay men want and are rarely able to see beyond their own prejudice and vanity. Not surprisingly we don't see so many older gay men on the scene. This is because – in many ways – it's served its purpose and is no longer of any use to them. They have simply grown up, moved on and have got themselves a different and more varied life. Since first impressions and appearance are often the factors which determine whether we approach men, what older men have to offer is sometimes not immediately apparent. The deeper qualities are more likely to emerge over a drink, a meal or a one-to-one encounter. But if this is not what you want, it costs nothing to be polite and courteous when declining.

Of course, you will see men in their late 50s, 60s and 70s who still use the scene, and while it may be difficult for some men to understand their motivation, it's perfectly possible that they're happy, well-adjusted and getting on with their lives. You'll probably also find that they won't be making the kind of crass and juvenile assumptions younger gay men make about them.

Age differences

A five-to-ten-year age difference between partners is not unusual and can add a valuable dimension to relationships. However, if you find that your relationships are short-lived, or just don't materialise, you should carefully examine the reasons why a younger or older partner is important to you. Major sources of disagreement between partners with 15 or more years between them can range from money, holidays, and careers to socialising, food and even the little things like when you go to bed! Attempting to realise a desire or fantasy for a much older or younger lover is often disappointing and unhealthy (for both of you). Although healthy relationships between older and younger men do exist and can work — you should think carefully before embarking on what might be a fruitless quest.

Further information and contacts

- **Caffmos** Website for older gay men www.caffmos.co.uk
- **Stradivarius** Website for older gay men www.stradivarius-london.co.uk
- **National Friend** Counselling, helplines and support groups for lesbians and gay men BM National Friend, London, WC1N 3XX.
- **London Lesbian and Gay Switchboard** with details of Regional Switchboards 020 7837 7324 / www.gayswitchboard.org.uk
- **The internet**

finding a place to live

Whether we're looking for a shag pad or a show home, most of us want a place we can call our own. It's where we eat, sleep, relax, invite friends and have sex and, in many ways, it's the cornerstone of our lives. When we're younger, we tend to move around but we still need a base – even if we pop back home for a few months. As we get older, many of us want a home whether we're by ourselves, living in a house or getting to grips with living with someone.

This chapter is aimed at guys looking for rented private accommodation and should only be used as a guide. Housing law rules and regulations are a complicated area and if you have concerns, worries or questions about your housing you should seek professional advice. The Citizens' Advice Bureau, or your local council/authority are good places to start and the internet has many sites with help, advice and information.

If you are fit and healthy and single or in a relationship, you will have to make your own arrangements to find somewhere to live. It can be difficult and take a lot of time and energy but the keys to success are planning, patience and persistence.

Renting privately

There are several types of accommodation to rent privately:

- Self contained flats with your own room, kitchen, bathroom, etc.
- Rooms or bedsits – where you have your own room and share a kitchen, bathroom, etc.
- Sharing with a landlord – where you rent a room and share facilities with the landlord.

Being homeless, vulnerable and/or at risk

Are you homeless, or within 28 days of being homeless? Do you fall into one of these groups:

- Have a serious physical or mental health problems.
- Are vulnerable in some other way, eg age.
- Lost your home through fire, flood or other disaster.
- Have dependent children.

If so you hsould contact your local council or get someone to do it on your behalf now! They may have to provide accommodation for you. If you don't fall into any of the above groups your main option is to rent privately, or investigate the following options:

- Housing associations or housing co-operatives.
- Buying or shared ownership.
- Hostels or hotels / bed and breakfast / guest houses.

When you start hunting, remember:

- If you have any doubts, concerns or queries, get professional advice.
- Read all contracts and agreements carefully – including the small print.
- Get written receipts for all transactions between you and the landlord.
- Keep notes and write stuff down.

Where to look

When looking for private accommodation, the following places should be helpful:

- Gay press, other newspapers, magazines and radio.
- Gay friendly shops and cafés with noticeboards.
- Accommodation agencies, letting agents, estate agents.
- College/university notice boards and accommodation offices.
- The internet

When you're hunting...

- Try to be as clear as you can about where you want to live and why.
- When looking at the property, go with a friend and get a second opinion (make sure your friend is sensible!).
- Find out what you have to pay on top of the rent and if the bills are shared.
- Don't be afraid to ask questions. It's going to be your home.
- If you're seeing more than one place, it can be easier to compare them if you devise a check-up list for each property.
- Can you honestly afford the rent? Make a complete budget of all your income and outgoings.
- Most landlords require references, often including one from your bank. Try and arrange this before you start looking.

You may be entitled to help with your rent – ask your local council. If you require any further advice ring your local council housing advice centre.

Accommodation agencies

These agencies may be able to help you find a place to live owned by a private landlord. You are likely to be asked about the type of property you're looking for, how much rent you're willing to pay, details of your job and income and references from your employer, bank, or a previous landlord. You will also be asked to register with the agency. An agency can only legally charge you a fee when they have successfully found you somewhere to live. However, an agency cannot refuse to register you if you are unemployed, or on benefits, or because of your sexual orientation or any disability, for example. In most cases it is illegal for an agency to discriminate on grounds of race or sex – even where the landlord has stated this clearly. Once you have signed a contract and accept the tenancy of a property, the agency can charge a fee – it is therefore vital that you determine all costs in advance. However, it is against the law for an agency to ask for payment for:

- Putting your name on its list
- Taking your details.
- Providing a list of properties available for renting.
- A deposit which will be returned if no suitable accommodation it is found.

A relatively new form of help comes in the form of accommodation information services, many of which take advantage of the internet and offer up to the minute information on houses, flats and flat shares. They match tenants and properties using computer systems more akin to dating agencies, but rarely undertake the more traditional role of viewings, referencing and contract negotiations associated with estate agents and agencies. By all means check them out, but check out the fees involved as well.

If an accommodation agency or service offers you accommodation you should inspect the property first and read through the agreement thoroughly before signing anything.

Tenancy agreements

Many tenants have a written tenancy agreement, but a legal contract exists between you the landlord whether anything has been written down or not. It may involve a conversation between you and the landlord which may seem fine at the time but can be difficult to enforce later especially if there were no witnesses to the agreement. Wherever possible it is important to get a signed agreement in writing.

Tenancy agreements vary but should usually contain the following:

- The type and terms of the tenancy agreement.
- The rent you will have to pay (and whether it includes other charges, eg services, fuel and water).
- How much rent you have to pay in advance, eg premium and/or security deposit.
- The start date of the contract (and finish date, as required).
- The name and address of the landlord.

Before you sign anything, make sure you understand what it is you are agreeing to and what it is you are responsible for. If you have any concerns, doubts or queries – however small – check it out first with an independent organisation such as a CAB or local housing advice centre. When you're ready, the contract should signed and dated by you and the landlord or the representative of the landlord.

Rent

Rent is the money paid to your landlord in return for the right to occupy a property. It can be paid weekly, fortnightly or monthly, as agreed between the landlord and yourself. If you pay your rent weekly you are entitled to a rent book which must have the name and address of the landlord or agent on it and it must be provided by them. Remember – most landlords want four weeks' rent as a deposit and four weeks in advance. This may be negotiable, so don't let this put you off. If you disagree with the rent or an increase and you are unable to negotiate a mutual level with your landlord, then you can apply to the RAC (Rent Assessment Committee) within 28 days.

Deposits

The most usual type of deposit is paid to the landlord as security against rent arrears, damage, or removal of furniture. The security deposit is usually returned in full when you leave. If you paid it originally by cheque you will probably get a cheque and if you paid cash you should get cash. Check this out beforehand, because if you need the cash for a new place waiting for a cheque to clear can be frustrating and may delay your move.

Deductions are usually made for damage, fuel bills (for which you are responsible) and any outstanding rent that might be due – the landlord should tell you in advance if this is the case. Consequently, you should carefully check the condition of the property (including fixtures and fittings) when you move in because you could be held responsible for loss or damage and lose some or all of the deposit.

Occasionally, you may have to provide a 'holding' deposit when you have agreed to rent a place but have not signed the contract. The amount is usually set against the security deposit. Before you make any payment like this, you should make sure that you want to live there as holding deposits are not usually returned unless you are unable to move in for reasons beyond your control.

Right of entry by the landlord

In general, a landlord should give you 24 hours' notice of their intention to enter the property but they should always ask your permission and give a minimum of 24 hours' notice. However if you are a lodger, and there is an agreement to provide a room cleaning service, the landlord can enter without permission. The landlord does not have a right to enter in any other circumstances unless they have a court order.

A landlord has a right to 'reasonable' access in order to carry out maintenance and repairs. Reasonable depends on why access is required. For example, if the ceiling is falling down, immediate access will be needed. On the other hand, if fixtures or fitting need replacing this should be done at a mutually convenient time.

Harassment

All tenants are entitled to live safely and peacefully in their homes and harassment by your landlord or a person instructed by your landlord is an offence. Harassment can be in several different forms such as:

- Entering your home without prior warning.
- Changing the locks.
- Cutting off your utilities, such as gas, water and electricity.
- Tampering with your mail or possessions.
- Threatening you verbally or physically.

Keep a record of any instances where harassment has occurred, names of witnesses or anyone who may have become involved, doctors, police, etc. Also get advice from your local council as soon as possible – they may be able to advise or help you further.

Condition of property

Whether it is furnished or unfurnished, you should inspect the property and record its condition and contents. Landlords have a legal responsibility to ensure that the gas supply is safe and that any upholstered furniture complies with the fire safety regulations. It is your responsibility to check that other appliances are safe and clarify with the landlord what you are responsible for.

If the property is unfurnished, it's still worth making a record of the condition of the decoration, fixtures and fittings. For example, you don't want to be held responsible for cigarette burns on the carpet, a cracked pane of glass or loose bathroom tiles if you have noticed them before occupying the property. The cost of a disposable camera is a small price to pay to prove you didn't burn a hole in the camera (placing a dated newspaper in the picture).

If the property is furnished, an inventory (list of contents) should be provided by the landlord which should include a description of everything you're going to use with their age and condition. As the tenant, you're usually required to check it and sign it. If there isn't one make one up yourself and get it signed by an independent witness. If you damage anything you should inform the landlord and agree how/when repairs, replacement, and/or any payment will be made but you are not responsible for 'normal wear and tear' of furniture, fixtures and fittings.

Should something happen which could be dangerous, eg faulty electrics, a spring through a sofa or a wobbly banister the landlord should undertake repairs as quickly as possible. This should also include cookers and or washing machines which have been working at the beginning of your tenancy (unless you broke it).

Locks

If you are not sure about who has keys, change the locks. What's to say a previous tenant with a spare set of keys can't return? Unlikely, but it's been known to happen.

Television licence

If you have a TV or video recorder in the property you are responsible for getting a current TV licence, unless the landlord has installed the set – in which case you should check that a current licence exists by contacting the TV Licensing Records Office. If there is no licence and you're caught – you can be fined up to £1000.

Damage

The landlord is usually responsible for external and structural repairs. You are usually responsible for internal decoration and for making sure that any furniture and fittings are not damaged through negligence on your part which you will have to pay for. However, your exact responsibilities should be described in the tenancy agreement. You should also inform the landlord about anything which could cause damage to the property, eg a leaking roof.

Eviction

Landlords must follow the correct legal procedure to evict a tenant. In most cases this involves serving a notice requiring possession. If you have been illegally evicted you should seek legal advice. You have the right to apply for a court injunction to be allowed back into your home and your landlord can be liable for an unlimited fine and/or two years imprisonment. The landlord can evict you if he can prove to a court that one of the mandatory grounds for possession is satisfied.

If you want to leave

Generally, you you and the landlord both have to give the same amount of notice to end the tenancy agreement. If you leave without giving proper notice, the landlord may be entitled to charge rent to the date of notice when the agreement should have expired

Leaving stuff behind

Property left behind still belongs to you and should normally be returned to you when you ask for it. If you leave stuff behind after you have given up the tenancy, the landlord may charge for the cost of clearing it out of the property.

Further information and contacts

- **Citizen's Advice Bureaux** Housing advice   www.ncab.org.uk
- **Stonewall Housing** Housing advice 020 7359 6242 / Unit 2A, Leroy Business Centre House, 436 Essex Road, London N1 3QP
- **Local Council / Authority** Housing advice and details of local CABs
- **Outlet** Accommodation service for Lesbians and Gay men in London. 020 7287 4244 / homes@outlet.co.uk / 32 Old Compton Street, London, London W1V 5PA
- **Internet** Search under heading, related words
- **Press** for accomodation, eg The Pink Paper, Time Out
- **Search** on the Internet, eg letonthenet.com
- **GLAD** Gay legal advice 020 7837 5212 (Mon-Thu 7pm-9.00pm)

employment

This chapter gives basic guidelines about rights at work. Employment law is a complicated area so don't rely solely on anything contained here – always get advice first. In addition to a range of organisations listed at the end of the chapter Lesbian and Gay Employment Rights (LAGER) specialise in legal and employment issues for lesbians and gay men.

Starting work

- **Contract** A contract of employment comes into existence as soon as you start work. It can be verbal or written. It is always better though if terms and conditions are written down. As well as specific terms all contracts of employment contain 'implied' terms that are broader, such as a duty of 'mutual trust and confidence'.
- **Written statement of terms and conditions** Employees are entitled to this by law within two months of starting work. It must include details of pay, hours, holidays, sickness and notice.
- **Notice of termination of employment** Your contract may tell you how much contractual notice you are entitled to. However, everyone is entitled to the minimum statutory notice – your contract may give you longer.
- **Hours/pay** New laws set out minimum rates of pay and maximum hours of work. Does this affect you? Find out by getting in touch with your local CAB or calling LAGER on (020) 7704 6066.

First signs of trouble

- If you think you're being badly treated or discriminated against, don't wait until things get out of hand; contact your local CAB or LAGER straight away. You can discuss the situation with them and get advice about action you could take.
- Write everything down; it's easy to forget crucial dates and details. Keep a record of comments, events and action taken by your employer or colleagues that you think are unreasonable, unjustified or discriminatory. If appropriate, get this record signed by a witness.
- If your employer asks you to accept a change in terms and conditions of employment which you find unacceptable, and which alters your written or verbal contract of employment, don't agree without getting legal advice. Don't sign anything, and don't start work under the new conditions; this might indicate that you have agreed to them. Ask for time to consider the change. Ask your employer what will happen if you don't accept the change. Try to put these questions in writing and get written replies, or get a friend or trade union rep to be a witness. If you object to the change but feel that you have no choice, let your employer know in writing that you are working under protest. Keep a copy of this letter and send it recorded delivery.
- Don't take action or walk out of your job without getting legal advice.

Dismissal

- If you are sacked get legal advice as soon as possible since there are tight deadlines for taking action.
- If you are in a trade union contact your shop steward or representative straight away.
- If your employer asks you to resign, get legal advice first. As well as finding out if you would be able to make a claim to an employment tribunal, you need to be aware of problems getting benefits (although resigning doesn't automatically mean no benefits).

If you think that your employer sacked you unreasonably you can take a claim of unfair dismissal to an employment tribunal. To take this action you need to have been in the job for at least one year, unless your dismissal was to do with race, sex or disability discrimination, trade union membership, or for trying to get rights that you were entitled to by law. There are other exceptions, so always get legal advice. An unfair dismissal claim needs to be submitted less than three months after the date you were sacked. Discrimination claims need to be submitted less than three months after the last act of discrimination that you experienced.

Constructive dismissal

If you have been employed for at least a year, and your employer has acted so badly that you want to resign, you may be able to claim 'constructive dismissal.' Again, you need to get legal advice before doing so, since a successful claim requires certain conditions to have been met. Your employer's bad treatment must be shown to be a 'fundamental', ie serious breach of your contract – although this could be an implied term as mentioned above, as well as a specific term. Failure to stop harassment is an example of a breach of an implied term. You also need to tell your employer in writing exactly why you are resigning.

Discrimination

Discrimination is less favourable treatment on grounds of disability, race or sex. This can occur whilst in employment, during recruitment or in rare cases after leaving a job. An employer has a duty to make reasonable adjustments to enable disabled people to get or stay in employment. If an employer has tried to make these adjustments but been prevented from doing so by cost or other factors, he/she may be able to justify the discrimination in an employment tribunal. Employers with less than 15 employees are not covered by the Disability Discrimination Act. People who are HIV-positive may be able to claim disability discrimination. The law in this area is complex. Get legal advice!

Sexual orientation discrimination

There is no specific law to stop employers from treating lesbian and gay employees less favourably than heterosexuals. Within the next three years the government will have to remedy this and the Human Rights Act means that, already, existing laws are having to be reinterpreted. If a person who experiences discrimination has longer than 1 year's employment, they may have a constructive dismissal claim. The law is complicated and is constantly changing, so always get legal advice.

Equal opportunities policies (EOP)

Many employers now have EOPs that include lesbians and gay men, especially public sector and large private employers. It is easy to find out before applying for a job what the employer's EOP includes. If the EOP is incorporated into your contract you might be able to rely directly upon it.

Trade unions

Think about joining a trade union, whether or not your employer recognises them. You will receive support and legal advice. If you encounter discrimination a trade union's support can protect you where the legislation does not. A number of motions passed at TUC conferences have made it clear that all affiliated unions should adhere to equal opportunities for lesbians and gay men. If your employer recognises more than one union, contact their headquarters to check which is the most progressive on lesbian and gay issues; some produce specific material and some have lesbian and gay groups.

Further information and contacts

- **LAGER** Help with all legal and employment related issues for lesbians and gay men. 020 7704 6066 (11am-5pm Mon-Fri) / Unit 1G, Leroy House, 436 Essex Road, London N1 3QP
- **Stonewall** 020 7881 9440 stonewall.org.uk / 46-48 Grosvenor Gardens, London SW1W 0EB
- **Rank Outsiders** Advice and information for people in the armed forces 0870 740 7755 www.rank-outsiders.org.uk BCM Box 8431, London WC1N 3XX
- **Citizen's Advice Bureaux (CABs)** Employment advice www.ncab.org.uk
- **Libraries** Details of local CABs
- **GLAD** Gay legal advice 020 7837 5212 (Mon-Thu 7pm-9.00pm)
- **ACAS** Employment advice and information 020 7396 5100 / www.acas.og.uk / Brandon House, 180 Borough High Street, London SE1 1LW
- **DTI** Employment advice and information 020 7215 5000 / www.dti.gov.uk / DTI Enquiry Unit, 1 Victoria Street, London SW1H 0ET
- **Trade Unions** eg TUC, Unison
- **Local Council/Authority** Contact for details of local CAB and employment services

debt and **credit** problems

Debt is an increasing problem in the United Kingdom, affecting people of different ages, backgrounds and incomes. The nature of the problem means that, once started, the cycle of debt and poverty can be difficult to break. Debt can lead to problems at work, relationship breakdowns, loss of personal assets, county court judgments, or in extreme cases criminal prosecution. Debt can arise in many forms, from credit cards to mail order catalogues, from hire purchasers to mortgages and not having a basic understanding of domestic finance.

Is this you?

Look down this list. If you can relate to one or more of the points below, then this chapter should be able to help you better manage your money, and help you get out of debt.

- Anxiety, stress and/or depression related to money matters
- Unopened or hidden bills
- Repeated requests or threats from your landlord for rent
- Ducking the landlord or sleeping with him to pay the rent
- Threat of disconnection of utility services
- Ignoring the telephone or monitoring calls from creditors
- Bumping into guys to whom you owe money – and making lame excuses
- Afraid to open the front door
- Worried about losing your home
- Wondering where you can get £5

- Dreading the arrival of the post
- Court summons
- Threats of legal action
- Threat of bankruptcy/liquidation
- Bailiffs at the door
- Income and tax demands
- Multiple debts
- 'Robbing Peter to pay Paul'
- Tax and VAT demands
- Avoiding the bank
- Never can get cash out of the cash points
- Withdrawal by your bank of services
- Turning to prostitution solely to pay off debts

When it starts to go wrong

Debt or borrowed money comes in all shapes and sizes. Properly managed credit can – and does – work for many people. But, we all have periods when it can be difficult to manage on the money we have coming in. That's life. It can be particularly difficult if we have fallen on hard times, for example, through health problems, an unexpected period of unemployment, redundancy or a change in personal circumstances – even a delayed benefit payment can seem to tip the balance against us. But, ever hopeful that the money will somehow 'miraculously appear' or 'just turn up', the need to comfort ourselves and spend what we don't have can be overwhelming. For some, it's a comfort meal here, a small treat there and a few extra CDs. For others its 'plastic' holidays and party, party, party. Then it's a matter of patching up the problem with increased spending limits, new credit cards and ignoring the problem by spending more. It's a classic gay man's dream until is goes horribly wrong. This behaviour triggers the debt problem from which point we compound the problem by not dealing with it. These are the sorts of things that <u>can</u> happen:

- You miss regular payments, 'rob Peter to pay Paul' and take out additional loans which lead to multiple debts and increased pressure to pay it all back.
- You promise to repay creditors – usually unrealistic amounts due to fear/guilt/pressure – then break

promises resulting in increased pressure (e.g. debt collectors).

- This is followed by legal pressure: letters from solicitors, court summons (often ignored) court orders often leading to bailiffs' action and then agreeing to unrealistic repayments.
- Finally, furniture/equipment are seized by bailiffs, utility supplies can be disconnected, you can lose your home and face potential imprisonment.

Underlying this, there is often denial, depression, frustration and anger accompanied by relationship breakdowns domestic violence, deterioration of physical health, problems at work, mental breakdown... if they haven't already happened. It's a miserable and frightening existence and so sorting debts out sooner rather than later can reduce the likelihood of it happening in the first place.

Sorting out debts

When sorting out debts, the first few steps are often the hardest, but should soon make a difference. Acknowledge there is a problem and seek professional advice immediately. The longer you leave it, the worse the debts become and the more difficult they are to deal with. Eventually, you'll have run out of places to hide the post! Many local authorities and some voluntary organisations provide debt advice and the majority of creditors are prepared to assist you if you communicate with them. The ostrich mentality of sticking your head in the sand only worsens the situation and obliges creditors to take legal action.

Prioritising

All debts are important but it can be useful to break them down into priority and non-priority debts. Priority debts are those that, if unpaid, lead it to criminal prosecution and/or eviction. This includes, but is not necessarily limited to: unpaid fines, council tax, rent or income tax. Non-priority debts will be all remaining debts that may not lead to such serious consequences. It is important to note that failure to pay non-priority debts can still lead to a summons in a County Court, which, in the event of a judgment against you, may affect on your credit rating. Whether you're managing your debt though a debt advice service or you're dealing with creditors yourself, the following advice should be helpful.

Communication

Communication is the key to successful negotiations with creditors. Do not ignore their letters. Answer them promptly by letter or by telephone. If you promise to contact someone by a certain date, make sure you keep your promise and contact them even if only to tell them when you are going to make a payment to them or advise why there is a delay.

Mind your manners

It never pays to get angry with anyone, even when you feel justified in doing so. Always be polite and courteous even when being treated rudely. It takes the wind out of their sails. If someone is acting negatively with you and you react negatively, it always makes the situation worse. As a debtor your objective is to persuade someone to be sympathetic to your circumstances.

Don't take any nonsense

Don't take any nonsense from anyone. A hundred years ago we had debtors prisons in the UK. If this was the case now we would not have enough prisons to house even a small proportion of debtors. The worst that can happen is that a creditor will obtain a judgment against you and take money from you on an involuntary basis, which you can avoid. If you are being harassed by a creditor or a company employed by a creditor take the name of the individual and report them. Many companies have codes of conduct.

Get it in writing

Always create a paper trail. This starts with your records such as invoices, credit card statements etc. Keep a record of every telephone call, letter written/received and offers made. Always make a note of the date and time and to whom you have spoken and if necessary confirm all conversations or offers in writing.

Don't bluff

If you make an offer, make sure that you can fulfil your promises. Don't tell creditors what you think they want to hear. Tell them what you really can do and make sure you follow through.

Don't threaten creditors with legal action

Most creditors and their agents hear these types of threats every day. It is a form of stonewalling that hinders negotiations. Creditors are likely to become more aggressive and their standard reply is 'go ahead and file'. There is a way to do this indirectly in the context of portraying adverse financial circumstances, with an inference that bankruptcy is a possible alternative in the event that the creditor does not accept your offer.

Make your offer brief

Explain the reasons for your current financial difficulties and then come to the point and make the offer. Make the terms of the offer precise. Do not leave things open ended such as 'things should pick up during Christmas and I will increase my payments if I can'.

If you get into trouble

If you get into trouble after you have negotiated an offer and you can't stick to the arrangement, contact the creditor in advance. Attempt to send a portion of the funds you promised with a proposal to make up the balance, or renegotiate the entire proposal. Do not wait to contact the creditor until after you have missed a deadline for payment.

Protect yourself

If you receive court or official papers, protect yourself. Make sure you know how much time you have until a legal response is required to be filed with the Court. This is usually set out on the court or official papers. Consult with either a Citizens Advice Bureau or similar organisation or insolvency practitioner/solicitor regarding your rights or the means to resolve the claim without going to court. If you contact the creditors or their agent and start negotiating the claim, make sure the response deadline is postponed to a date that you can keep to. This postponement must then be confirmed in writing.

Be realistic

Always be realistic with your offer. Only offer what you can actually afford. Ensure you complete your statement of means as accurately as possible. Do not insult your creditor by overestimating your expenses, such as entertainment, dining out etc. The majority of creditors are fair and they will expect realistic payments within your budget.

Top tips for getting out of debt

- **Don't bury your head in the sand**
  The problem will not go away. The longer you leave it the worse it gets.

- **Do not be tempted by consolidating your loans**
  Take advice, especially on secured second loans. You could end up losing your home.

- **Make sure you pay your priority debts**
  eg mortgage, council tax, fines etc.

- **Contact your creditors immediately,**
  Either phone or write to them. You will be amazed as to how helpful they can be.

- **Check your entitlements**
  ie benefits, insurance claims etc, to work out your income/expenditure and an offer of repayment.

- **Keep a paper trail**
  Note every telephone conversation, letter, date, time and name of person to whom you spoke.

- **Do not accept rejection**
  Creditors are like any business, they are only as good as the staff. If you find a member of staff unhelpful, ring back and speak to someone else, you may be amazed at the difference.

- **Do not ignore court papers**
  Courts actually work to your advantage as much as the creditor's. The majority of court judgements are issued by default because the debtor doesn't respond!

- **Always attend Court hearings**
  There is no jury and you will not be sent to jail, (unless you are a criminal of course).

- **Disclose all information**
  Always declare all debts and income/expenditure. Do not underestimate or exaggerate your expenses.

- **Keep in regular contact with your creditor**
  If you promise to return a call, make sure you contact them before they have to contact you again.

Getting credit

Lenders use a number of methods to decide whether or not to give credit. If you are told you cannot have credit you can apply again either with the same company or another one. You have no right to be granted credit or to be given a reason why credit has not been granted, although some creditors may give this information.

Credit scoring

This is a method used by most lenders to profile their applicants. You score points (or lose points depending on the system) for certain criteria. Some are basic, some are very sophisticated. Things like having a phone, having credit cards, length of residence at the same address are all examples of credit scoring criteria. The lender is obliged to tell you if they use a system but not details of the system or why you may have failed it. This is because if you knew the criteria it would be tempting to alter your application to suit.

Credit reference agencies

A credit reference agency builds up information on an applicant's financial position from the electoral roll, county court judgments, bankruptcy details, payment record in previous agreements etc. The payment record may include details of other people living at the same address and their record may affect whether or not the applicant is given credit.

If you have had your application for credit refused because of information on a credit reference agency's records you can ask the creditor which credit reference agency it used. You can then get a copy of the record from the agency. You will have to pay a fee for this. You can ask for the record to be corrected if it is incorrect or misleading. There is, however, still no guarantee that credit will be given.

Bank references

A bank requires your authorisation before it can supply a reference on your account, and they are allowed to charge you for this, and being banks you can be sure that they will! You have a right to see the reference, but obviously this could delay your application.

Credit reference agencies

The two main companies in the UK that supply credit reference requests are:

Experian Consumer Help Service PO Box 8000, Nottingham N61 5GX

Equifax (Dept 16) PO Box 3001, Glasgow G81 2DT

Write to the above companies including your existing and all previous addresses over the last six years, including postcodes (which can be obtained at **www.royalmail.co.uk.**) Together with a cheque/postal order for £2.00. You should hear from them within 14 days with a detailed report of your credit history.

Common sources of debt

Credit Cards

A credit card entitles the holder to use the card to purchase goods and services from organisations that have arrangements with the issuers of the card. Holders are permitted to purchase up to a set credit limit. Credit is sometimes available interest free for a few weeks (except for cash withdrawals). Statements are issued monthly by the credit card company to the holder and must be paid in full to avoid interest charges. Payment is by monthly instalments. Minimum payments required are normally 5% of the outstanding balance.

Credit card budget account

The customer is provided with a credit card and a credit limit is fixed. Repayment is by fixed monthly instalments. This operates as a running account agreement.

Catalogues/mail order

Catalogue buying is very popular, not only for purchasing clothes but also for obtaining consumer goods. Catalogue companies produce a glossy brochure or catalogue featuring their products. Payment is made by weekly instalments until the cost of the goods purchased is paid off. This is generally a fixed-sum credit agreement.

Charge account

The customer is provided with a credit card and a credit limit. Repayments will be by flexible monthly payments. This is a running account agreement with an interest rate likely to be higher than other credit cards.

Hire purchase

A hire purchase agreement is a hire agreement that contains an option to purchase clause. It is normally an agreement where a customer selects goods from a supplier who then sells them to a finance company which hires them to the customer under the HP agreement. Payments are usually made monthly. The goods subject to HP agreement remain the property of the creditor until the final instalment and the option-to-purchase fee have been paid. Until this has been done the debtor may not dispose of or sell the goods and may be liable to criminal prosecution if this is done without the creditor's permission. However, this will often be given if the debtor undertakes to remit the proceeds of sale.

Mortgage

A mortgage is given by a building society or bank to buy property. An extra mortgage on the property, called a second mortgage, can be given, for example, for home improvements. The lender may charge a higher rate of interest on the second mortgage. If you do not keep up repayments you are likely to lose your home.

Personal loan account

The customer is offered a personal loan with a fixed rate of interest built in at the beginning of the loan. Repayment is by a fixed monthly payment over an agreed period of time. The interest rate on all the above is relatively high. You will need to check whether it secured or unsecured on your property or the goods purchased, eg car.

Loan sharks

It is a criminal offence to loan money without a credit licence. There has been a great deal of publicity about 'loan shark' creditors who charge extortionate rates of interest (from 500% into the millions), use harassment and threats of violence to enforce payment or take benefit books as security for loans. Any creditor indulging in these practices should be reported to both the police and the local Consumer Protection/Trading Standards Department but borrowers/clients who complain should not be named without their specific consent.

Pawnbrokers

Recent recessions have given this old-fashioned business a new lease of life. Goods are taken in as security and called 'pledges'. There is still a class difference in the pawn-broking trade. Those operating up-market and charging low rates of interest for valuable 'pledges' are known as 'city pawnbrokers' while those operating down-market are historically known as 'industrial pawnbrokers'. It is another fixed-sum agreement typically costing between 25% – 200% APR. Goods are sold off if not purchased back with an agreed period of time.

Store Cards

Most of the high street shops now offer credit facilities to customers wishing to purchase goods from them. If customers cannot pay cash, they are encouraged to use one of the store's credit facilities. There are a number of different forms of credit used.

Unsecured loan

A separate loan account is opened for the customer. Interest is built in from the beginning and repayments are paid on a monthly basis from their current account by Standing Order to the loan account. An early settlement rebate will normally be available where the loan is repaid in full before the expiry of its agreed term.

Bargain tip (and we've all been there)

'Don't borrow money unless you can afford to pay it back!'
'Don't lend money unless you can afford not to get it back!'

Further information and contacts

- **Citizens Advice Bureaux (CABs)** Debt advice   www.ncab.org.uk
- **Money Advice Association (England & Wales)** Free information and advice 01476 594970
- **Money Advice Association (Scotland)** Free information and advice 0141 572 0237
- **National Debt Line** Free information and advice
  0121 359 8501 (10am-4pm Mon-Thu and 2pm-7pm Tue-Wed)
- **GLAD** Gay legal advice 020 7837 5212 (Mon-Thu 7pm-9.00pm)
- **Libraries** Details of local CABs
- **Local Council/Authority/council** Debt advice and details of local CABs

body stuff

When it comes to sex, many of us are aware of our basic anatomy but we often over-simplify what goes on beneath the surface of our bodies. Some of us still talk about things 'down below' and while there's a certain quaintness about using such terms they are inaccurate and misleading. An informed working knowledge of the parts of the body used for sex can give greater control over what we do sexually and help put sexually transmitted infections (STIs) and other problems in context. For example, did you know that pain while getting fucked is often due to the cock 'prodding' nerve endings at the base of your spine or sensitive arse muscles inside your body? The pain will often go if you change the position or relax the muscles. This section takes us back to school to look at the areas most associated with sex:

- The cock and balls
- The mouth and throat
- The digestive system (arse and rectum)

The cock and the balls

The cock

The cock is made up of three inflatable cylinders of a honey-combed spongy tissue, two on upper side (as you look down at it) and one on the underneath. When your cock is soft the cylinders are like long flat balloons. The vein that you can see running down the top of your cock pumps blood into these balloons when you get an erection. Down the centre of the cock is the urethra, the tube through which we piss; more of this later.

85

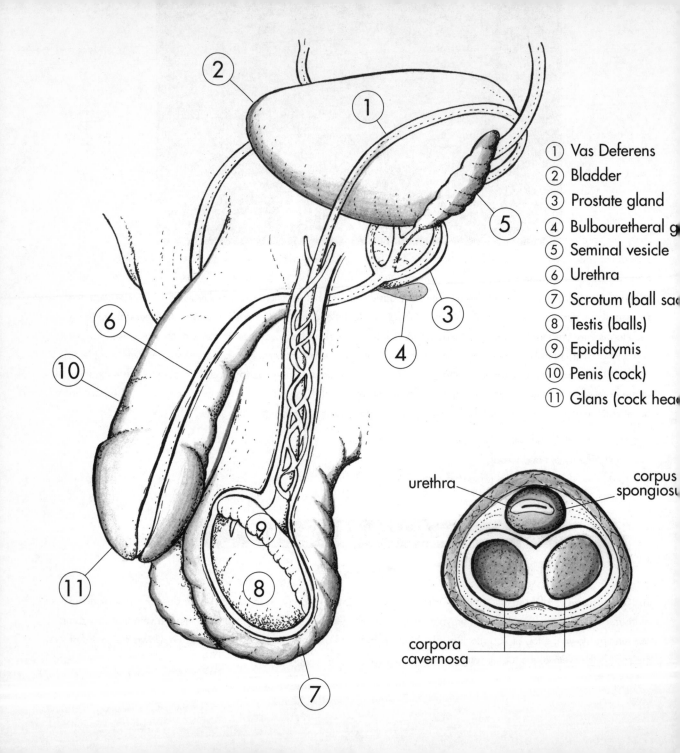

1. Vas Deferens
2. Bladder
3. Prostate gland
4. Bulbouretheral g
5. Seminal vesicle
6. Urethra
7. Scrotum (ball sad
8. Testis (balls)
9. Epididymis
10. Penis (cock)
11. Glans (cock hea

urethra

corpus
spongiosu

corpora
cavernosa

The foreskin

The end of the cock is covered by a sleeve of stretchy skin called the foreskin. It protects the cock while soft keeping it moist and sensitive. When we are born, the foreskin is usually stuck to it until we are about 3-4 years old when it starts to peel back by itself. By the time we are in our teens it can be pulled back and forwards without any problems.

Smelly white stuff smegma

Stale piss, bacteria, yeasts and discarded skin cells accumulate under the foreskin to form a white, smelly, cheese-like substance. This is called smegma. If it's allowed to build up, it can cause irritation and soreness which is why you should clean beneath the foreskin (gently but thoroughly) at least once a day. As a child, you may remember bath times where we were taught to clean beneath the foreskin as part of our personal hygiene regime (together with potty training). Having said that, Mummy didn't tell us that some guys are turned on by smegma and will leave it to ferment for days, even weeks before finding a willing partner to lick it out.

Tight foreskin phimosis

Some guys are unable to pull the foreskin back over the head of the cock without discomfort of pain. This is caused by a condition called phimosis and is usually accompanied by balantitis, a swelling and tenderness of the head of the cock. Treatment for balantitis usually involves antibiotics but in some cases circumcision is required. A related condition, paraphimosis is when the foreskin gets stuck in the pulled-back position causing pain and swelling. Again, circumcision is often required.

Some larger foreskins catch piss as it comes out of the urethra where it can then remain trapped and lead to dribbling when you think you've finished. Getting into the habit if pulling the foreskin right back every time you piss followed by a thorough shake and squeeze is the obvious solution but occasionally circumcision is required.

Circumcision

When men are circumcised (usually as new born babies) the foreskin is surgically removed. While the principle reasons for this are religious grounds and to improve personal hygiene, as was mentioned earlier, men with excessively large or tight foreskins are often treated by circumcision. Although the vast majority of American men are circumcised, more recently, circumcision has decreased in popularity and, in the UK, circumcised men are in the minority. After circumcision, the head of the cock loses its soft moist texture and becomes darker, tougher and dry becoming more like normal skin. Understandably, men can lose some sensitivity and it can take a long time to cum (not that it's necessarily a problem). If required, techniques can re-develop a circumcised foreskin particularly if the foreskin has been mutilated by poor circumcision. A specially shaped plaster will encourage the skin to re-grow (over several years) and skin grafts can also restore the foreskin.

Cock size

Well let's be honest, we're obsessed with cock size. Cocks come in all shapes and sizes, although they vary less in size than we would like to believe. When measured from the base to the tip (along the top or upper side) the average erect cock is 16cm (6.3 in). But, contrary to popular belief, the high majority of men fall between 14.5cm (5.6 in) and 17.5cm (7 in). Given that only the first two to three inches of the arsehole are touch-sensitive, a shorter or thicker cock can be just as good at stimulating those nerve endings as anything larger.

While big long cocks can have your arse poked skywards in seconds, they can knock into the rectum wall and sphincter muscles causing discomfort and pain. So the moral of this tale is quite simple: don't ignore smaller cocks and beware of bigger ones in the hands of dickheads who think they know what they're doing. Later on in the book describes how you can reduce the risk of pain and potential damage – and how to order him a taxi!

Erections

An erection (hard-on, stiffy, boner) is not under our voluntary control in the same way as we can pick something up or wiggle our toes. It is caused by emotional, physical and hormonal signals in the form of electrical impulses which pass near the spinal cord and trigger an erection. As we grow more sexually aware and experienced we accumulate a library of triggers or reminders which turn us on sexually: a look, body odour, being stroked, or the sight of a shaved head, for example. What turns us on is very personal to each of us, and during our sexual lives most of us will have at one time or another been surprised by something which, unexpectedly, has given us a raging hard-on.

When you get an erection, the cylinders in your cock fill with blood making it hard. Minute valves regulate blood into the cock when you get an erection, locking the blood inside while it's stiff, and releasing the blood back into the body when it goes soft again. There is also a misconception that as you get older you lose the ability to get or maintain an erection. It's true that it can take longer to get turned on, and that physical reasons why you might not get one are more likely the older you get. But many men don't see this as a problem and recognise that as we go through life our body and its needs change.

Curved erections Peyronie's disease

Some guys get an erection that curves. This is caused by excess fibrous tissue on one side of the cock preventing it from becoming fully erect. The expansion of the cock on the other side then forces the erection to bend one way. In cases the curvature is minimal and doesn't cause any discomfort or problems – it just looks as if it's got a mind of its own. Cast your eye back over a few dicks and you'll probably remember a few bananas requiring some oral massage! However, the curve can be so severe that it causes pain and fucking is not possible. The angle of curve can decrease without treatment but medication and/or surgery may be required.

Persistent erections priapism

A persistent erection – not connected with sex – is called priapism. The condition can be extremely painful and usually occurs when blood fails to drain out of the spongy tissue inside the cock. In some cases the cock will start to go blue! Urgent medical treatment at an accident and emergency department is usually required immediately. (An overly tight cock ring – which you can't remove – while you have an erection can cause similar symptoms. If it's made of rubber you can cut it off – carefully. Metal cock rings, however, are more problematic and the fire service has been known to have been called out. (Trying to remove it with a blow torch is not advised!)

Impotence

Not being able to get an erection is usually referred to as erectile dysfunction or impotence and, particularly since the launch of Viagra, men are finally beginning to talk about the condition. The truth is, however, that most men will experience impotence at some time or another. It's a fact of life, it's not uncommon and it's often temporary. However, it's important to separate physical and psychological impotence.

Physical impotence

This is usually the result of exhaustion, recreational drugs or too much alcohol but other reasons include:

- Certain prescription medications, eg sedatives and anti-depressants.
- High blood pressure and/or high cholesterol and heart disease.
- Other illnesses, eg diabetes, Parkinson's disease and multiple sclerosis.
- Faulty plumbing in your cock and/or traumatic injury and surgery.
- Smoking and /or being overweight.

Psychological impotence

If you can get an erection but not necessarily when you want to, the problem is likely to be a psychological one. Reasons are likely to include lack of sexual stimulation, fear of performance, low self-esteem, stress and depression.

It may sound obvious but if you're not turned on you're not likely to get an erection. For example, you may not find someone as attractive as you used to, or something which once aroused you sexually may have lost its allure which is one of the reasons why we experiment sexually. The significance we place on sex, performance and physical perfection creates high expectations – of ourselves and our partners – which can be impossible to meet. Consequently, a fear that we cannot perform adequately can affect our ability to get a hard-on, although it doesn't mean you don't feel horny. This can make the situation doubly frustrating. Physically, if we're uncomfortable with our bodies or the way we look, or if we don't feel good or relaxed about ourselves, getting an erection can be a major problem. Ironically, beauty is in the eye of the beholder, and what turns you off about yourself can easily turn someone else on.

Steps to solving impotence

Acknowledging that there is a problem is the first step. In the first instance, it can be helpful talking it through with a friend or your partner, difficult though this may be. Then, you should see your sexual health clinic, GP or one of the contact organisations in the back of this book. Embarrassment prevents many men from seeking help, making them miserable and putting strain on their personal and social life. Determining the source of impotence will determine the treatments, which and include changes to existing medication, prescription drugs eg Viagra and/or counselling/therapy.

The balls

Your balls hang together, at slightly different heights, in a small stretchy sac. Their purpose is to produce and store sperm and testosterone. They are positioned away from the body, allowing air to circulate around the sac keeping the sperm-making facilities at their best, 5°C lower than the rest of you. Your balls are so clued up and manoeuvrable that they have the good sense to pull themselves into your body when it's cold, stretch themselves away when you're hot and have time to enjoy themselves being sensitive to licking, sucking and smacking

Inside each ball are 500 metres of coiled up spaghetti-like tubing in which sperm are produced at a daily rate of 400 to 500 million. When they are ready, they are moved and stored for action in the epididymis situated behind each ball. The balls also produce testosterone, a natural anabolic steroid hormone, which increases at puberty and causes the characteristic changes, eg stubble, breaking of the voice, etc.

Cum spunk or semen

Cum or spunk is made up of sperm (made by the balls), the fluid in which they swim (made by the prostate gland) and a milky-creamy thickening agent (made by the seminal vesicles and bulbourethral glands). The fluid contains nutrients to keep the sperm alive and kicking as they battle their way towards the female egg – they're on a lost cause there then! These include zinc, potassium, glucose, and vitamin C which give cum its sweet, salty and very individual taste. As you're preparing to shoot your load, muscle contractions pump the cum from the epididymis, along the vas deferens, into the uretha which runs along the inside of your cock. Each time we cum, we release about 2-5ml (half a dessert spoon) which contain between 50-150 million sperm. When we cum repeatedly, we produce more fluid, less sperm – which is why it tends to be clearer and more liquid.

The prostate gland

Situated next to the wall of the rectum, the prostate gland is about the size of a chestnut, and is connected to the bladder by one tube and to the urethra by another. While its purpose is not fully understood, amongst other things it produces the milky fluid in which sperm swim and live (making up about 30-40% of semen volume). It also produces substances which give semen its characteristic smell and help pump the cum towards the end of the cock. It's packed full of sensitive nerve endings which is why getting fucked or fisted can be a big turn-on.

Piss urine

Our body continually produces waste some of which is filtered out in liquid form as urine. Each of us produce about 1.5 litres (2.6 pints) a day which is sent from our kidneys to the bladder, a globe shaped organ, which holds about 400-800ml of urine. Sensitive receptors send signals to our brain as it fills up which we translate as 'I need to piss soon/now'. When we're ready, it's channelled through the prostate, along the urethra, and out of the end of the cock through a series of muscles which control the flow.

The mouth and throat

The mouth is the beginning of your digestive system. The throat is situated behind the mouth and joins the pharynx to the oesophagus, the tube which takes food to the stomach. The mouth is covered with soft mucous membrane and smooth muscle generally resilient to bacteria and other infections. The tongue is a multi-skilled muscle which helps us to speak, taste and position food for chewing before moving it to the back of the throat for swallowing. But like, every muscle, it can grow tired with over-use and can be strained, which is why prolonged cocksucking can be exhausting and no longer a pleasure. Our tongue is covered in taste buds which can determine four primary taste sensations: sour, salt, bitter and sweet. All other flavours such as chocolate, pepper and coffee are combinations of these four, accompanied by the sense of smell. The tongue has three taste zones: salty and sweet (to the front and tip of the tongue), sour (to the sides) and bitter (to the back and centre of the tongue).

Saliva

The mouth contains three pairs of saliva glands: beneath the tongue, on either side and to the top of the mouth. Chemically, saliva is 99% water and 1% a digestive enzyme and (in addition to chewing) helps to break down and lubricate food before swallowing. Saliva also destroys bacteria to protect the mucous membrane from infection and the teeth from decay. Saliva is produced continuously to lubricate the mouth and to keep the tongue and lips moist. During stress, the production of saliva decreases to conserve water. A dry mouth contributes to the sensation of thirst and drinking will not only moisten the mouth but also help restore the body's water and chemical balance (homeostasis).

Gagging, coughing and choking

Sensitive muscles to back of the mouth detect sharp, rough or large objects and will trigger the gagging reflex to prevent them from passing into the throat. The coughing reflex also aims to remove foreign or unwanted objects from the throat and oesophagus such as large or sharp pieces of food, dust and pollen. Consequently, deep throat sucking comes with practice as you re-programme your brain not to reflex.It's also worth remembering that when we swallow, a small flap (the epiglottis) in the oesophagus usually closes the opening to the larynx which leads to the lungs. When food or drink 'goes down the wrong way', the flap doesn't close in time and we start to cough to get it out of the airway and back on track down the oesophagus to the stomach. Choking, on the other hand is when we don't get enough air and our body reflexes, demanding more.

The digestive system and your arse

Your arse is just the beginning – or rather the end – of your digestive system, which extracts nutrients and goodness from the food we eat. What's left is waste which we get rid of as shit. Many people believe that the digestive system is just a small tube linked to the stomach where shit sits waits for the rectal express to the toilet. In fact, from mouth to arsehole, it's a nine metre (30 foot) rubber-like tube, lined with muscles which massage the food and waste along, regulated by a series of locks and chambers.

The stomach

After swallowing, food travels down the oesophagus to the stomach – a 'J' shaped organ about 30cm long – where it stays for up to 6 hours. Here, acids and enzymes digest food until it becomes a semi-liquid soup which you have probably seen as vomit (with diced carrots). The speed at which food moves on from the stomach depends on what you've eaten and what's going on further down the line. Nerves which connect the arse to the stomach transmit messages to control the flow of food and waste. For example, you may experience discomfort or pains in your stomach if you are constipated or being fucked or fisted. Conversely, when you eat, you often want to go for a shit.

1. Oesophagus
2. Stomach
3. Duodenum
4. Small intestine
5. Colon (ascending)
6. Colon (transvesse)
7. Colon (descending)
8. Sigmoid colon
9. Rectum
10. Anus (arse hole)

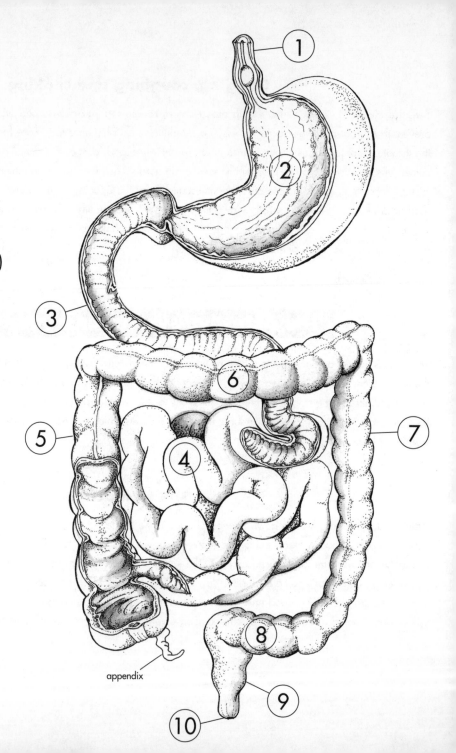

appendix

The small intestine

In a semi-liquid form, food is passed along the duodenum to the next stage of digestion: the small intestine, a long rubbery tube, 2.5cm (1″) across and some 6.5m (21′) long. It's here that the nutrients and goodness in food are extracted.

The large intestine

What remains resembles a rich vegetable soup, which passes into the large intestine. This is rather like an inverted 'U' shaped pipe which joins the small intestine at the bottom right-hand corner, near your appendix. This is made up of the ascending, transverse, descending, and sigmoid colons. It is here that the waste becomes more solid as the water and salt is absorbed back into the body. The sigmoid colon is best described as the final packaging and holding bay for shit. The rectum is the dispatch area and the anal canal to your arsehole is the main exit. By the time shit leaves the sigmoid colon and reaches the rectum, it is normally produced in discrete turds of a good consistency and reasonable size.

The rectum, anal canal and arsehole

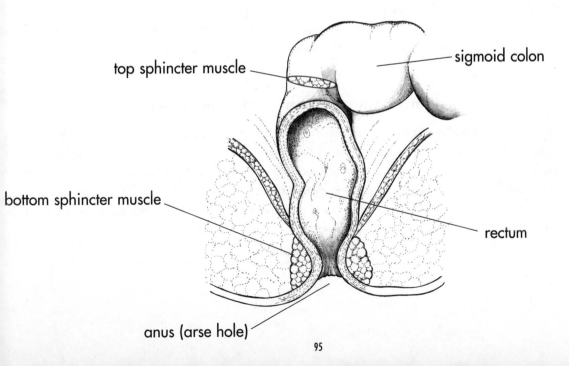

Around the connecting tube between your sigmoid colon and rectum is a ring of muscle that angles the tube in such a way as to close it off. This sphincter muscle regulates the shit leaving the sigmoid colon; without it, your rectum would fill up continuously and you would be shitting all the time.

Your rectum is a stretchy four to five inch (10-13cm) muscular tube that can stretch to the size of a clenched fist (when full of shit) or a hand. Below your rectum is the anal canal, 1-2 inches (2-5cm) long which ends in your arse hole. The surface of the rectum and the anal canal is usually covered with a thin layer of mucus or natural lubricant designed to help with shitting and which also helps offer protection from infections. If you rub the surface, you quickly exhaust the supply of mucus which is why you need additional lubricant when putting anything up the arse.

At the bottom of the anal canal is another sphincter muscle made up of two smaller interconnected rings of muscle. One of them is not under your direct control but responds to internal body messages when the rectum is full or when you cough – the muscle tightens. When the muscle doesn't work properly you leak. You have more control over the other muscle which you can relax or tighten at will. Try it now – you see control is everything!

Shitting

The weight of shit stretching the sides of the sigmoid colon signals the top sphincter muscle to relax briefly allowing a measured amount into the rectum. This is also called a movement. If you're ready to go and sitting on a toilet, the bottom sphincter muscle relaxes and lets the shit down the anal canal and out through your arsehole.

Sensation to enlargement, pain and touch

The rectum only senses enlargement and stretch, while the anal canal can sense temperature, touch and pain. This makes the anal canal more fun to play with than the rectum which will only notice if you stretch its walls. Above the rectum there are no receptors to sense pain or injury so penetration beyond this point is more risky. Located to the front of the rectum (tummy side) is your prostate gland, doughnut-shaped and about the size of a chestnut. Stimulating or rubbing during sex can be a big turn on which is why getting fucked in the right position can be so pleasurable. However, the prostate is very sensitive to pressure and harpoon guns!

Complications

There are many factors involved in shitting properly and some of these can go wrong. If your sphincter muscles don't seal properly then you may leak or shit yourself. Ulcers or a split in the anal canal may mean you get pain and a tighter sphincter muscle. If you regularly use laxatives, you may damage the nerve supply to this area and then either get diarrhoea or constipation. If you experience anything out of the ordinary or have any concerns, go to a doctor. Prevention or early treatment is preferable to suffering, or getting serious complications needing surgery.

Diarrhoea

Diarrhoea is usually caused by an irritation of the intestine lining or infection in your small or large intestine. Quite simply, your body wants to get rid of the problem and, if it can't vomit it out, it will shit it out as quickly as possible. The muscles which massage food through the digestive system go into over-drive (which is what can cause stomach aches, pain and cramps). To help flush out the problem, the locks and valves regulating the flow open up; however, this also means that there isn't enough time to extract the water from the waste and it's at times like this that your bowels just open to release that all-too-familiar brown sludge. Oddly enough, we sometimes underestimate our body's ability to deal with situations like this. Generally, speaking, it is best to let nature take its course – not forgetting to drink lots of fluids (containing salt and sugar) to help wash out your digestive system and prevent dehydration. However, if symptoms persist, get it checked out.

Constipation

Constipation may be caused by spasms in the large intestine, insufficient bulk or roughage in your diet, lack of exercise or stress. Shit passing through the colon, which extracts just enough water to turn the sludge into solid turds, can get stuck there and continue to dry out until they become hard and knotted. Shitting is then painful as the hardened turds rub abrasively against the walls of your colon, rectum and anal canal.

Haemorrhoids Piles

Haemorrhoids are veins near the surface of the bottom part of your anal canal that have become inflamed, forming pockets or mini-bags of blood. Initially, they'll stay inside the anal canal but can, over time, get larger and are pulled towards your arsehole by the downward motion of shitting. If constipated, straining makes them much worse. Sometimes they split open and can bleed, often quite profusely. Sometimes the blood work itself out of the bags back into the body and the haemorrhoids heal themselves. Suppositories (bullet shaped tablets which you slide up the anal canal) or creams (which you rub onto the entrance of your arsehole) will often alleviate the discomfort and pain of shitting. However, if symptoms persist, it's important that you get yourself checked out by a sexual health clinic or by your doctor.

Diet

Lowering stress levels, taking regular exercise and eating a balanced diet all play important roles in ensuring that your digestive system works well and is problem-free. Dietary advice to prevent constipation is based on the effects of certain foods being able to resist digestion. Such foods increase the weight (and volume) of shit, and are also able to bind water more effectively, forming a turd that is softer and easier to shit from the body. Fruit and vegetables, both cooked and raw, whole-grain cereal products such as brown rice, wholemeal bread, flour products and wholewheat breakfast cereals are excellent turd-bulking agents and the maxim is the more the merrier. Pulses, such as lentils and beans, are also known to be effective, although the novice may become rather farty and will need to adjust intakes accordingly. The addition of bran to the diet (along with sufficient fluid intake) can provide some relief from constipation, although this should not be a substitution for a healthy diet. Foodstuffs which are more likely to lead to constipation include dairy products, fatty foods and foods which have little or no fibre. If you experience pain, discomfort, if you're not shitting softish turds regularly or if you have any concerns – visit your doctor. Some GUM/STI clinics offer advice and information on diet and healthier living.

doing it

While our desire to have sex is built into our DNA, we must thank testosterone for delivering the goods. When we reach puberty the pituitary gland, located in the brain, releases gonadotrophin hormones which go straight to the balls and starts shouting 'make testosterone now!' For much of our lives, we produce minute quantities of this natural anabolic steroid each day and – amongst things – the breaking voice, the balls dropping , dick growth, stubble and body hair are all due to this little miracle-worker. There are several theories as to why we're attracted to men: some believe it's rooted in childhood while others believe that a genetic marker, Xq28 (the so-called 'gay gene'), has a role to play. Some suggest it's a combination of the two, while others say: what the fuck does it matter!

Feeling horny

What makes us feel horny and fulfils us sexually varies from person to person but several factors are usually involved. The fact that we are designed to have sex, the sexual experiences with other men, and the associations we make with them all have key roles to play. For example, if you had wild and horny sex with a guy who had a certain build, who wore a certain type of clothing or who had a particular scent about him – the next time you saw that type of chest, jeans or aftershave, for example, you'd probably be up there like a rat up a drain pipe! We make the connections that trigger the memories – even if it's a different man, in a different place, months or years later. We are not programmed to respond in certain ways but throughout our sexual career we accumulate a fantastic library of memories and triggers that help to guide us though pleasurable and satisfying experiences. Conversely, we should bear in mind some men can become understandably nervous if they recognise something from a negative sexual experience – they don't want to go there again and the associated memory is warning them accordingly.

Fetishes

A fetish is an object, substance, or part of the body that turns us on but which is not necessarily sexual in itself. Despite what you may think we all have them… or at least one… however small. The list is endless, and here are a few examples: aftershave, alleyways, arse cheeks, athletic men, beards, beefy men, beer, biceps, boots, trainers, boxer shorts, braces, calves, cashmere, changing rooms, check shirts, chubby men, clubs, cock cheese, cock rings, corduroy, dark rooms, dirty underwear, DM boots, dog collars, ear rings, ears, enemas, eyebrow piercings, flared jeans, gas masks, jeans, feet, fingers, goatee beards, hair, chests, hands, harnesses, jockey shorts, jockstraps, jogging pants, lean men, leather waistcoats, Levi jeans, nappies, nipple rings, nipples, nurses uniform, sweat shirts, piss, plastic, rubber vests, rubber, shaved balls, shaved heads, shit, showers, sideburns, silk, skinheads, sports logos, stocky men, stubble, suits, sweat bands, sweat, tall men, tattoos, thighs, thin men, toes, toilets, water, white socks and work boots. These are just the tip of the iceberg. You are challenged to find not one of the above a turn on! While gay men don't have exclusivity, we have used fetishism successfully to re-define traditional aspects of masculinity. Of course society sends a message that fetishes are unusual or wrong – even perverted – but that's never bothered us before. Just think of them as additional opportunities for sexual enjoyment. Fetishes can also encompass sex – guys who are turned on in a major way (sometimes exclusively) by a particular practice – sucking cock, nipple play or fisting, for example. While this may seem to restrict their sexual repertoire, it's a personal choice which they have chosen to acknowledge and use to their advantage and if they're getting the pleasure they desire – then that's their business.

Fetishes can also extend to dress codes such as military or skinhead uniforms, rubber, leather and plastic clothing. Clubs cater for an increasing range of fetishes such as big guys, sports and gym wear, rubber and S/M with strict dress codes to attract aficionados rather than a generic crowd. This can be disappointing because you don't have to belong to any type of dress code to enjoy fetishes! Some men wear the gear just because it's comfortable and makes them look good and because dressing a certain way will get them into clubs where they are more likely to find the guys they find attractive. As to where fetishes originate – there are theories about early childhood and sexual experiences and stuff like that, but a satisfactory explanation has yet to be found. Besides, does it really matter?

Sometimes it can be difficult to tell a partner about a fetish – there's always a possibility that they might laugh, find it absurd, be turned off or refuse to participate. Given that we all have something the reticence is understandable but absurd. It's a little like 'I'll show you mine if you show yours'… but no one's prepared to make the first move. While some guys will share fetishes it's more usual that one guy will have a particular fetish while the other is relatively neutral. That's not to say that the neutral party can't be swayed or intrigued but it's a considerate guy who is prepared to indulge his partner. If he's happier, then you're happier and you both get something out of it. Besides, who knows what might happen? The important thing is not to over-analyse it, spare yourself unnecessary guilt and be true to yourself. Denial can only cause frustration and disappointment although coming to terms and accepting what really gives us a buzz can be difficult particularly if there's a loaded moral perception that it's unnatural or not normal. While meeting guys on the scene can be a hit-and-miss affair, personal advertisements, phone lines and the internet provide increasing opportunities to be honest and explicit about what you're into and reach someone with whom your fetish or interest resonates.

Body scent, odour and pheromones

Each day, the body gets rid of two to three litres of water through two million sweat glands and so it's not surprising that body scents and odours occur naturally. Our natural body scent – often a musky smell on the skin – is an individual fingerprint of who we are. In moderation, it's generally regarded as pleasant and we respond and get turned on by the right scent in others. Body odour is when sweat turns stale – a reaction between fats and proteins in the sweat and bacteria that live on the surface of the skin. Having said that, some men prefer a strong ripe body odour to a less aggressive body scent.

Pheromones are substances released in minute quantities by humans and other animals, to affect behaviour in others of the same species. In humans this seems to be centred around attracting a mate. As to whether gay men can simply differentiate between male and female pheromones or have to re-learn how to recognise male pheromones (once the attraction to other men has been established) is uncertain. However, many of us can smell for ourselves the difference between our day-to-day body scent and what kicks in when we're horny, picking up, and having sex.

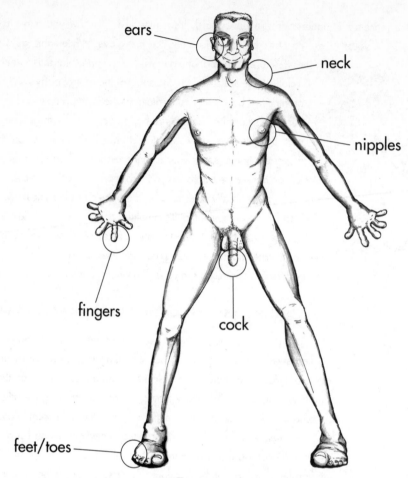

ears

neck

nipples

fingers

cock

feet/toes

Erogenous zones

These are parts of the body – often associated with sex and sensuality – where higher concentrations of nerve endings are located. When these are stroked, rubbed, licked, nibbled, or bitten we can be made to feel very horny. These areas include ears, lips, cock, balls, nipples, armpits, the neck and spine, the soles of our feet, toes and the arsehole. When we get turned on our sense of sight, touch, hearing and smell become sharper, we become more aware of our surroundings and these zones play a major part in our sexual arousal. Everyone's a little different, and other parts of the body, which we might not ordinarily consider sexy, can also become sensitive and highly charged. Knowing whether you or he's hit the mark is usually not difficult: just listen for those sighs, grunts, groans and whimpers.

Kissing

For many of us, kissing another man is a powerful expression of our sexuality and identity. A kiss can signal a beginning or an end, a need or a desire. It can persuade, reassure, tantalise or hurl us into a pit of uncertainty as we wait impatiently for the little bugger to ring. While our kissing technique is as individual as we are, most of us learn directly from others. We can kiss someone virtually anywhere although the mouth is the most common place and the most complex to interpret. For example, does a gentle kiss on the lips say 'I want to... but I'm shy' or 'this is a far as I want to go'? Or, does a aggressive kiss mean 'I'm so fucking horny' or 'I'm taking control.' While different types of kissing usually indicate levels of intimacy, a gentle kiss at the right moment can be as effective as an aggressive open-mouthed kiss with tongues and tonsils. We're invariably communicating what we feel at that moment as well as what we want or desire next. Obviously, kissing is accompanied by other signals, and as we grow more experienced we learn – most the time – to understand what one kiss means in relation to another and what our intentions are when we kiss someone else. Like a longitude and latitude, that first kiss – whether you are in a backroom, bedroom or on a first date – provides a direction in which you can both go, at least in the first instance. Lips and tongues are extremely sensitive so, when you kiss, remember to receive, absorb and enjoy his attention. A long mutual deep kiss can often develop a satisfying rhythm of its own and if you feel you are inexperienced or could improve your technique, follow someone else's lead. However, there are men who don't like to kiss. It might betray an existing relationship or face them with the reality that they might be gay. Alternatively, they could have appalling bad breath and are just being considerate. You'll probably never know.

Noise

For many of us, it's essential to make noise when we're having sex. Grunts, groans and whimpers are all part of a primal language which communicates effort... enjoyment... pain... and more... It's a fantastic stress-reliever and we should never leave home without it! Granted, some of the noises might warrant a knock on the door from a jealous flatmate or a call to the police, but who cares? Talking dirty, however, is in class of its own. Remember that such classics as 'fuck me baby', 'get that ass' and 'pussy boy' can either electrify the moment or kill it in its tracks. Of course there are those of us who don't make a noise at all. You know who you are. You say things like 'Shusssh!' or 'Keep quiet!' or use pillows when we're about to shoot our load. You don't make so much as a whimper as you thrash around the bed or leap majestically in and out of the sling – but you make us ask questions like 'Have you cum yet?'

Nipples

Nipples are one of our erogenous zones and contain many additional nerve endings. When stimulated they can be very sensitive and become hard and erect as the body provides them with additional blood.

Tit play ranges from licking, sucking, and rubbing to pulling, pinching and biting. With repeated attention nipples often become increasingly responsive, give greater pleasure and increase in size. Unless you've been given instructions, start off slowly to find out whether your guy likes it. Moans and whimpering usually indicate you're on to a good thing. If not, it does no harm to ask him how he likes it. While moderate tit play is a real turn-on for many of us, a surprising number of guys (a) just assume it's what other guys want, (b) start playing – aggressively, and (c) don't think about how they're doing or how they're doing it. If you've got a guy clamped to your tit, ask him to slow down and tell him how you like it. If he won't give up: push him off, they're not radio buttons.

Some guys have their nipples pierced with rings or bars, which can increase sensitivity or be purely decorative. They have been known to be swallowed by eager partners but they usually pass through the digestive system without any problems and a reassuring clunk 12 hours later. If you have any concerns – get yourself to an accident and emergency department. If you've got nothing better to do – buy a metal detector.

For some guys, the more attention their nipples receive the more they want and it can quite a revelation to discover how hard he wants you to play with them. More advanced play will include tit clamps, which pinch the nipples tightly, or stimulation with extremes of heat and cold. However, over a period of years, overuse often leaves nipples looking more like cow's udders rather than pert tits. You've been warned.

Massage

Massage is a powerful relaxation technique which involves rubbing, stroking and kneading the body, particularly muscle areas which accumulate tension. For example, head massages can relieve tension headaches and a foot massage can make you feet feel wonderful. While qualified masseurs will maintain (quite rightly) that it is a skill in its own right, massage can also be a big turn-on and a sensual prelude to sex.

In our desire to get our rocks off, we can sometimes forget the intimate pleasure gained from getting to know someone's body without fucking them rigid... well at least not immediately. And so, given its benefits to de-stress, relax and produce a positive feeling of well being, its not surprising that massage is used to set the mood. Buy some massage oil available from chemists, the Body Shop, and some health shops. Experiment with different scented oils. Bear in mind that once massaged you will pong (lovely though this may be). Oils damage condoms. If you intend to use them later all traces of massage oil should be removed. However, massage is not recommended if you have a skin condition, or thrombosis (varicose veins) and Karposi's Sarcoma which can be aggravated by massage.

- Keep some towels to hand.
- Oils can be difficult to wash from sheets and clothing and in some cases can stain.
- Unplug the phone, turn off mobiles/pagers and turn off the TV.
- Relaxing music will often compliment the massage.

- Be sure the room is comfortably warm.
- Dim the lights or perhaps use candles.
- Above all don't rush, take time. (If you're that horny just fuck him).
- Don't talk unless it's necessary but do listen to your partner.
- Your guy should be naked with a towel over the groin (tummy to thighs); if he's totally naked this can be prematurely distracting.
- Making sure your partner is comfortable, place him (in the first instance) on his front.
- Place a teaspoonful of oil into the palm of one hand and warm it up by rubbing your hands together.
- Where you massage is up to you but think about the scalp, head, neck, shoulders, back (remembering the sides which can be ticklish), small of the back, thighs, ankles feet and toes... in fact anywhere. But, if you're after maximum stimulation don't forget the nipples, ears (lobs), the soles of this feet and the cheeks and crack of his arse (without losing your hand).
- With firm circular stroking movements – developing a smooth and constant rhythm – knead and rub the skin moulding your hands into to the contours of the body. As you massage use different parts of your hands. Your technique should be purposeful but reassuring.
- Use your thumbs and fingertips to apply deep pressure and relax tense muscles, eg in the shoulders and neck. You should be able to increase the pressure slightly over larger areas, eg the back and legs, but don't push or leave your partner out of breath. If an area proves ticklish increase the pres sure or move to a different area.
- One hand should be in contact with the body at all times using your other hand if you need more oil.

Wanking masturbation

Wanking, jacking off, masturbation, beating your meat, jerking off (you Americans are sooo... funny), beating off, – whatever you want to call it – crosses cultures and continents and is probably the most practised sexual activity in the world. Past centuries have described as depraved, undesirable, heinous, frightful, unclean and abominable which all seem like pretty good reasons to get into it. Today, it is accepted as a natural, healthy activity – and don't we know it! Of course it has its critics, but they're probably still doing it behind the bike shed.

Most of us start wanking in our teens, sometimes earlier, learning from friends or books as we discover the sensations of rubbing and playing with ourselves or being touched for the first time by a mate. Some guys see wanking as

inferior to 'real' sex, but they have a lot to learn. Whether alone or with a partner wanking allows you to create and exercise your own fantasies. You have total control whether it's planned, impulsive, stress-relieving or you do it just because you're horny. Best of all, you can do it as much as you like. Your body will tell you when it's had enough for the time being – your dick will be sore or you won't be able to get a hard-on. There's no proper way. We all learn and develop our own style and it can be fab watching someone else. Techniques vary from tugging, pulling, massaging up and down, rolling between your hands, lying on your back, standing up, on your front, on your knees or on the toilet. Some guys may use lubricant or spit to help improve technique, movement and sensitivity. While some of us prefer to use a particular hand others are equally adept with both. Some guys can only jack themselves off. It addition to giving loads of pleasure, wanking can also familiarise yourself with your body, develop your sexual techniques, better manage your ability to cum or to hold off and practise using condoms. If you feel guilty about wanking, remember that this is usually the result of negative, moralistic prejudice which demonises a natural and healthy activity. Ignore all that – and just do it!

Cocksucking

There can't be many gay men who haven't sucked a guy off or been sucked off. Known also as a blowjob, giving head and oral sex, cocksucking is as common as it is versatile and can be done virtually anywhere and in any position. While it can be a prelude to fucking, it's also immensely satisfying in its own right. If you're short of time and fancy a 'quickie, you don't have to get undressed which is why it is often the preferred choice for sex in cruising areas and back rooms. Cocksucking should be a pleasure and not a chore and if you don't enjoy it (either way) then it's something guys notice quite quickly.

- Guys being sucked will usually send out signals to what feels best: grunts, groans, sighs... and verbal instructions if he's pushy.
- It may not always be possible to take a whole cock without gagging, a perfectly natural reflex to rid yourself of something 'stuck' in your throat. Eventually your body learns that in this particular instance this is an exception.
- An erect dick stands about 45° upwards and the angle between your mouth and throat is about the same. This is one reason why it can be difficult to take a dick in your mouth particularly if you're on your knees in front of the guys. If circumstances allow (if you're in bed for example) turn yourself around so that the dick offers less resistance in the mouth and throat.
- Cocksucking uses muscles that don't get much other use: with practice you'll last longer. If you get tired, take a break, have a Kit-Kat, and suck his balls instead.
- Your tongue can also stimulate the shaft and the head of the cock although some guys can find this overly sensitive.
- His dick is not a snack: ensure that you don't use your teeth. The cock is tender and can be scratched and cut by teeth, braces, and sharp fillings. If you're wearing dentures, make sure they are fixed.
- Putting a thumb and forefinger around his dick will give you some control over how much you suck at any on time. Some guys will just want to fuck your mouth and this can be uncomfortable particularly if they put their hands around your head and pull you (repeatedly) on to the dick. If you're not ready or if it's not what you want, this can be a real turn off as his dick plays jack-hammer.
- Knowing if your partner wants to cum in your mouth can be difficult to assess but if you hear pre-cum moans or something along the lines '...I'm gonna cum baby, take my load', you can take it as read. Such a warning allows you disengage – but get out of the way, or he may cum over your face or in your eyes, which will sting.
- And finally, some guys also like having their arsehole played with while they're given a blow job.

How safe is oral sex?

It's fair to say that the question of HIV transmission through cocksucking has given HIV prevention workers more headaches than any other sexual activity. While the risk is generally described as 'low' or 'very low', transmission has occurred. More recently, experts are now saying that there is an increased risk of HIV transmission from oral sex particularly if oral gonorrhoea is also present. Quite understandably, two of the most frequent questions asked are: is there a risk and how risky is it?

Let's go back to basics: for HIV transmission to occur, the virus has to be present and it has to get into the bloodstream. Your mouth is lined with a membrane which is usually waterproof and protects us in very much the same way that skin does on other parts of our body. However, we all get cuts and nicks in our mouth and there are times when we have sores, ulcers and bleeding gums, particularly after we've brushed our teeth. If HIV is present in cum or pre-cum, it can pose a risk of infection. So the answer to the first question is yes, there is a risk.

HIV transmission from oral sex is much less frequent than from unprotected fucking, but it's impossible to know exactly how much lower. Factors to consider include how much of the virus is present, its strength and the presence of cuts, sores, or abrasions in the mouth and throat. These are impossible to measure unless, by chance, you have a laboratory in the bedroom which is why sexual health advice on cocksucking is based on reducing the risk involved.

The following guidelines reduce the risk of HIV and other sexually transmitted infections such as gonorrhoea and hepatitis.

- Clean and floss your teeth regularly and properly – but not directly before sex. Brushing your teeth just beforehand increase the likelihood of bleeding gums or cuts.
- Bigger dicks are more likely to graze the membrane lining your mouth and throat.
- If you have a sore mouth, bleeding gums or mouth ulcers, don't suck until it has healed.
- Attend dental check-ups at least twice a year.
- Attend sexual health check-up at least three times a year.
- Don't let him cum in your mouth.
- Consider pulling out if you taste pre-cum.
- Bigger dicks are more likely to graze the membrane lining your mouth and throat.

Puttings things up your arse

The arse is one of the most sensitive parts of the body, and putting things inside it can be very horny. However, your arse is delicate: you should treat it with respect as something that you wish to keep in good condition for years to come both for sex and shitting. Not all gay men use their arses for sex – some don't and have wholly satisfying and fulfilling sex lives. But the majority of gay men use their arses for sex in one way or another whether it's a tongue, finger, cock, dildo or fist.

Why it can feels so good

- The arsehole and anal canal are sensitive to touch.
- The rectum can sense movement and can stretch.
- The prostate gland (which is very sensitive) can be stimulated through the wall of the rectum.

Shape, size and texture

Warm, flexible, smooth-edged and dildo-shaped objects which can slide in and out easily are the best things to stick up your arse – which is why cocks are so wonderful. With care and practice larger cocks and dildos and fists can eventually be accommodated. Conversely, cold, hard, rough and angular shaped objects can graze or cut the inside of the arse and cause bleeding, bruising and serious damage. Glass objects tend to break or shatter under pressure, and for this reason it does not make sense to insert light bulbs, glasses, bottles or chandeliers.

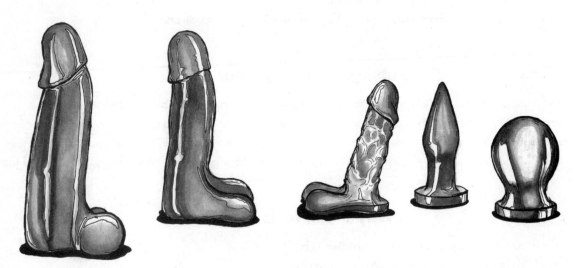

Force

Sphincter muscles are closed for a very good reason: to stop shit from falling out. They only open (usually) when we're sitting on the toilet. If we're to open them for different reasons, sphincter muscles need to be gently massaged, teased and coaxed open before they'll let anything through by choice. Obviously, there's a guy attached to these muscles who will want to feel comfortable and relaxed before he's likely to tell them to chill out and relax – quite literally. If you try and force a dildo, a cock or even a small finger through closed sphincter muscles, nerve endings will register discomfort – in many cases pain – and contract immediately. A classic example of this happening is when a dick is rammed into an unsuspecting arse taking the muscles completely by surprise. The pain can probably be best described as the 'pain of pains' and you can never quite work out whether you want to nurse yourself, hit him or throw him out first.

Loss and retrieval

All sorts of things can go in but not all of them come out as easily. When an object gets 'lost' up a person's arse, it's usually slipped into the rectum and the bottom sphincter muscle has closed behind it. If there's blood, discomfort or pain you should go to casualty immediately. If not, you may be able to retrieve it yourself by:

- Relaxing the sphincter muscles again (with lubricant and/or poppers)
- Massaging the arsehole to 'tease' it open.
- Shitting it out.
- Using a few fingers to ease it out.

Understandably, a person can be anxious (which can tighten the arse muscles) and may need to be calmed, relaxed and reassured. If none of these techniques work then you should go to casualty immediately.

Retrieval becomes more difficult when the object is an awkward shape – a little like a lobster getting into a lobster pot but not being able to get out. Vibrators can slip out of your hands and up an unsuspecting arse. The novelty value of buzzing your way into an accident and emergency department runs out very quickly and probably before the long-life batteries. Glass objects can be sharp and shatter and trying to retrieve light bulbs, apples, cock rings, and golf balls at 3am in casualty, ceases to be sexy after about two minutes.

Blood and injury

During or after sex, you may see a little pink in the lubricant or arse mucous. This usually means that small blood vessels running close to the surface of the rectum or sphincter muscles have ruptured. While it may be no more than a graze on the skin, there are no nerve receptors to register pain and you cannot see the injury to make an assessment. Consequently, all suspected injuries should be taken seriously.

While you should stop what you're doing, the reality is that if you're having a good time and there is no pain or discomfort it's possible you'll carry on – albeit with greater care. However, it needs to be made clear that physical damage has already been done. Furthermore, if gloves have not been used and your hands aren't in perfect condition, there is a risk of STI transmission.

If the blood becomes thicker or darker in colour – stop what you're doing immediately. No ifs, buts or maybes. If you don't feel the need to seek medical help, rest up and see how you're feeling in a few hours as it can take a while before you realise that harm has been done. Indications that there is a problem may include a temperature, persistent pain or discomfort, sweating, feeling nauseous or weak.

If there is pain, discomfort, nausea, or continued blood loss, or if you don't feel any better, go to a casualty department immediately. If you don't know where to go phone the police who will be able to tell you the nearest hospital; you don't have to tell them anything.

The effects of arse play

On one hand, in addition to the risk of HIV and STIs, putting stuff up our arse can mean a gradual reduction in the elasticity and co-ordination of the sphincter muscles which can result in permanent damage. This can lead to problems in shitting and incontinence. Certainly there are gay men with arses the size of the Grand Canyon which have probably resulted from over use. On the other hand, by taking sensible precautions, risks from HIV and STIs can be reduced significantly (or in some cases eliminated). Like many other parts of our bodies, with practice and care, we can tone up and improve our sphincter muscle control. Furthermore, by gaining an understanding of our digestive system and the workings of our arse, we are better able to manage and care for them and recognise problems. It's difficult to imagine us not using our arses for sex in some way and so, in the absence of any clear information about the effects of arse play, the following guidelines are a compromise between overdoing it and not doing it.

- Don't abuse your arse: treat it with care and respect.
- Listen to what your body has to say.
- If you're not comfortable or relaxed – don't.
- If in doubt – don't.
- Adopt good techniques in arse preparation and play.
- Don't do anything that causes pain or discomfort.
- Respond quickly to any problems or complications.
- Go for regular sexual health check-ups.
- Arse play is also thought to contribute to or aggravate Irritable Bowel Syndrome (IBS).

Sex toys

Made from rubber or latex, the most common dildo looks like an erect cock and is put up the arse for sexual pleasure. They vary in length and width and often taper from the base to a cock-shaped head with designs and contours which are often exaggerated. Butt plugs are related to dildos but are smaller, stumpier and less penetrating. They are a gentler option to dildos, and while many guys are happy with them, others use them as stepping stone to dildos named Maximus, Gargantuan and Jeff Stryker. Dildos and butt plugs have thicker bases to give you a good grip and make sure you don't lose it up there.

Since sex toys come in all shapes and sizes, you would do well to consider what you want to get out of their use before you get one. For example, broader based dildos tend to stretch and stimulate your anal canal. If you want to excite your prostate gland you'll probably need one that's longer. While they usually come with a base for grip, it's easier to keep hold of dildos with a ball shaped base.

Maintenance

Dildos and butt plugs are easy to maintain. (1) Soak them in a one-to-ten solution of household bleach and water for a minimum of two hours. (2) Wash them off in hot soapy water. (3) Rinse off thoroughly – you don't want bleach or soap residue up your arse. Finally, using condoms will reduce cleaning times.

Hands and fingers

Fingers and hands are sometimes overlooked as a source of infection and transmission during sex. Here are some tips to help keep the risks to a minimum.

- Hands should be in a good condition; skin should be unbroken and have no cuts, sores or abrasions.
- Fingernails should be clean, short, and filed to remove any rough edges. Cuticles (that's where your nails join your fingers) should be smooth and unbroken.
- Rough or dry hands can be softened with a moisturiser, although oil-based moisturisers damage condoms.
- You should wear gloves if your skin is broken or has cuts, sores or abrasions, or if cuticles are torn or split, or if fingernails are damaged, ragged or raw. This is because damaged or broken skin is more likely to provide routes for infection to get into the body.

Risk of infection

If you are sharing fingers, dildos or fists between arses or mouths (very possibly covered with traces of blood, cum, shit or piss) this can put you or your partner(s) at risk from STIs. Generally, we don't cover our fingers when we put them up our own arse but they should be washed thoroughly if they are then going up anybody else's. The same applies if you finger someone else first and then want to finger yourself. Alternatively you can use a finger-cot (a condom for your finger) with a new cot used on each partner. You may only be able to obtain these from sexual health clinics and chemists. If you are using condoms, your cock should only go up one arse with each condom. If there's more than one arse on offer, use a fresh condom. Similarly, if you're using gloves a new glove should be used with each partner. The same applies to dildos and toys. Getting into the habit of always using a condom on a dildo (whether you're by yourself or not) will also give you repeated opportunities to practise putting on and taking off condoms.

Irritants like soaps and laxatives cause diarrhoea, and their long-term use will damage your arse. Blood, cum, and shit may be infected with HIV and other sexually transmitted infections like hepatitis, gonorrhoea, syphilis and herpes.

Fucking

For the high majority of gay men, what we do with our dicks defines us and – love it or loathe it – fucking is inextricably linked with that. However, there is an assumption by many gay men that all gay men fuck and it's the sexual practice around which everything revolves. Even if it's true it doesn't mean you have to fuck or made to feel there is something wrong if you don't. There are guys have never tried it and really don't care if they don't, and some guys who have tried it and don't like doing it. There are those who think it's overrated or just feel that the risk of HIV is too great. Not fucking doesn't mean that you can't or don't have a fabulous sex life. So, ask yourself the question: do you really want to fuck?

If you're getting fucked you get the pleasure of getting your arse massaged from the inside and your prostate gland taken on an all-expenses-paid holiday to the destination of your choice. If you're fucking – you get to have your cock rubbed and massaged into heavenly oblivion. We can change roles and start again. Not bad really. It is emotional and we can be overwhelmed. It brings us together and we can feel as one. It allows us to dominate and to submit. It releases us and tells us who we are. It can be some of these things, all of them or something else. Even better.

Oh, I thought you wanted to fuck me...

If you're fucking with a new partner it may be sensible to agree who's doing what. Some guys use hanky codes and keys as a clue to what they want, but they're not always accurate. Some of us can be upfront and ask; others, particularly if they're versatile, will simply go with the flow. Granted, there is something to be said for not asking 'who's going to do what?' on the way home – it can seem planned, predictable, and tacky. Equally, if you only want to fuck or get fucked and your partner wants likewise then you either have some serious negotiation to do or you may as well put the kettle on.

Positions

Exactly how we fuck or get fucked is a matter of personal choice, although we usually have a favoured position derived from five basic positions:

- Lying on the stomach with the other lying (partially / fully) on top.
- On the knees (doggy style), bent forward, with the other kneeling behind.
- Lying on your back with legs raised either side of the other or resting on his shoulders.
- Both lying on your side one behind the other.
- Sitting on top (and/or slightly raised) of the other guy who is lying on his back.

Sitting astride your partner who's lying beneath you allows greater control, while other positions can make the person getting fucked more vulnerable. You can always change later. Make sure condoms and lube are to hand unless you have talked through the issues and taken the decision not to use them.

- To help relax you and your arse, ask your partner to lubricate his finger and gently massage the entrance to your arse. When you're ready, say so – he can then slide a finger into the arse hole and massage the anal canal, eventually putting two fingers inside.

- Sit astride your partner placing his cock against the entrance of your arsehole. At this point, he should do nothing more than nuzzle or rub the opening gently. Stay in this position until you feel suitably relaxed.
- Ideally lower yourself on to his cock, drawing it into the anal canal. This can be made easier by pushing down as if you are opening your arse to shit. It may not sound it, but this can be very horny for both of you.
- The anal canal can stretch greatly but will contract automatically when pain occurs. This will happen if he enters too quickly and it's said that a considerate partner can be gauged by the care he takes when entering someone. If you encounter any pain or discomfort, lift yourself off completely, catch your breath and decide whether you want to try again.
- Once he's inside you, ask him to lie still until you get used to the feeling of his cock inside you. You may to wish to tighten your bottom sphincter muscle around it. This can be an intense sensation for both of you. He may lose his erection – this is quite natural. Take time to help him get up some steam again.
- You'll probably begin with slow movements. If you want him to do the work, you may need to raise yourself slightly to give him enough room to move his cock in and out of your arse.
- At this point, the cock will be stimulating the anal canal which is touch-sensitive, and the rectum which can sense movement. Depending on the depth and angle of the thrusts your partner will be able to stimulate your prostate gland on the other side of the rectum wall.
- The thrusts will usually become deeper and faster but they don't need to. Develop your own rhythm and communicate to each other what you want.
- Combined with what's already going on in your anal canal and rectum, stimulating the prostate gland may encourage you to cum. This may be exactly what you want but you may also find that you cum too quickly.
- Remember you can take a break or stop at any time.
- Longer cocks will sometimes knock into the top sphincter muscle causing some discomfort or pain. Relaxing the top sphincter muscle will allow the cock to pass through into the bottom part of the sigmoid colon.
- If you're being fucked on your back, the cock can knock against some of the nerves around the bottom of the spinal cord, which again can cause discomfort to the person being fucked. Similarly, if the cock knocks into the prostate gland, the same will happen.
- Not everybody who fucks has to cum to enjoy them selves.
- If you're getting fucked, your erection may come and go. This is quite natural.

Barebacking

The term 'barebacking' first appeared in a 1995 edition of Steam magazine. In an editorial Scott O'Hara, a gay man with HIV, said: 'I'm tired of using condoms and I won't, and I don't feel the need to encourage negatives to stay negative.' Like a tinder-box to brushwood, a fire swept across the USA with accusations split between 'irresponsible idiots ' and 'condom Nazis!' – with not much in the middle – and it wasn't long before the issue jumped across the Atlantic and landed on European shores.

What's clear is that most of us understand barebacking as some kind of fucking without condoms. Most men use condoms most of the time. That said, condom-less shags are nothing new – they were going on before HIV, they will be going on tonight, and there is no reason to think they won't continue tomorrow. It can be difficult to measure up to expectations created by ourselves, other gay men and HIV prevention workers. If two guys decide to fuck without condoms there will always be someone who will be critical or damning. However, we should be mindful of their informed decision.

Some UK HIV prevention agencies have responded to this new word, producing campaigns and resources which talk about it. Unfortunately, this is a prime example of ill-thought out campaigning since a clear definition has not been forthcoming. If they haven't actually worked out what they really mean – how can they communicate their concerns intelligently? This lack of clarity has only served to confuse gay men.

It's too easy to think of men who fuck without condoms as stupid, foolish or irresponsible. Lots of us have lots of reasons for having sex without condoms. Sometimes this leads to HIV and STI infection and sometimes it doesn't. The point is we need to talk about our desires, fears and concerns, explaining what we really mean. Otherwise we risk talking at cross purposes and that seems to be what is happening at the moment. The barebacking debate is set to continue with plenty of fuel to add to the fire as some HIV-positive, HIV-negative and untested gay men continue to openly seek condom-less shags. We need to ask ourselves why we might want to fuck without condoms, what the risks might be and whether we are prepared to taken them.

Fucking without condoms

More often than not we don't use condoms:

- **Because of who we are with**
  eg someone we love, someone we think is more attractive than we are, someone we assume is HIV negative or HIV positive, like us.
- **Because of where we are having sex**
  eg a rush job in the club loos.
- **Because of how we are feeling**

eg 'when I'm sad I want him to show me how much he loves me,' 'because I'm up nothing bad can happen to me.'

- **Because of the situation we find ourselves in**
  eg 'he's taking the lead, I can hardly ask him to use a condom.'
- **Because we've been drinking or doing drugs**
  eg 'it'll be okay, anyway I don't care, I can't remember what a condom is!'

Often it isn't until later that we begin to worry about it. We can blame it on the sunshine, the moonlight or even the boogie, but whatever the reason, it was your decision.

So what could unsafe sex mean for you?

- A whole range of sexually transmitted diseases can be passed on by unprotected fucking.
- It puts you more at risk of getting, or giving HIV.
- If you are HIV positive, getting an STI is the last thing you need. They are often difficult to treat, they increase your viral load and put a greater strain on your immune system.
- If you fuck with someone on anti-HIV therapy you may become infected with a strain of HIV which is resistant to some of the anti-HIV drugs (and there aren't that many drugs available).
- If you are HIV positive already, it puts you at risk of re-infection with a more serious strain of HIV.

There may be times when sex without condoms is less risky, what you need to know is when and how.

Times when you might consider not using condoms

If you are both HIV negative, you might consider that you have nothing to protect each other against. But to be absolutely certain of your HIV status you have to take a test at least three months after your last risky sex; just guessing isn't enough. And even if neither of you has HIV, you might expose yourself to other STIs. You'll need to be completely honest with each other about whether or not you've had sex with anyone else, and this requires a very high level of commitment and trust. Think ahead and talk it through: how would one of you feel if the other had unprotected sex with someone else?

If you are both HIV positive, you might decide not to worry about the risks to your health from reinfection with other strains of HIV.

If you fit into either of these scenarios and accept the risks that they involv then, in theory, you could have unprotected sex with your partner. However, there are times we don't use condoms when we feel that we should. So what can be done? Here's a step-by-step guide:

- Ask yourself 'Do I really want to put myself at risk?'
- If you answer no, you are halfway there, you've made a commitment to the idea of safer sex.
- Now, think of occasions when you've had unsafe sex. What were your thoughts, and feelings at the time? What events lead you to think and feel that way?
- Are there any situations when you find it more difficult to have safer sex? For example, out cruising or with someone you really care about.
- Now you know some of the things that might cause you to have unsafe sex. If any of these feelings or thoughts surface when sex is on your mind, you could be heading toward an old pattern where unsafe sex is more likely.
- Think about how you would feel if you or your partner became HIV positive because of that sex. Would it really be worth it?
- When you're about to fuck, remember your thoughts and feelings about unsafe sex. Either tell your partner that you want to stay safe, or go right ahead and get the condoms and lube ready, make sure he sees what you are doing, or knows what you are up to.
- Put the condom on (him or you) before you get close to fucking, that way you'll be ready in the heat of the moment.
- If you have unsafe sex, don't hate yourself – learn from it. Think about what happened and see how you could change this in the future.
- Finally, if you find it too difficult to make your sex safer on your own, speak to a health adviser at a sexual health clinic. Many clinics offer counselling and support sessions for men in your situation.

There are all sorts of reasons why we end up having unsafe sex, but it's nearly always our choice. Our reasons are totally understandable but, at the end of the day, who is responsible for your health if it isn't you?

Douching

At a very young age we are taught to dispose of shit neatly and we are not encouraged to talk about one of life's messy taboos. And yet, while the anal area exemplifies – for some – everything that's dirty and unclean it is also one of the most sensitive and enjoyable parts of the body. Consequently, for many of us, shit is not something we deal with very well. Ironically, many gay men are forced to come to terms with shit as the arse plays such key role in the sex we have. There's probably been a time in our lives when we have shit ourselves during sex or seen our partner do the same. How we deal with the situation can make or break that hot date!

A solution is douching, which means washing out the anal canal, rectum and/or sigmoid colon with water. Although never fool-proof, it makes fingering, fucking, using dildos and, in particular, fisting much cleaner. Whether you're learning to drive, use a computer, or put in your first set of contact lenses, the first experience is often uncomfortable or daunting. Douching for the first time is no different. Like many things in life, with practice and familiarity we can get it right. Quite apart from cleaning you out, douching's a good way for you to get to know your arse, how it feels and works. While shit can be unpleasant to some people, douching helps to put it into perspective and over time it becomes little more than an occupational hazard. There are several types of douche equipment which we'll deal with in turn.

Hose (tap/bath/shower) attachments

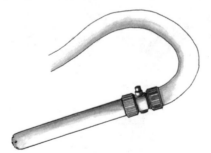

Hose douches provide a continuous stream of water under pressure and is an effective way to clear out the rectum, the sigmoid colon and further up. Attaching one end of the hose to the shower or bath/sink taps and making sure that the water pressure and temperature are correct, you slide the nozzle up up anal canal into the rectum and further as required. Unless you have any preferences, water should be body temperature to luke warm. Gauging the correct pressure comes with practice, but as a guide turn the head of water upward like a fountain – it should be no more than one or two inches high.

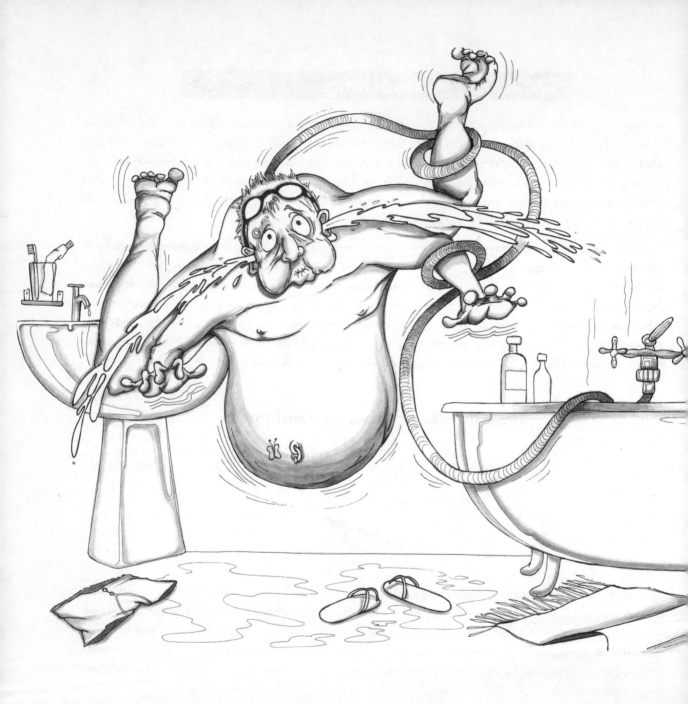

Some hot water systems are not able to provide warm water at this low rate of flow and the only way you'll get water at the right temperature is with a higher fountain. Just be careful. If the water pressure's too high, this is the classic way to perforate the rectum or colon wall, but this is very rare and monitoring flow and temperature will significantly reduce any risks. This type of douche (or direct plumbing hook-up) also runs the risk of unexpected changes which can be uncomfortable or even dangerous.

A hose is more likely to wash away the protective mucus lining your arse than a gravity or bulb syringe douche. Any infections taken into your rectum (eg: dirty douche equipment) or which are already present can be taken further up where they can be difficult to treat. Again, anecdotal evidence suggests that this is rare, but it does happen and good hygiene will significantly reduce any risks.

Many hose douches comprise a standard flexible metal hose to which a shower nozzle is usually attached. The shower attachment can then be unscrewed and replaced with a douche nozzle, usually aluminium, purchased from gay shops (£10-15). You can also use a 'Y' shaped plastic shower hose which is attached to the hot and cold taps, but controlling the temperature and pressure is more problematic. Furthermore, when you take off the shower nozzle it is not advisable to simply stick the pipe up your arse as the end of the tube can be abrasive. A simple solution is to attach the smooth-edged nozzle from a gravity feed douche.

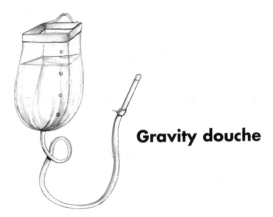

Gravity douche

Given some of the cautionary points raised in the previous section, gravity feed douches are slower but seen by some as safer. Gravity feed douches will clear out the rectum, sigmoid colon and further with patience. Douche kits of this type usually consist of a plastic two litre (three to four-pint) bag, a one metre (three foot) tube, a 12cm (five to six-inch) nozzle and a small on/off tap to control the flow. The bag is filled with lukewarm water and hung about two metres (six feet) on a hook above the toilet. The water pressure increases the higher you raise the bag. Gravity carries the water down the tube, through the nozzle, into your rectum. One bag of water may not be enough; to avoid running out, an extra jug of water is handy. As a rough guide, it takes about 15-20 minutes, but longer if your shit is loose.

Bulb/syringe douche

If you don't have facilities to use a hose or a gravity feed douche, a bulb syringe is a practical alternative. The size of a bulb syringe douche will restrict how far you can douche. They are used to clear out the bottom part of the rectum, although larger ones will clear out the rectum fully. This method is unlikely to clear out your sigmoid colon. The equipment consists of bulb-shaped container made of rubber and a plastic or rubbery nozzle that you either screw on or push into the top. They vary in size holding between 125-250ml (3-8fl oz). You fill the bulb with water, insert the nozzle up the anal canal and squeeze the bulb gently to pump the water into your rectum.

How far to douche

What you want to do sexually will determine how far to douche. The further up you douche the longer you will usually remain clean. Douching to the depth you require comes with practice. Factors to consider include the position of the nozzle, the amount and pressure of water and how long you keep the water inside before releasing it. You have sphincter muscles above and below the rectum and you need to bear in mind that there is sometimes shit above both of them. When douching the rectum, the nozzle or the build-up of water can accidentally stimulate the top sphincter muscle which may relax and let a dump of shit down from the sigmoid colon. This often means that you have to douche again. What was to be a 10-15 minute douche now takes much longer as you have to wash out the area above the top muscle as well as the rectum. With practice, however, you can improve your muscle control and sense how long your douche will take.

Staying clean

It's difficult to gauge how long you will remain clean. As a rough guide, a light douche (rectum only) may keep you clean for four to six hours. A heavier douche (rectum and sigmoid colon) is effective for up to 12 hours, maybe longer. Factors to consider include what and when you last ate, to what extent you've douched and whether you have any diarrhoea, irritation or infection. The digestive system moves everything along and will affect the time you will remain clean. Occasional muscle reflexes from the rectum to the stomach and small intestine can cause symptoms such as tummy upset and cramps which can affect the speed food is moved towards the rectum.

What to do

If you're new to douching be gentle, take your time and never rush. Follow these guidelines to ensure that you do the job as well as possible and keep the risk of complications or infection to a minimum.

- First of all, decide where you're going to douche. The toilet is usually the best place but wherever you do it remember that pushing lumps of shit down a shower or bath plug-hole isn't much fun and can upset hotel staff, flatmates or your mother. Some people find it easier to shit naturally before douching but this not essential.
- When you're ready to start, wash your hands thoroughly.
- You may wish to lock the door (unless you want someone to watch).
- Using lukewarm water will make douching easier and more comfortable. Let the water run through for a few seconds to make sure it is at the correct pressure and temperature. Make sure metal douche nozzles are warm. Using cold water is like throwing your arse into a freezer – the muscles clamp up and can send you into shock.
- Smearing a little lubricant on the inside of the entrance of your arse and on the nozzle end will help it slip inside. (As you continue to douche you might need to re-lube).
- Relax your sphincter muscles and gently slide the nozzle up the anal canal into the rectum. Without straining, close your sphincter muscles. As you feel your rectum filling with water, you'll feel the urge to shit. Without straining, take inside as much water as you can before relaxing your sphincter muscles to let out it out together with any shit. Repeat the process until you're flushing out clear water.
- You will probably need to hold the nozzle in place with your hand while you're douching. When you let the water and shit out, your hand is very likely to come into direct contact with it. This may come as a bit of a shock to you but, however, unpleasant as it may seem, shit is nothing more than the remains of digested food.

If you hurry your douche by perhaps thrusting the nozzle inside or banging it against a sphincter muscle, your arse will register the pain by tightening up or prematurely emptying out the water and shit. These spasms or cramps may mean you'll experience some discomfort but this is not so much dangerous as unpleasant. Your muscles usually settle down after a few minutes. When you've finished you may feel that there is some excess water caught inside. Depending on how much is there, the urge to shit it out sometimes goes away as the colon absorbs the water back into the body. Douching is never fool-proof. Sometimes you can clear yourself out and then find yourself wanting a shit an hour later. There will be other times when you'll remain clean longer than you anticipated. Practice and experience are your best guides.

Irritation and infection

Douching by itself can cause irritation as the water washes away friendly bacteria and the protective mucus lining. Rough or careless douching technique can bruise the wall of your arse, and breaks in the surface are more susceptible to infections which can be difficult and unpleasant to treat. Furthermore, if your arse is damaged, this can provide a route into the body for cum, blood, piss and shit, possibly infected with HIV and other STIs. You can minimise these risks with good technique, and by maintaining your douche equipment.

Keeping equipment clean

Ideally, clean your equipment before and after use. Flush it through with one part bleach to ten parts water (kitchen Flash with bleach is a good alternative). But remember, bleach or bleach derivatives can cause rubber to perish. Finally, rinse it thoroughly with water or the next time you douche you may flush bleach residues up your arse. Finally, make sure your douche is in good condition and check the equipment regularly for nicks or cracks which are havens for infections.

Etiquette

Make sure the area is clean when you or your friends have finished particularly if the bathroom/shower area is shared. If you've taken someone back, make sure they know where to douche, and what they should and shouldn't use by way of bathroom douche and shower utensils. (Remember the fluffy towels).

Recreational drugs

If you've taken drugs your ability to make judgements may be impaired. For example, you might injure yourself when inserting the douche and there have been horror stories of bathrooms resembling sewage farms. Better still, there's always the one about the guy who douched on acid and was inspired to paint the bathroom... the hallway... and the bedroom... a fragrant brown.

Fisting

Some of us get turned on by taking as much of a hand as far inside the arse as possible. Practice is the name of the game and – although you might never want to fist – almost everyone can accommodate at least a few fingers. To get a fist in and out safely does require more effort, time and concentration on the part of both partners. In this section the term 'fister' has been used for the person giving the fist, 'fistee' the person receiving.

While there are obvious benefits to fisting with an experienced partner, learning with another novice can be just as safe and horny. It's advisable to take some time to get to know each other, and to try and discover each other's fantasies. Whatever happens it is important for both of you – but particularly the fistee – to feel relaxed and comfortable.

Foreplay should never be underestimated in helping develop a sense of rapport, trust and humour. Codes or 'stop/start rules' are essential and should be agreed beforehand. 'Stop' from a fistee means stop immediately and 'out' means out, albeit very slowly and with extreme care. The important thing is to talk about what you want and not to assume or guess. If a person allows you deep into their body, they are putting a tremendous amount of trust in you. Be extremely gentle and cautious and take all movement slowly. Sudden movements can be painful, can tear the rectal wall and cause serious injury. The more you go in, the more you will find yourself pressing against your partner's organs, so take great care. If the fistee wants you to be up there, he will encourage you.

If you fist beyond the rectum you may encounter several problems. There are no receptors to register pain above the rectum. Perforations and subsequent bleeding can go unnoticed for several hours. You're more inclined to press against and bruise other body organs. You may damage the upper sphincter muscle so that it doesn't close properly (but still has to regulate shit passing between the sigmoid colon and rectum) which can result in leaks or shitting yourself.

If you're fisting...

Firstly, if you're into controlling others in sex or if your trip is power, then don't fist unless it is part of an agreed scene. When you're buried inside someone else, it's the fistee that allows you the privilege of being there. They are putting trust in you that you will respect their vulnerability and together create a combined energy that neither of you could ever create on your own. A good fister is totally focused on the needs of the fistee and is aware that each partner is different physically and mentally. There is no best way to do anything and using a particular technique on one person may not work on another. Before you start, choose which hand you're going to use. A combination of fisting and then wanking with the same hand could increase the risk of infection both ways. Remove all rings, jewellery or sharp objects which may cause damage or just get lost!

Entry

Cover your entire hand and partner's arsehole with a generous coating of lubricant. Then slowly press in and out with one finger. When there is no resistance, increase to two. Try using just a thumb, using its base to broaden the opening further, twisting slowly. When your partner is ready, gently work in three fingers until you find yourself in to the knuckles. Each time you come out add more lubricant making sure there's lubricant ahead of you. This will prevent drying out which can cause major discomfort for both of you. Initial opening up is often a slow process. Never rush, savour the moment and take your time. Do not assume that gaining entrance (past your knuckles) to the rectum will be quick and easy. It is often the greatest challenge for fisters and the most likely point when inexperienced fistees will want to have a break or stop altogether. Before gaining full entry into the rectum, find an angle of approach that fits most comfortably and try to avoid pushing against any bony structure.

Often the most sensuous moment of the session is the gentle slide of your hand into the cavity. If they take them, some fistees like their first hit of poppers at this point. Enter just as slowly as possible allowing your partner to savour the moment. Once inside, rest a few seconds until your partner's body has had time to adjust. To confirm adequate relaxation, it may be appropriate to come out completely, slowly and carefully, and re-enter again. Above all, be sensitive to the needs of your partner and you'll know what to do when you get there. Your hand is now situated in your partner's rectum which will expand on stretching.

Having entered the rectum you should curl your fingers to make a fist with your thumb inside, although practice will provide variations on this. Once you've settled inside, a gentle in-and-out motion (without pulling out of the cavity) will usually help your partner relax. Taking cues from your partner, allow yourself to be subtly creative, changing the speed, twist and depth.

As you gently work yourself inside, allow your hand to open slowly. Then go slowly – and gently – feeling your way deeper into the passage. Your partner will probably let you know with groans and moans whether to proceed or stay right where you are. Also he will tell you when it's time for a break perhaps having cum, or being sore, or exhausted, or just in need of a rest from the overwhelming experience and emotion. Sometimes you'll be the one who initiates the break, realising that your partner is overdoing it or that your hand is getting dry. Sometimes, you will reach orgasm or just run out of energy. Your break may be for a few seconds or may signal a major rest period, or perhaps your partner may have had enough for that session. As you become more experienced with each other, fisters will be able to gauge how much the fistee can take in a session. A thoughtful fistee will also make sure to see to their partner's needs.

If you're getting fisted...

In theory, almost anyone can take a hand inside the rectum although few people have the ability to relax enough to do it easily or at will. The technique is about learning to relax and let go rather than stretching the anal canal – allowing your arse muscles to accept entrance from the outside with the same ease they allow release from the inside.

Practice

You can loosen up by using increasingly larger dildos and butt-plugs. A more effective way is to increase control of your sphincter muscles by exploring your arse with your own fingers, (clean and lubed of course). Once again – practice is the name of the game. Explore gently, see how this part of your body reacts to deep breathing or thoughts of fear and relaxation.

Remember: go slowly, take your time and don't push. It's not a race or competition. If your arse feels threatened or attacked it will react in fear and tighten up. (As mentioned earlier douching will help familiarise yourself with your arse – getting a sense of where things are and their dimensions). With greater control dildos and butt-plugs will be more pleasurable and give you experience in stretching and taking more and more inside you. A fistee needs to remain relaxed which is helped by practice. Breathing deeply, rather than holding your breath, will often help. You should be pulling or willing your partner in so that there's no need to push. Sometimes pushing out, as if shitting, then pulling in can make a difference.

As a fistee you have a responsibility to let your partner know if you're okay. You should also be aware that your partner may need a break and has needs of his own which a considerate fistee will attempt to meet. If you sense or feel discomfort or have pain tell your partner to slow down, take a break or stop. It's your body – if it's telling you something, listen.

Pain could mean that you're going to be sore later. More importantly, if your partner isn't listening or thinks he knows better, question whether he's suitable and maybe suggest he takes his frustrations elsewhere. Ultimately, it is trust – the absence of fear – that not only makes taking a hand possible but makes it the great experience it can be. You also have a responsibility to let your partner know when it's feeling good. Support them all you can: maybe talk, moan or groan, or if you can touch him respond to movements you can feel inside.

Blood, soreness, pain and damage

A little soreness is common and usually goes away in an hour or so. It may also indicate that your partner went in or came out a bit too fast. The most common feeling is that your arse feels like it is purring (à la Eartha Kitt). Sometimes air will have worked its way into the system but this will feel no different from standard gas pain and will work its way through in time. Once the prostate and bladder have been stimulated, it's also common to feel the need to piss afterwards and often not be able to do so easily.

There are risks associated with fisting, including perforations in your lower intestine. These may be little fissures or splits or can range from bleeding to a prolapsed rectum requiring surgery. You should not underestimate any of these problems or complications. This is usually as a result of the fister being unnecessarily rough or the fistee being too drugged-up to recognise their limitations. A tear or perforation may not be noticed for an hour or two. Internal pain (that often increases over time) and/or undiluted blood is an indication of damage.

Don't hesitate to seek medical help immediately. Try not to be embarrassed or apologetic if you have to go to an Accident and Emergency Department. Although hospital staff may think what you've done is strange, they should deal with you professionally and will have very possibly seen it all before. If you have perforated your bowel going to hospital can save your life.

Afterwards...

Douching after a session is not a good idea as this can aggravate any minor cuts or abrasions. In the remote possibility that there are minute perforations or tears, douching is likely to make them more severe. After your session, you may feel the need to shit out the lube and any mucus, and this is not unnatural, given what you have just been doing. Take your time, and don't strain. You may also feel sick, drowsy or perhaps a little confused. Between heavy breathing, smoke from candles, incense, cigarettes and poppers you may have used up much of the oxygen in the room. All you might need is to open the windows or go for a short walk. Alternatively, you may just want to sleep! You may also feel hungry, so if you can, plan ahead and have something ready. Even if you don't have the munchies, make sure you drink lots of non-alcoholic fluid.

Watersports

Watersports, also known as golden showers involves pissing on one another or drinking someone else's piss. It also has the added advantage that you can usually piss more often than you can cum. Piss on unbroken skin does not pose a risk but pissing into the eyes, in the mouth or up the arse can pose risks of hepatitis and gonorrhoea if they are present. Drinking large quantities of beer or water will make piss more plentiful and will reduce the aroma. Piss can carry a strong smell and becomes ammonia-like if it's left to stand. High protein diets make it more acid, vegetables increase alkalinity, and eating asapargus makes piss particularly acrid and unpleasant. If you don't clean a designated area regularly and properly it will start to smell really unpleasant as it reacts with common household bacteria in carpets or porous floor coverings.

Points to remember

- You may wish to cover the bed or designated area with a rubber or water proof sheet.
- It is worth giving some thought where you do it and where you might be later (in a car or on a bus for example).
- Before you start, cover open cuts and sores with a waterproof plaster.
- Keeping your eyes closed and not taking it in the eyes or up the arse will significantly reduce risks from sexually transmitted infections.

Pornography

Porn gives us a safe, fun opportunity to get turned on and explore our sexual fantasies. There are many forms of porn: magazines, videos and written stories and, more recently, the internet and websites. It has been video porn, particularly, which has introduced us to live-action sex from which we can learn and improve our own techniques. However, we should make allowances for grim story lines, a disproportionately large number of over-sized dicks and seamless action which is a far cry from the reality of what we actually do. Today, video cameras allow us to create our own porn videos and can transmit live action across the internet. If you own porn or are thinking about starting a collection, remember:

- Magazines are for men over 18 years old.
- It may be appropriate to put any away porn when family visits which can mean pictures, videos, magazines, photographs and books which are easy to forget.
- If you have a camera connected to your computer (and left on) it can be activated without you knowing.
- Taking porn through customs is not advisable. If you're caught, it's usually confiscated.
- Be careful what you acquire – particularly off the internet. Some imagery, eg extreme SM scenes and child pornography can lead to prosecution and jail sentences.
- Think carefully whether you want to be included in a porn video whether it's for cash or through a sexual encounter. If you're in doubt, don't do it – or discuss it first with a friend (who will most likely disapprove).

Telephone sex

Telephone sex usually means wanking off while talking or listening to someone on the phone. For a time at least it became very popular as the ultimate safe sex but today, while it still has a niche, needs and technology have moved on. The numbers in the gay papers will usually put you through to a chat line or recorded story. While they offer uninterrupted wank potential their cost can be prohibitive and will be recorded on your telephone bill.

Sadomasochism

Some guys might be horrified if they thought they were into SM but if you have enjoyed nipple play, squeezing or tugging balls, spanking and giving/carrying out orders the likelihood is that you have already been there.

Most of us have imagined or fantasised about bondage, or other situations involving some level of dominance and submission. SM is about exploring and realising those fantasies in a safe, sane, consensual and fun way. Not all SM is overtly sexual although, for many, it is an integral part of sexual enjoyment and lovemaking. Traditionalists will probably say that pure SM is sexual excitement and enjoyment caused by inflicting or being subjected to pain. While accepting this view, sadomasochism is much broader and includes dominant and submissive role-playing, bondage and physical restraint, humiliation, verbal abuse and punishment. In some cases, these practices don't involve pain, but what they all share is the exchange of power between partners. Sometimes this is dramatic, at other times it can be more subtle, but the degree to which power is exchanged is not impotant so long as the experience is consensual and enjoyed. It is also said that SM practices involving pain heighten a sexual experience through the release of endorphins in the body. Many men say this experience is far more intense than that of 'vanilla' (non SM) sex. Punishment, torture, bondage, and humiliation are the most common SM practices, although they often they overlap.

Before you get into activities with an obvious potential for harm, such as whipping, torture, heavy restraints, learn what you're doing first. If you're interested in SM and don't know where to start, SM Gays is a non-profit making social and educational group for gay men interested in consensual sexual sadomasochism. Run by volunteers its aim is to encourage safe and lawful SM practices through sharing of information among peple with similar interests. Amongst its activities, it holds events in Central London, produces resources and information sheets and runs courses to introduce people to safe consensual SM. They can be reached by post at **SM Gays, BM SM Gays, London, WC1N 3XX** or through the internet at **www.smgays.org** (their website is excellent), email **info@smgays.org.**

Roles

Depending on the scenario or type of SM relationship, the active or dominant partner is usually known as the top or master while the passive or submissive partner is known as the bottom or slave. Some men have a preference, others will swap roles while others will only take on one. Generally men adopt these only during sex but, occasionally, two men may form a relationship in which they have taken the decision to stay in these roles. For the purposes of this section and simplicity the dominant partner is referred to as the 'top' and the submissive partner as the 'bottom'. The key ingredient of SM is the contrasting roles of a top and the bottom. Here are a few examples:

Being the bottom	Being the top
Being spanked	Spanking him
Being tied up	Tying him up
Having your nipples squeezed and pinched	Squeezing and pinching his nipples
Being fisted	Fisting him
Being pissed on	Pissing on him
Being a naughty schoolboy	Being the schoolmaster
Being verbally abused	Verbally abusing him
Carrying out orders and instructions to the letter	Giving orders or instructions
Being the patient	Being the doctor

Passwords

Guys usually agree to use a password which, when spoken, says stop and means stop. It may seem like stating the obvious but don't choose words like 'stop'. Often, during sex, we can say 'stop' when we're really saying 'slow down' or 'go on'. Ideally, passwords should be simple and non-sexual, eg: apple, rainbow, or Ann Widdecombe.

Experimentation

If you and another inexperienced man want to experiment with SM , go ahead. Just use some common sense. You can wrestle and spank each other to your heart's content and not get hurt. You can tie your partner down and wank him off. You can administer light pain with tit clamps or clothes pegs. Just remember that the pain that seems erotic before orgasm will feel like ordinary pain again afterward. Be ready to remove clamps and uncomfortable restraints quickly.

Hanky codes

Hanky codes evolved in the early 1970s as a means of distinguishing specific sexual interests and practices. A hanky or, more usually, a coloured bandana is worn in the back pocket of your jeans so that other men can see it. While the hanky's colour and/or pattern determines the practice, its location in either the left or right pocket determines whether you are active or top (doing it), or passive or bottom (having it done to you). Where this is not possible, eg if you're wearing a pocket-less outfit, hankies are usually worn on the left or right arm. If you don't want to pre-determine a role, the hanky is worn around the neck. Over the years, some of the better-known colours are used as code words in contact ads, eg: '…seeks guys into red'. Colours are also used in speech, eg: "I'm into yellow" rather than "I'm into watersports," although the logic behind this is uncertain. While so-called definitive lists are endless, there are a few colours, such as black, red, grey, brown, yellow and dark blue which are the most widely recognised and used today. UK and USA versions of hanky codes contain differences and, in some cases, contradictions. More 'obscure' codes seem to be more fanciful than real, but you never know. It can be difficult to see hanky colours in dimly lit venues or in filtered lighting that change a colour's appearance completely!

Colour/pattern	Worn on left (top, active)	Worn on right (bottom, passive)
Air Force Blue	pilot/flight attendant	likes flyboys
Apricot	two tons of fun	chubby chaser
Aqua	sex in the shower	same, cold water
Beige	wants to be rimmed	likes to rim
Black	heavy SM top	heavy SM bottom
Black Leather Gloves	fist fucker	likes to be fisted
Black Strap	strapper	strappee
Black Velvet	has/takes videos	will perform for the camera
Black/White Check	safe sex top	safe sex bottom
Black/White Stripe	likes black bottoms	likes black tops
Brown	scat top	scat bottom
Brown Corduroy	headmaster	student
Brown Lace	uncut	likes uncut
Brown Satin	cut (circumcised)	likes cut
Burgundy	likes razors	like to be cut

Patriic Gayle

Camouflage	military discipline top	discipline bottom
Cat-o'-nine tails	whipper	whippee
Chamois	rides a motorcycle	likes bikers
Charcoal	latex fetish top	latex fetish bottom
Coral	suck my toes	shrimper
Cream	cums in scumbags	sucks it out
Dark Grey	rubber top	encase me in rubber
Dark Pink	tit torturer	tit torturee
Dark Red	two-handed fister	two-handed fistee
Dirty White	looking for dirty old man	dirty old man
Doily	tea room top (pours)	tea room bottom (drinks)
Electric Cord and Plug	electro/tric torture, top	electro/tric torture, bottom
Fake Fur	teddy bear	likes hairy men
Fuchsia	spanker	spankee
Gold	two looking for one	one looking for two
Gold Lamé	likes muscle boy bottoms	likes muscle boy tops
Grey	bondage top	bondage bottom
Handcuffs	steel restraints top	steel restraints bottom
Handy wipe	gives hot motor oil massage	wears it well
Holstein	milker	milkee
Hounds-tooth	likes to nibble	will be bitten
Kelly Green	for rent/hustler	looking to buy/'john'
Keys	negotiable	definitely bottom
Kleenex	stinks	sniffs
Lavender	likes drag queens	drag queen
Lemon	catheterizer	catheterizee
Leopard	has tattoos	likes tattoos
Light Blue	wants head/blow job	expert cock sucker
Light Pink	dildo fucker	dildo fuckee
Light Blue/Black Dots	likes black/Latino suckers	likes to suck blacks/Latinos
Light Blue/White Dots	likes white suckers	likes to suck whites
Light Blue/White Stripe	sailor	looking for sailors

143

Light Blue/Yellow Dots	likes Asian suckers	likes to suck Asians
Magenta	suck my arm-pits	likes armpits
Maroon	enema top	enema bottom
Mauve	likes navel worship	has navel fetish
Medium Blue	cop	cop sucker
Mosquito Netting	outdoor sex top	outdoor sex bottom
Mustard	has 8" or more	wants 8" or more
Navy Blue	fucker	fuckee
Oil Pump	Can give slime	receives slime
Olive Drab	military top/wears uniforms	military bottom/likes uniforms
Orange	anything anytime	nothing now
Paisley	wears boxer shorts	likes boxer shorts
Pale Yellow	gives spit	takes spit
Piece of Black Leather	gives leather sex	receives leather sex
Pump	pumper	likes to be pumped
Purple	piercer	piercee
Red	fist fucker	fist fuckee
Red Sock	foot fucker	foot fuckee
Red/Black Stripe	furry bear	likes bears
Red/White Gingham	park sex top	park sex bottom
Red/White Stripe	shaver	shavee
Rope	bondage top	bondage bottom
Rust	cowboy	his horse
Salmon	likes toes sucked	shrimper
Sheer Material	voyeur	exhibitionist
Steel Grey	gives hot wax	likes hot wax
Sweat Band	wrestling, no rules	wrestling, rules
Tan	smokes cigars	likes cigars
Teal Blue	cock and ball torturer	cock and ball torturee
Union Jack	skinhead top	skinhead bottom
White	jack me off	will do us both
Yellow	pisser/watersports top	pissee/watersports bottom

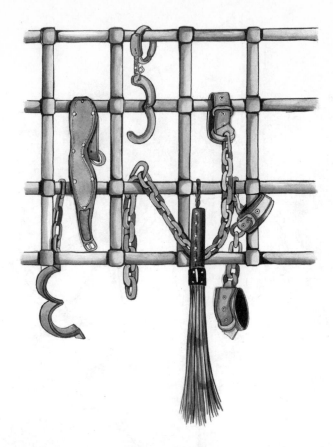

Further information and contacts

- **SM Gays** BM SM Gays, London, WC1N 3XX **/** www.smgays.org
- **Gay Press** Scene and club stuff
- **Internet** Search under heading, related words

dietand**nutrition**

When it comes to eating a healthy diet, most of us have an idea of the basics but are often confused by an endless supply of nutritional advice and the mythology of carrot sticks, treadmills and low-calorie foods. Everyone seems to have an opinion on what we should and shouldn't be eating and a new generation of health and fitness magazines for men – whilst broadly welcome – have created narcissistic expectations of what we should look like. Consequently, taking the first steps towards better health can be difficult.

- You may be disappointed about the way you look and feel, believing that it's just not worth it.
- Lack of time, work pressures and expense are common barriers.
- Brought up to believe that they should hide their feelings, men generally put on a brave face, even if it's at the expense of their health. Gay men are no exception.
- Gay scene culture perpetuates images of hunky, healthy-looking, fit men and for many of us the gap between what we are and what we're expected to become is just too great.

But... if you want to feel fitter, fuck longer and love better, a positive attitude and realistic expectations will help towards:

- Enjoying a better quality of life – particularly as you grow older.
- Better stress-management, work and relationships.
- More energy and stamina for clubbing, shopping and sex.
- A lower risk of heart disease and some common cancers.
- Stronger, more toned muscles for a more active life.

So don't feel left out or feel that being healthy is reserved for brain-dead Muscle Marys. This chapter provides some common-sense stuff to help you get there.

lots of these

lots of these

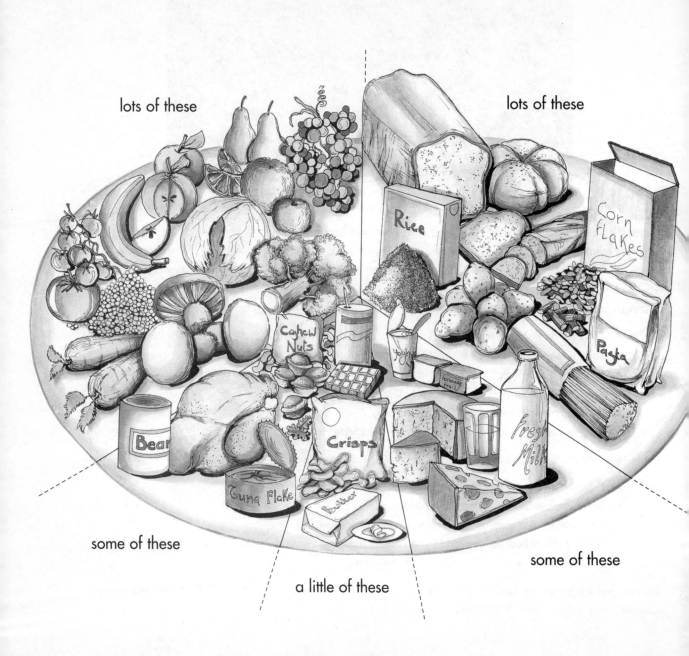

Rice

Corn Flakes

Pasta

Beans

Cashew Nuts

yoghurt

roman fruit

Crisps

Fresh Milk

Tuna Flake

Butter

some of these

a little of these

some of these

We need the energy provided by food to keep the organs and cells in the body alive and active and to supply the raw materials used for growth, maintenance and repair. A healthy diet provides the right combination, quantity and quality of food to achieve this and supplies the necessary nutrients to maximise physical, mental, emotional and spiritual health. Conversely, an unhealthy diet means eating too much of the wrong combination of foods or taking in more food than the body needs. Excess energy is then stored as fat, and while it isn't neccessarily a bad thing – it's needed for insulation and an energy reserve – but you need to have the right amount. Common storage areas include the stomach, waist and arse. But what you can't see is the excess fat that is carried in the blood and which can clog up the arteries of the heart, making it more difficult to pump blood around the body.

Fat is also attracted to internal organs such as the heart, making it harder fror them to work efficiently. Combined with other factors, a diet that is too high in fat can lead to obesity, heart disease, diabetes and sleep problems. Conversely, those people who eat too little (or whose diet doesn't contain enough of the right nutrients) can feel tired at best, and at worst become malnourished.

Our relationship with food is lifelong and what we eat is influenced by years of programming which affects our body shape, day-to-day health and social lives. While food should be enjoyed, what we eat, how much we eat and when we eat are also powerful responses to our emotions. When we're unhappy, stressed, depressed, or lack confidence, food can be the great comforter. It's instantaneous and you can eat what you want when you want. Unfortunately the comfort factor is usually short lived and the guilt and misery which follows often perpetuates a common cycle: I don't like the way I look… I feel miserable… I eat to comfort myself… I don't like the way I look, etc. This example is one of a range of behaviours that includes binge-eating, excessive dieting or excessive physical exercise. The two most common disorders are anorexia nervosa and bulimia. Anorexia nervosa is characterised by severe weight loss, the avoidance of food and an intense fear of becoming fat. Bulemia sufferers typically binge-eat and then induce vomiting; however, the condition can also include laxative abuse and extreme or excessive excercising. While both conditions are often associated with women, they can also affect men. We can become quite expert in punishing ourselves for not being what we think we ought to be. Perhaps surprisingly, this applies whether we think we're overweight or feel that we already looking great but should look better.

If you're used to eating what you like and have never had any warning signs or symptoms, the motivation to change the habits of a lifetime may seem exaggerated and unnecessary. Furthermore, if you think you're in relatively good shape now – whatever your age and whether you exercise or not – you probably believe you'll be as you are now in ten, 20 or 30 years. It's possible, but it's more likely, that you'll have less energy for clubbing and sex, less confidence, feel less attractive to yourself and others, be more stressed, have reduced physical stamina and a less enjoyable quality of life. Then, of course, there's the increased risk of obesity, heart disease, cancer, diabetes and sleep problems. Bit of a bummer really but it's your call. Combined with regular exercise, even moderate changes now will help you achieve the benefits detailed at the start of this section.

What the body needs

In order for the body to function efficiently, it needs:

- **Protein** for body growth, maintenance and repair. Protein also provides the raw materials for tissues and fluids and helps maintain the chemical balance in the brain, spine and intestine. Sources of protein include meat, dairy products, eggs, fish, chicken, pulses, nuts and seeds.
- **Carbohydrates** provide the body's main source of energy. Carbohydrates exist in two different types: simple sugars and complex carbohydrates such as starch. The majority of the diet should be made up of the latter. Sources of these include bread, pasta, rice, fruit, potatoes and other vegetables, and pulses.
- **Fat** provides essential fatty acids for production of substances such as hormones and heat and is used as a concentrated energy source. Fat is found in most foods although butter, cheese, lard, margarine and oil all have exceptionally high fat contents.
- **Fibre** has almost no nutritional value but has several key functions. It helps the digestive system

absorb water from food and bulks shit so that it can pass more easily through the body. Foods containing fibre fill you up without piling on the calories. It can also help in lowering fat levels in the blood. Sources of fibre include wholegrain bread, cereal, oats, fresh fruit and vegetables and pulses.

- **Vitamins** are essential to tissue-building, hormones, nerve and muscle function and protection against illness and disease. Needed in small quantities, they are vital to the diet because they cannot be made by the body. Most foods are packed with vitamins but many of them increasingly lose their value the more the food is refined and cooked.
- **Minerals** help regulate the body's water balance, and the acidity level of body fluids. They assist in body growth and repair. Like vitamins, they are needed in small quantities but are usually found in most foods although they lose their value the more they are cooked.
- **Water** is the body's most important component, in that it makes up nearly two thirds of our bodies. All organs and tissues are dependent on water, and, without sufficient quantities they will stop working. Blood, which is made up mainly of water carries dissolved nutrients and oxygen to the body's tissues and carries away waste products including carbon dioxide.

So, to meet the body's nutritional requirements, your diet should ideally contain a balanced mix of foods from the following groups and approximately two litres of water taken throughout the day

Fruit and vegetables – ideally five portions a day	**30**
Bread (preferably wholemeal) pasta and rice – eat plenty of these, making them the main part of every meal	**30**
Milk and dairy foods – eat moderate amounts choosing lower fat versions whenever you can	**15**
A balance of meat (white rather than red) and fish, and/or eggs lentils, pulses, nuts and textured vegetable protein (TVP) – eat moderate amounts whenever you can	**15**
Foods high in fat and sugar – eat these in small amounts or not very often	**10**
	100%

You may also find the 'traffic light' guide helpful when making changes to your diet. You can eat as many green foods as you like, yellow foods should be eaten in moderation (choosing lower fat versions wherever possible) and red foods should be avoided or eaten sparingly. Wherever possible choose lower fat, wholemeal and organic products.

Green foods

Apples, beans, beetroot, cabbage, carrots, cauliflower, cottage, cucumber, fish, fruit, fresh herbs, lentils, lettuce , mange-tout, sugar snaps, skimmed milk, mushrooms, onions, peas, peppers, sweetcorn, tomatoes, spinach, bread, pasta, bananas, cereals, dried fruit, fruit juice (unsweetened), rice.

Yellow foods

Avocado, baked beans (unsweetened), cheese, honey, semi-skimmed milk, mayonnaise (low fat/diet), nuts (unsalted), potatoes, meat (red and white), semi-skimmed milk, pulses, eggs, prawns, cheese, yoghurt (low fat).

Red foods

Alcohol, bacon, biscuits, butter, cakes, canned drinks, cereals (sweetened), chips, chocolate, cream, crisps, doughnuts, fatty meat, fried foods, fruit juice (sweetened), full-cream milk, ice cream, jams or conserves, marmalade, mayonnaise, oily salad dressings, pastry, paté, peanut butter, puddings, salad cream, salami, salted nuts, sauces, sausages, sour cream, sugar, sweets, syrup.

Daily calorie requirements and food allowances

The basic unit for measuring energy is the scientist's calorie. This is the amount of energy needed to raise the temperature of one cubic centimetre of water by 1° centigrade. When talking about food and human energy, the measurement most commonly used is the kilocalorie – 1000 times greater – often written as kcal or calorie. Kilojoule (kJ) is the international unit of energy. Approximately 4200 joules or 4.2 kilojoules is equal to one kilocalorie. These measurements are used to provide the nutritional information found on the back of food packets.

The chart on the next page shows the daily calorie requirements for men who lead inactive, active and very active lives. For example: a 25 year old will need about 2500 calories a day if he doesn't exercise and a 40 year old man will need about 2900 if he leads an active life. However, these are average values. The daily calorie requirement depends on a number of factors including your height, weight, age and body composition (how much muscle compared to fat you have) and your activity level through the day.

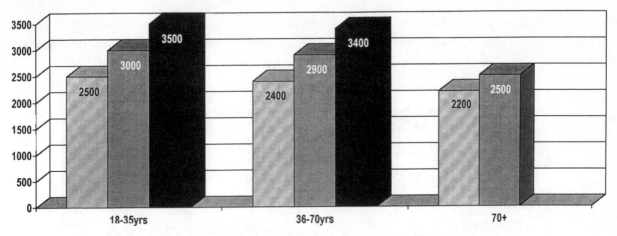

□ Inactive: sits at a desk all day, watches TV at every opportunity and does fuck all exercise
▨ Active: takes exercise at least 3 days a week and dances when clubbing
■ Very active: loves exercising and/ or gym bunny, dance crazy and fucks for hours... bless

Advice as to how much of any one food type we should eat varies, but the following can be used as a guide:

- 18-25g of fibre.
- 70-80g of fat.
- 55g of protein.
- 50g of carbohydrates
- 5g of salt.
- 1-2 litres of water.

Minerals and vitamins should be included in the food you eat although occasionally supplements are required.

Nutritional information

Many foods today are labelled with nutritional information and usually include energy (kcal/calorie), protein, carbohydrate, fat, fibre and sodium (salt) content. Below are two examples of the type of information you are likely to find.

250g Pack of Butter

NUTRITIONAL INFORMATION	
Typical values per 100g	
Energy	2970kJ/720kcal
Protein	0.4g
Carbohydrate	Trace
Fibre	Nil
Fat	80g

375g of Breakfast Cereal

NUTRITIONAL INFORMATION	
Typical values per 100g	
Energy	1565kJ/369kcal
Protein	7.9
Carbohydrate	75.9
Fibre	6.2
Fat	3.8

100g (40% of the pack) of butter will provide about 720 kcal which is about a quarter of your total daily calorie allowance. Furthermore this is equal to your entire fat allowance for a day and provides no protein, carbohydrate or fibre. It may taste yummy but almost all of it will head for the waist. Alternatively, 100g (a bowlful) of cereal will provide about 369 kcal which is about 12% of your total calorie allowance – it's low in fat (3.8g) and provides 15% fibre, 14% protein, vitamins and minerals – and is within your daily allowance of carbohydrate (75%). Unfortunately, a good dollop of cooking oil can provide 30% of your total calorie allowance and that's before you've even taken into account the food. It's easy to pile on the calories and fat without knowing it or thinking that a little here and a little there doesn't make a difference.

Food should be pleasurable...

It's important not to get carried away with figures. A healthy diet is a balance of the food groups detailed earlier and the 'traffic-light' chart can help you decide which choices to make. There is no doubt that nutritional information can be helpful in telling you whether you're overdoing it or not, but once you start depending on the figures the 'science' can take over the fun of enjoying your food and experimenting.

A little bit about fats

Fats can be very confusing but in short there are good and bad fats and generally we tend to eat too much saturated fats which are not good for us. There are different types of fat which affect us in different ways:

- **Saturated fats** are not required by the body because it makes its own. However, they do add flavour to foods such as butter, cheese, lard, fatty meats, bacon, sausages, cakes and chocolates - which is why we like them. Unfortunately, too much can lead to obesity, heart disease and cancer.
- **Trans fats** are not essential in the diet and are found in foods such as meat and meat products, dairy products, processed or refined foods such as crisps, biscuits, cakes, savoury pies, and margarines. These fats in processed foods have been linked to heart disease. Frying food in re-used cooking fats/oils will generate an increasing amount of trans fats which are not good for you.
- **Monounsaturated fats** can have a beneficial effect on blood cholestrol levels when replacing saturated fats. Examples include olive oil, rapeseed oil, avocados, nuts and seeds.
- **Polyunsaturated fats** (omega 6) are necessary for healthy growth and development and are found in vegetable, corn, and soya oils. Insufficient amounts of these fats can affect the immune system and lead to skin disorders. Polyunsaturated fats (omega 3) can be helpful in treating heart disease and arthritis and inflammation and are found in oily fish such as sardines, mackerel and herrings, and walnuts and grapeseed oil.

Salt and sugar

Many processed foods are packed with salt, which contributes to high blood pressure. (The World Health Organisation recommends no more than 5g a day.) Try to avoid salty foods and choose lower salt versions whenever you can. When eating: don't pile on the salt before even tasting it – it's unhealthy and very rude. Current advice suggests that crisps are preferable to sweets but you should aim to choose varieties with lower amounts of fat and salt.

Sweet foods and sugary drinks, particularly when eaten between meals, can lead to tooth decay. If you have a sweet tooth try to keep your intake of surgary foods and drink to meal times. Chew sugar-free gum or have a small piece of cheese at the end of the meal. This will neutralise the acid and help protect the teeth from decay. Although sugar contains the same amount of calories as starch, you can eat more before you feel full. Therefore an excess of sweets, cakes and biscuits can lead to an excess calorie intake which causes weight gain.

Fibre

Fibre is essential to the digestive system. It swells the bulk of food left after the nutrients have been removed, giving it shape and a dough-like consistency. Without it, your daily turd will come out slimy – like a wet fish, and diets with insufficient fibre can result in irritable bowl syndrome, constipation, haemorrhoids and piles. Western diets tend to be low in fibre because we eat so much processed and refined food. Fibre comes from vegetables, high fibre breads and fruit. You should aim to have 18-25g a day. Even if you're on the go, there are easy ways to increase your fibre intake, although too much fibre can lead to constipation if taken with insufficient fluid. Switch to a higher-fibre breakfast cereal, eat brown or whole-meal bread and change your snacking habits – replacing chocolate, pastries, and biscuits with fruit and vegetables.

Top tips

- Making improvements to your diet can mean changing or breaking lifelong habits. Some of them may be difficult but they can be made.
- Changes don't have to be wholesale. They should be gradual and easy to maintain.
- Set yourself realistic targets so that you are less likely to feel 'on a diet' or that you are being deprived of foods you want but can't have.
- Eating more healthily is not a test, and punishing yourself for having 'that cake' serves no useful purpose and will only make you miserable.
- Don't be tempted to miss meals. Current thinking suggests that you should eat five times a day: two healthy snacks between three main meals (breakfast, lunch and dinner), evenly spaced. Particularly, don't miss breakfast: you'll feel hungry all morning and be tempted to snack on unhealthy instant sources of energy.

When you're shopping...

- Before you go decide what you're going to eat, make a list and stick to it.
- Avoid the temptation to pick up foods which 'look nice' or are on 'special offer' — many of them will be packed full of sugar and fat.
- Don't shop when you're hungry.
- For guidance, read the nutritional information on foods — but don't obsess!
- Many foods today come in low or lower-fat versions. For example, if you drink full cream or whole milk, switch to semi-skimmed. There are also a wide range of low(er) fat yoghurts, cheeses and salad dressings.
- If you usually eat red meat, try chicken, turkey or fish instead.
- Ready-made meals can be packed with fat. If you're buying them choose products containing no more than 5g of fat a serving.

When you're cooking...

- If you eat meat, trim off the visible fat and skin.
- Grill food rather frying.
- Avoid fried or sautéed foods.
- Don't add salt.

When you're eating...

- Eat calmly, taking time to enjoy the food: savour the tastes and textures.
- Chew your food slowly, rather shovelling it in and swallowing it whole.
- Try to make mealtime a 'no distraction' time. Eat from the table and not your lap and resist the temptation to turn your meal into a TV dinner.
- A glass of water with meals will aid digestion and make you feel more full.
- If you tend to pile your plate high – eat off a smaller plate. Eat until you are comfortably full – not bursting or bloated. Shovelling food can lead to indigestion and heartburn.
- Try to develop regular eating habits as this will help to regulate your appetite.
- Avoid piling on the salt and sugar.

And, if you're eating out...

- Choose plain grilled meat, fish and poultry and avoid gravies and sauces made with cream or butter.
- Avoid the temptation to smother a healthy meal with butter or high-calorie sauces.
- If you feel brave enough, ask if lower fat versions of meals are available.
- By all means have wine with your meal but remember it's not calorie free!

Further contacts and information

- **British Nutrition Foundation** 020 7404 6504 / www.nutrition.org.uk
  High Holborn House, 52-54 High Holborn, London WC1V 6RQ
- **British Society for Allergy, Environmental and Nutritional Medicine** 01703 812124 /
  P.O.Box 28, Totton, Southampton SO40 2ZA
- **British Heart Foundation** 020 7935 0185 / www.bhf.org.uk /
  14 Fitzhardinge Street, London W1H 4DH
- **Coronary Prevention Group** 020 7580 1070 / www.healthnet.org.uk /
  42 Store Street, London WC1E 7DB
- **Eating Disorders Association** 01603 621414
  Wensum House, 103 Prince of Wales Road, Norwich NR1 1DW
- **Food Standards Agency** 020 7238 6330 / www.foodstandards.gov uk /
  Room 6/21, Hannibal House, PO Box 30080, London SE1 6YA
- **Food Standards Agency (Northern Ireland)** 028 90417726 / www.foodstandards.gov uk /
  10B and 10C Clarendon Quay, Clarendon Dock, Clarendon Road, Belfast BT1 3BW
- **Food Standards Agency (Scotland)** 01224 285168 / www.foodstandards.gov uk /
  St Magnus House, 6th Floor, 25 Guild Street, Aberdeen AB11 6NJ
- **Food Standards Agency (Wales)** 029 2067 8918 / www.foodstandards.gov uk /
  1st Floor, Southgate House, Wood Street, Cardiff CF10 1EW
- **Healthwise Heartline** 0800 858585
- **Stroke Association** 020 7566 0300 / www.stroke.org.uk /
  Stroke House, 123-127 Whitecross Street, London EC1Y 8JJ

exercise

Regular exercise can provide relief from stress, more energy and stamina, a sense of wellbeing and a positive outlook. It can help you to enjoy a better quality of life and lower the risk of heart disease and some common cancers.

The heart

Just for a second, place your hand over your heart and feel it thumping. The heart is the body's engine room, beating continuously as it pumps blood around the body. This remarkable organ is a true lifelong friend – all it asks in return is nutritious blood to pump around your body. Situated left centre of the chest, the heart is about the size of a clenched fist and weighs around 250g/8oz. As long as it is supplied with oxygen and nutrients it will go on contracting, spontaneously, rhythmically and completely automatically. As you're reading this, it's beating between 50 and 90 times a minute, depending on your age, its condition and your level of fitness. During strenuous exercise, however, this may increase to about 180-200 beats a minute.

The heart is really two pumps. One receives oxygenated blood from the lungs and pumps it around the body. The blood leaves the heart down the aorta (which is the biggest artery in the body) distributing it to all organs, tissues and cells through a succession of increasingly small tubeways (capillaries). Compared to the width of the aorta (1cm), capillaries are tiny, barely half a millimetre across. Having delivered its oxygen and nutrients – and picking up carbon dioxide and waste products on the way back – blood returns to the heart via a system of veins. The other pump receives de-oxygenated blood from the body and sends it to the lungs where carbon dioxide is exchanged for more oxygen. This complex network of arteries, veins, blood vessels and capillaries carry blood to and from the body, in a continuous figure of eight circuit. Beating around 40 million times a year, each beat pumps _ pint (.15 litre) of blood in and out of the heart – a staggering 2000 gallons (9100 litres) a day, or 50 million gallons (227 million litres) in a life time.

Blood pressure

Despite the fact we seem perfectly happy to stick out our arm, and have it wrapped up in an inflatable lilo – many men don't know what their blood pressure is and what it means. Here's a brief explanation. Blood pressure is the pressure created by the flow of blood through the main arteries. The pressure rises and falls as the heart responds to the demands we make upon it, for example exercise, anxiety and sleep. (By the way, the lilo thing is called a sphygmomanometer). Two measurements are taken: the systolic or higher pressure records the heart as it beats, pumping blood around the body, while the diastolic or lower pressure records the heart between beats – as it relaxes. The sphygmomanometer measures the pressure in millimetres of mercury (mm Hg) and you can see the gauge go up and down as the doctor takes the two readings. A healthy young adult, for example, might be told that their blood pressure is '110 over 75' which is a systolic pressure of 110 and a diastolic pressure of 75. This often rises to around 130/90 as we get older.

Heart problems and solutions

If a kettle is not de-scaled regularly, it will fur up with limescale, affecting its ability to boil water and contaminating hot drinks with white-grey flaky deposits. Similarly, a lack of exercise, an unhealthy diet, excessive alcohol and smoking will fur up the heart, arteries and veins with sludgy deposits of cholesterol and blood clots. This furring-up makes it increasingly difficult for the heart to function properly, causing it to beat irregularly, slow down or in extreme cases stop completely. The results can be life-threatening and include conditions such as high blood pressure, heart attacks, strokes and angina. If you in you're in 20s, 30s or 40s, it's unlikely you'll give these illnesses a second glance... they happen to people you don't really know. You may hear about them on the news, or perhaps see them mentioned in health leaflets when you visit your GP, but you'll probably feel that don't apply to you (not yet anyway). In many ways, heart disease is about death by stealth. It's not until you get older that you find out that what you did – or rather didn't do – when you were younger, has contributed to your first – and perhaps last – heart attack. While you're partying away in your youth, you can also be laying down the foundations for a dead-cert heart condition later on. By taking the following steps and integrating them into your life, you can significantly reduce the chances of developing circulatory problems, a heart condition or heart disease.

- Give up smoking. Twenty cigarettes a day triple the risks of heart trouble.
- Check your cholesterol level through your GP, particularly if your family has a history of heart problems.
- Take regular exercise.
- Lose weight (if you have excess weight to lose).
- Get your blood pressure checked by your GP.
- Drink sensibly. Current research suggests that a glass of wine per day can protect against heart disease, but excessive alcohol use leads to its own problems.

Starting out

There are many everyday opportunities to improve your level of fitness but to begin with you should set yourself realistic goals. While many people start out hating exercise, most enjoy it sooner or later and learn to make it part of their everyday life. If you start exercising suddenly you will probably make yourself so stiff you won't want to try again. You could also injure yourself. So, if you're a little (or a lot) out of shape, start slowly to allow your body time to become accustomed to the new demands you're making on it. Even after a few weeks your ability to exercise will improve, and after a few months you should see an improvement in your stamina. A good way to introduce exercise into your life is to continue your everyday routine but in ways that require more energy. It's a simple and easy process that means you don't automatically have to join a gym or your local football club. Here are a few examples – which don't cost a penny.

- When you walk, walk a little faster (but try not to mince).
- Try a 15-30 minute walk, increasing it by a few minutes every week – as you feel able.
- Use the stairs instead of the lift – especially if it's only one floor up or down.
- If you use escalators – walk up instead of standing still.
- For short journeys walk or cycle instead of going by bus, underground or car.
- Get off the bus or train a stop or two early and walk the rest of the way.

Getting more adventurous

Before you start any regular strenuous physical activity, you should see your GP so that other health factors can be taken into account when planning what you aim to do. These factors include:

- Being significantly overweight.
- Being a smoker.
- Having back problems.
- If you have a chronic disorder such as diabetes, asthma or arthritis.
- An immediate family member has developed heart disease before 40.
- Being under medical treatment for high blood pressure, a heart condition, or other long term disease.
- Being over 35 and having done very little exercise for a few years.
- Being over 50 years old.

Choosing your exercise

The exercise you choose should aim to improve endurance (the ability to keep on exercising without stopping to rest), strength (the ability to use muscles to lift, carry, push and pull a load) and flexibility (the ability to stretch, bend or twist through a wide range of movements). Swimming and aerobics are good all-rounders promoting endurance, strength and flexibility; weight training focuses on endurance and strength, and jogging on endurance. Sex, on the other hand, provides an opportunity to improve your endurance, flexibility and strength and if you get it regularly, it's a useful indicator as to your overall level of fitness.

However, there will be factors which may limit how fit you can become like your genetic make-up, your natural body shape, musculature, flexibility and metabolism. If you are naturally muscular you may be inclined towards the gym and weight training. Alternatively, if you have a sinewy or lean physique you may be more interested in jogging or running.

Other things to consider:

- The type of exercise or sport that you would like to do, eg aerobics, walking, cycling, dancing, jogging, running, skipping, squash, swimming, tennis, joining a gym.
- Your short and long-term goals, eg to have fun, make friends, get fitter and feel better, increase stamina, lose weight.
- How you are going to exercise, eg by yourself, with a friend, as part of a team.
- When you will exercise, eg frequency, the time of day, having sufficient time.
- Injury costs, eg professional fees in the case of treatment.
- Any other costs, eg travel, fees, membership, equipment, exercise/sports gear.

Staying motivated

In addition to your goals (see above) here are few tips to help you stay motivated:

- Avoid measuring your fitness solely in terms of weight lost, the number of lengths you can swim or what you can lift. Also take into account the fun and exhilaration felt after exercise.
- If you're exercising alone, how about finding a partner to exercise with?
- Vary your routine to avoid becoming bored.
- Keep a record to monitor your progress.
- During repetitive exercises count backwards.

Exercising safely

Anyone who exercises or plays sport regularly is bound to pick up the occasional injury. It probably won't be serious ,but exercising safely is important to ensure that you can keep on exercising while reducing the risks as far as possible.

- Wear clothing that is comfortable and appropriate for the exercise or sport you are undertaking.
- Before you start, do a five to ten minute stretching routine to prepare you for the exercise itself.
- It may be helpful to seek professional advice from a coach, a more experienced person or manual.
- Use protective equipment available for a specific sport.
- Make sure that any equipment you use fits, works properly, and is the correct size.
- Replace exercise shoes which have become worn or that don't fit properly.
- Don't smoke, take alcohol or recreational drugs, or eat before exercising. Any of these could make you feel drowsy or dizzy or reduce co-ordination which in turn could lead to an accident or injury. However, you may need an energy drink to raise your blood-sugar levels.
- After exercise, cool down with muscle stretches and by continuing to move around for a few minutes to reduce stiffness and soreness.
- Stay warm – a sudden drop in temperature can induce a chill or shock.

Injuries, straining and illness

If you experience an injury or have any concerns or suffer any discomfort or pain, seek professional advice immediately. Most injuries (if you've not broken anything) involve minor damage to muscles, ligaments, tendons or the lining of a joint. If you have any injuries that remain painful or tender (or if you have any concerns about an injury) you should have them seen by your GP or a physiotherapist (or your nearest accident and emergency department if neccessary). Always ensure that you follow to the letter any advice or treatment that you are given.

Danger signs that you might be straining your heart include pain in the chest, neck or arms, nausea, dizziness, lightheadedness or feeling faint, severe breathlessness, extreme fatigue. Stop exercising if you suffer any of the above symptoms and get a check-up from your doctor before continuing. We all get ill from time to time and if you have a sore throat, temperature, swollen glands, a bad cough or mucus-producing cough, take a break from exercise until you feel better.

Further information and contacts

- **British Heart Foundation** 020 7935 0185 / www.bhf.org.uk / 14 Fitzhardinge Street, London W!H 4DH
- **Coronary Prevention Group** 020 7580 1070 / www.healthnet.org.uk / 42 Store Street, London WC1E 7DB
- **Healthwise Heartline** 0800 858585
- **National Back Pain Association** www.backpain.org / 16 Elmtree Road, Teddington, Middlesex TW11 8FT
- **National Sports Medicine Institute** 020 7251 0583 / www.nsmi.org.uk / Charterhouse Square, London EC1M 6BQ
- **Sportscotland** 0131 317 7200 / www.sportscotland.org.uk / Caledonia House, South Gyle, Edinburgh EH12 9DQ
- **Stroke Association** 020 7566 0300 / www.stroke.org.uk / Stroke House, 123-127 Whitecross Street, London EC1Y 8JJ
- **The Sports Council** 020 7273 1500 / www.english.sports.gov.uk / 16 Upper Woburn Place, London WC1H 0QP
- **The Sports Council for Northern Ireland,** 028 9038 1222 / info@sportscouncil-ni.org.uk / House of Sport Upper Malone Road, Belfast, BT9 5LA
- **The Sports Council For Wales** 029 2030 0500 / Sophia Gardens, Cardiff, CF11 9SW

sleep

We all have to sleep, and most of us will spend about a third of our life (250,000 hours) in a state of near unconsciousness, nonetheless aware of your environment. During this time, the body rests and undertakes maintenance and repairs. Sleep is essential for promoting physical and mental health; when you sleep, blood pressure drops, breathing slows down and the body releases growth and sex hormones (although this is dependent on age). If you can manage six hours' sleep or less then you're unusual; most men need around seven or eight hours, although we can usually cope with much less for a few nights.

Your sleep pattern is managed by your biological clock which co-ordinates other functions such as waking, sleeping, eating, pissing and shitting. It is thought this internal clock orchestrates the brain to stimulate and suppress various body systems. For example, it slows down piss and shit production until you wake up and are ready to go. Without sleep the body cannot rest or repair itself and after about ten days of total deprivation, death occurs. The brain can adapt to periods of up to three days without sleep but eventually lack of sleep causes irritability, irrational behaviour, confusion and hallucinations.

REM, NREM and dreaming

When asleep, two distinct patterns alternate throughout this time: NREM – a deep, dreamless non-rapid eye movement sleep, and REM – when rapid eye movement occurs and you dream. When you fall asleep you drift into NREM, spending about 90 minutes sinking through four levels and back up again. This is broken by a 10-15 minute burst of REM during which time the body is almost completely immobile except for the rapid flickering of the eyeballs. However, the brain is almost as active as it is when you are awake, and this is when dreams occur. It is thought that dreams are

the brain's way of sorthing through information and experiences gathered when awake. This pattern of sleep repeat itself throughout the night although the last REM before waking up can last up to an hour. During an eight-hour night, dreams take up about two hours, and although everyone has them, not everybody can remember them. If you're woken up in the middle of REM you are likely to remember the dream vividly. However, if you're woken up just five minutes after REM you will have a vague recollection of a dream; after ten minutes you're not likely to remember any of it.

Can't sleep, won't sleep

Reasons for insomnia are numerous, and include:

- Unfamiliar surroundings.
- Noise and too much light.
- Feeling cold or being too hot; inadequate ventilation.
- An uncomfortable bed; having bedding which is too light or too heavy.
- Anxiety, stress, depression, emotional upset, and overwork.
- Disturbed sleep patterns – grinding of teeth.
- Bad eating habits, eg eating a large meal late at night and indigestion.
- Drinking caffeine-based tea or coffee just before going to bed.
- Thirst (often made worse if you've been drinking alcohol).
- Lack of exercise during the day.
- Trying to sleep more than you think you need.
- A full bladder and waking for a piss in the middle of the night.
- A heart or lung disorder which may make breathing and lying down difficult.
- Pain and illness.
- Recreational drugs.

Sleepy bye bye

Whatever your ritual before you go to bed, try to develop a gentle and calming routine. Try to sort out insomnia naturally before considering sleeping tablets, which can leave you feeling groggy and disorientated in the morning. The following tips can help you get a good night's sleep:

- A firm mattress rather than some stuffing with a dent in it is less likely to give you back problems.
- Ensure that the bed and linen provide suitable cover and warmth.
- Open a window to ventilate the room. When it's cold, even a couple of centimetres can help.
- If you wear pyjamas (deepest sympathies) or some other clothing – make sure they're comfortable.
- If you're worried or stressed, making a things to do list or mini action plan can help.
- Have a warm bath or a shower to relax.
- Go to the toilet if you need to.
- Have a hot milky drink (a little ground nutmeg and honey is delicious).
- Read, listen to the radio or watch TV until you drift off – assuming the programme doesn't over stimulate the brain.
- Some relaxing sex or a wank can help.
- Have a glass of water by the bedside.
- If you've been drinking try and drink a glass of water for each pint or spirit. While you run the risk of having to get up for a piss, you should feel less dehydrated and hungover in the morning.
- Cuddle up to a hot water bottle (they don't snore or fart).

If you have to take sleeping pills under your GP's advice try a 'natural' variety from a health food store first. It is better to use pharmaceutical drugs only at times of serious or short-lived stress or emotional trauma.

Recreational drugs

Recreational drugs like ecstasy, acid, coke and speed are all likely to keep you awake and disrupt your natural sleep pattern. Partying all weekend – without sleep – and then going to work on Monday morning will make you feel like shit and bugger up your sleep pattern further. You'll go to bed shattered on Monday and wonder why you can't get up on Tuesday. After your drugs, set aside the next day to catch up on lost sleep even if it means taking Monday off to relax and chill out. Otherwise, the lingering effects of the drugs and the come-down, can fuck up the whole week. If you don't come down gently, the temptation is to take more drugs to help get over the wretchedness you can feel.

Further information and contacts

- **British Snoring and Sleep Association** 01737 557997 /
  The Steps, How Lane, Chipstead, Surrey CR3 3LT
- **The British Sleep Foundation** 020 7345 3317 /
  www.britishsleepfoundation.org.uk / 10 Cabot Square, Canary Wharf, London EH14 4QB
- **The British Snoring and Sleep Apnoea Association (BSSAA)** 0800 0851097/01737 245638
  www.britishsnoring.demon.uk / 1 Duncroft Close, Reigate, Surrey RH2 9DE

smoking

While cigarettes account for the bulk of tobacco consumption there are also cigars, pipe tobacco, snuff and chewing tobacco. Tobacco comes from the nicotiana tabacum plant and is grown around the world, with an estimated 8000 million pounds (3628 million kg) produced annually.

The major active ingriedient in tobacco is nicotine, a stimulant that acts on the body by causing it to increase its production of adrenalin, a chemical produced by the body in response to stress, fear or excitement, which acts by increasing the heart, pulse and breathing rates. Every time you draw on a cigarette it delivers a burst of nicotine to the body and brain and therefore stimulates adrenaline – giving smokers a buzz or high. By working in this way on the nervous sytem, nicotine can reduce tiredness and improve concentration, but you should never forget it is also the reason why smokers become dependent on tobacco. Smoking also provides rituals – lighting up, sharing a cigarette with friends – as well as providing a diversion in a stressful situation by giving smokers something to do with their hands. Nonetheless, smoking is still thought by many as sexy, cool, stress-relieving, a confidence boost, a tool with which to meet people and a tradition after a shag.

Smoking tobacco (in varying forms) has a long history but it is only in the last century, with the advent of the cigarette, that it achieved its status as a social activity (even to the extent of being promoted by doctors as a remedy to breathing problems in the 1950s). Today, however, smoking is widely accepted as being a major health hazard, with tobacco companies paying out billions in lawsuits to people who have suffered lung disease and cancer as a result of their habit. The damaging effects of smoking are often gradual, taking many years to appear, which is why the harm it causes can often seem inconsequential to young smokers.

What's in a puff?

Smoke enters the lungs as gases and solid particles which condense to form a thick brown tar; this lines the passages down which the smoke travels and then collects in the lungs. Tobacco is made from several hundred chemical compounds that fall into five main categories:

- Nicotine – one cigarette can deliver between 0.5mg and 2mg depending on how it was cured and how it was smoked (up to 90% if inhaled, and 10% if not).
- Gases – carbon monoxide at 300-400 times the level considered safe in industry and hydrogen cyanide at 160 times the safe level.
- Carcinogens, or chemicals capable of causing cancer – there are anything between 10-15 in a single cigarette.
- Co-carcinogens, or chemicals which don't cause cancers directly but which accelerate the growth of cancer.

- Irritants – substances which disturb and inflame the bronchial passages to the lungs, increase mucus secretion and damage the process for getting rid of it.

Today, the majority of cigarettes are filter-tipped which removes many of the harmful substances from cigarette smoke. Low-tar and low nicotine cigarettes will reduce the amount of nicotine and tar entering the body but some filter-tipped cigarettes allow more poisonous carbon monoxide into the lungs.

Does smoking damage my health?
No, we've just made this up

Around 50% of smokers will die from smoking related diseases including lung cancer, heart disease, strokes, arterial disease, chronic lung disease and cancer of the bladder, stomach, mouth and throat. Smokers' skin ages more quickly, they get indigestion and ulcers while their partners get lung cancer through passive smoking. However, here are the details of three particularly unpleasant and threatening conditions:

- Lung cancer is probably the best known harmful effect of smoking but there are other forms including mouth, lip, and throat cancer. For those of you who don't know, cancer is abnormal cell growth and can develop for a wide variety of reasons, smoking being one of the main triggers. Normal cells have certain limits to their growth, but cancerous cells continue to grow without controls, eventually causing serious and life-threatening damage to body tissues and organs.
- Coronary heart disease is the most common cause of death in middle-aged men in Western countries, and the risk to a young man who smokes over 20 cigarettes a day is about three times that of a non-smoker. Chemicals contained in cigarettes enter the bloodstream through the lungs and encourage the build-up of fatty deposits. These deposits narrow or block the arteries supplying blood to the heart, which has increasing difficulty in pumping blood. Eventually you feel like shite as the heart struggles to do its job. Sometimes it stops and that's it: a heart attack. If that wasn't enough, the deposits also damage arteries in other parts of the body including the brain (which can result in a stroke) and the legs which, in severe cases, can lead to amputation.
- Inhaling cigarette smoke damages the lungs and can severely reduce their capacity to function properly. Firstly, it irritates the passageways to the lungs which narrow, produce mucous and are more susceptible to infections. Secondly, the lungs are covered with millions of little sacs (alveoli) which are responsible for passing oxygen into the bloodstream and ridding the body of carbon dioxide. Smoke inflames the alveoli causing the lungs to become less elastic and efficient. Once

carbon monoxide passes from the lungs into the bloodstream – where it competes with oxygen – it combines with the blood and interferes with oxygenation of tissues. In the short term, this leads to shortness of breath, wheezing, coughing, and recurrent chest infections. In the long term, persistently high levels of carbon monoxide in the blood lead to a hardening of the arteries which, in turn, greatly increases the risk of a heart attack.

Killing others

Passive or secondary smoking is breathing in air contaminated with others' cigarette smoke. There is an increasing body of evidence that those in the vicinity of smokers (eg barmen) are at an increased risk of developing tobacco-related disorders, such as heart and circulatory diseases, bronchitis, emphysema and lung cancer. They also suffer from considerable immediate discomfort from eye irritation, sore throats, coughs, headaches, asthma and other allergic reactions, increased heart rate and breathing difficulties. Just thought we'd tell you.

Breaking the habit

If you need a cigarette when you wake up then it's more than likely that you're addicted and should make a serious effort to give up. If you're a social smoker – say one or two at weekends or at parties – you should still try and give up completely. The good news is that the benefits of giving up smoking start immediately.

- After 30 minutes circulation improves, blood pressure and pulse rate return to normal.
- Eight hours later, oxygen levels in the blood return to normal, chances of heart attack start to fall.
- 24 hours later, carbon monoxide is eliminated from the body, lungs start to clear out mucus and other crap.
- 48 hours later, nicotine is no longer detectable in the body and the ability to taste and smell improves.
- 72 hours later, bronchial tubes relax and breathing becomes easier, energy levels increase.
- Two to 12 weeks later, circulation improves throughout the body, making physical activity easier.
- Three to nine months later, breathing problems such as coughing, shortness of breath and wheezing decrease, overall lung function increases by 10 to 15%.
- After five years, the risk of heart attack falls to half that of a smoker. After ten years, the risk of lung cancer falls to half that of a smoker, and the risk of heart attack falls to the same as a non-smoker.

Quitting

Breaking any habit is difficult, and success depends on determination, planning, and will power. The benefits to health far outweigh the possible discomfort of a week or two, and the additional rewards of considerable financial savings should also keep you going when things get tough.

Many smokers are physically dependent on nicotine and so when they stop smoking the craving to have a cigarette continues and will take time to die down. Withdrawal symptoms are varied and can include mood swings, depression, restlessness, anxiety, difficulty in concentrating, and sweating. Some people find that they put on a few pounds after they give up smoking. This is partly because they are no longer taking in nicotine (which stimulates the body's metabolism) and because their appetite has increased. However, if you only nibble on healthy snacks, you're unlikely to put on more than a few pounds which is not as bad for your health as continuing to smoke.

There are many different ways you can give up smoking: group sessions, individual medical care (through your GP), therapy, acupuncture and hypnotism, although the act of self will is probably the most popular method used. Nicotine replacement therapies (NRT) such as Nicotinell and Nicorette don't stop you from smoking but provide a much-reduced level of nicotine to help control the physical withdrawal symptoms. NRT supplies controlled levels of nicotine that allow you to gradually reduce your intake. NRTs are usually supplied as chewing gum, patches, or as a nasal spray available through your chemist. The new kid on the block is Zyban – a nicotine-free pill to help smokers to quit. A prescription medicine available only from your GP, it helps reduce the urge to smoke, lessens symptoms of withdrawal and makes quitting more bearable. Zyban is thought to affect chemicals in the brain, although exactly how and why this works we're not actually certain.

Ten-point plan

- Make a date to stop smoking and stick to it. Let others know and get as much support as you can. Maybe a friend might like to give up with you.
- Bin your ashtrays, lighters and fags.
- Drink plenty of fluids (not vodka) and keep a glass of water or juice close by.
- Get more active. Increased exercise helps clear the shit from your system.
- Expect withdrawal to be irritating. It's a sign your body is recovering from the effects of tobacco. Irritability, urges to smoke, and poor concentration are common – don't worry, they usually disappear after a couple of weeks.
- Change your routine, eg try to avoid the shop where you usually buy cigarettes.

- Bear in mind any drama in your life might get you reaching for just one fag to get you over it. How are you going to cope with that?
- Reward yourself. Use the money you are saving to buy something special.
- Be careful what you eat: snack on fruit, raw vegetables, sugar-free gum or sugar-free sweets, not fatty foods.
- Take one day at a time. Each day without a fag is good news for your health and your pocket, remember to celebrate your success. If this doesn't work, don't beat yourself up, you can always try again later.

Further information and contacts

- **Quitline** 0800 002200 Victory House, 170 Tottenham Court Road, London W1P 0HA
- **Action on Smoking and Health** 020 7739 5902 www.ash.org.uk
  102 Clifton Street, London EC2A 4HW
- **Nicorette** www.nicorette.co.uk
- **Nicotinell** www.nicotinell.co.uk
- **Zyban** www.zyban.co.uk
- Refer to the chapter on Alternative and Complimentary Therapies page 276.

alcohol

There are two types of alcohol: methyl alcohol (methanol or wood alcohol) is highly poisonous and is used as a fuel and solvent, and ethyl alcohol (ethanol), the active ingredient of alcoholic drinks. Ethanol is also used in medicine as an antiseptic and as a base in which other ingredients are dissolved. Ethyl alcohol is produced by fermentation – the chemical reaction between bacteria and starch such as maize, barley, rice, potatoes, hops and grapes. Malt and barley make beer, and grapes make wine but only a 10-15% level of alcohol is possible by this method. Spirits such as gin, brandy, vodka, whisky and liqueurs which have a higher alcoholic level require distillation as well as fermentation. This means that the water is evaporated, leaving the alcohol in greater concentration. Distilled alcohol is also added to fermented drinks to strengthen them, eg sherry, port and other fortified wines.

What it does

Alcohol affects the body in several ways.

- It depresses and slows down the central nervous system; this is what leads to a reduction in tension, anxiety, and inhibitions.
- It provides energy (but also tons of calories) that usually head for the waist. Burn it off through exercise and you're okay but from a nutritional perspective, it's pretty useless.
- It affects liver function. After heavy drinking, as much 50% of the liver can be 'immobilised' although it is usually recovers within a few days.
- It makes you piss. With heavy alcohol intake the body loses more water than it takes in and you become dehydrated.

"It's my round I think."

The liver

The digestive system absorbs about 30% of any alcohol drunk. This is carried around the body by the bloodstream and reaches the liver, one of the largest and most important body organs. The liver makes and regulates many of the body's chemicals and helps break down and eliminate toxins and other poisonous substances from the blood. It is here that alcohol is broken down, at a rate of one pint of beer or 30cc (1oz) of whisky per hour. This process breaks down around 90% of the alcohol into carbon diioxide and water, the remaining 10% being processed through the lungs and as sweat (which is why you may smell rotten the morning after).

Units and limits

Units are measurements of alcohol consumption and can be used to help calculate the amount of alcohol contained in a drink. However, although most of us have heard of them, surprisingly few people actually know how to calculate them, so here is a quick guide to help you:

- One pint of ordinary lager, beer or cider.
- Half a pint of strong lager, beer or cider.
- One small glass of wine (100ml.
- A single pub measure of spirits (25ml).
- One small glass of sherry or fortified wine (50ml).

Drinks poured at home are usually more generous and should be scored double. Also, score twice as much for extra-strength beers. The healthy maximum is currently accepted as 21 units a week, which equates to:

- Ten pints of ordinary lager, beer or cider.
- five pints of strong lager, beer or cider.
- Three bottles of wine.
- 21 single spirit drinks, with or without mixers eg coke, tonic.
- 21 single drinks of sherry or port.

Spread your allowance throughout the week as this level and frequency of drinking is not likely to harm your health. However, people's tolerance to alcohol varies enormously and even the recommended amounts may be too much. You should aim for at least one or two alcohol-free days a week. Don't save up your allowance to blow it over one night at the weekend because it puts excessive strain on the body and liver especially.

The risk to your health and safety increases, the more you drink. If you drink over 36 units a week you are running the risk of liver damage, accidents and alcohol dependency. It's not only your physical health that's affected: your drinking could lead to social and legal difficulties, eg drink/driving offences, problems with your friendships and relationships or the loss of your job. It's when we're tanked like this that we behave badly at parties, become aggressive and argumentative and take very risky decisions when it comes to sex...

How your behaviour changes

Even small quantities of alcohol have effects on the body which are noticeable (particularly in someone who doesn't drink often or hasn't done so for some time). It's surprising how after a single drink – 20-30 minutes later – people can become more relaxed. Problems occur when people don't take into account the effects of alcohol on behaviour when socialising or tasks requiring co-ordination such as talking, walking , or driving. When you are drunk, you are also more susceptible to assault, rape, theft and abuse. Prolonged heavy drinking that stops short of dependence may still cause liver and health problems. Dependence (alcoholism) can cause early death and is a major factor in absenteeism from work, accidents and relationship breakdowns. Changes in behaviour depend on the amount of alcohol reaching the brain, which are determined by several factors apart from the quantity of alcohol drunk.

- The rate at which the alcohol is drunk.
- The size of the person, eg the larger the person the greater the diluting effect of the blood on the alcohol consumed and the more it takes to produce the same effect.
- Whether alcohol is consumed on an empty stomach or not. The effect will be much more immediate (as little as five minutes) if the stomach is empty. Food in the stomach slows down the rate at which alcohol is absorbed into the bloodstream.
- The size and condition of the liver.

Taking into account the above factors, your behaviour from your first to last ever drink will look something like this: a sense of warmth – friendliness – flushed face – talkativeness – increased social confidence – reaction time slows – further sense of mental relaxation and general wellbeing – trip over words – tendency to be loud and talkative – inhibitions about to jump out the window – confused and disturbed thinking and co-ordination – irritability – reduced self-control – irresponsible talk and behaviour – unsteady on feet – slurred speech – unpredictable, exaggerated emotions or (aggressive) behaviour – extreme confusion and disorientation – difficulty remaining upright – drowsiness – nausea – shitting yourself – delayed or incoherent reaction to questions – coma (a state of deep unconsciousness from which you cannot be aroused) – followed by death.

The hangover

The body reacts to large quantities of alcohol in several ways although this usually takes several hours. The lining of the stomach and lower parts of the digestive system are irritated; the body is dehydrated while the level of alcohol in the blood stream exceeds the livers ability to process it; and the nervous system is shocked and needs time to recover. Symptoms include headache, nausea, stomach-ache and cramps, vomiting, dizziness, and irritability. This is the twilight world of the hangover. We've all been there: stumbled into a cab… staggered on to a bus… rolled into bed… and fallen into a nauseous sweaty sleep. The next day you wake up with a throbbing headache, a furry tongue, a mouth which tastes… interesting and breath you could bottle and sell as paint stripper. The best cure is not to have got in to this sorry state in the first place. When you get a hangover you have in effect poisoned the body – albeit temporarily – and it needs time to recover. However, there are practical steps you can take
to ease symptoms and aid recovery:

- Drink as much water as you reasonably can throughout the day. This rehydrates the body and helps you to piss out the toxins.
- Drinking other liquids can help the body re-hydrate, tea and coffee which contains caffeine will stimulate the nervous system but are also dehydrating. Sugar can be taken to provide energy. Fruit juices, honey and a vitamin C are also known to help and fizzy drinks may have a soothing effect upon the stomach.
- Drag your sorry arse out of bed, take a shower or bath. Take a walk to get the blood circulation going. This will help provide fresh supplies of oxygen and sugar to the brain and stimulate endorphins, the body's natural painkillers.
- Settle down in front of the TV or a video and relax.
- The stomach can be relieved by something to eat but anything fatty or rich may make you feel nauseous.
- Aspirin or other pain relievers should only be taken after you have eaten something. Your body will be further irritated if they are taken on an empty stomach.
- Another alcoholic drink – a 'hair of the dog' – will kick start the nervous system and can make you feel better… for a while. However, this only postpones the original hangover with a second one on the heels of the first.

The gay scene

For many years, gay pubs were the only places where we could meet other men without fear of abuse or assault. Today, while we can meet guys through a much wider range of places and activities, pubs, clubs and bars are still central to the gay scene. Also, since the main reason for going to bars is quite often to meet other guys, you'd be forgiven for not thinking about the risk of alcohol dependence. It's not difficult just to have a few beers – three or four times a week – and you've reached the recommended limit before the weekend has even started. A drink or two can dull the sense of loneliness as you stand by yourself in a bar trying to look confident. A drink or two will often provide the necessary confidence to go up to another guy and ask him whether… he'd like a drink. A further drink or two will also dull the sense of rejection after he tells you that he's not interested or he's got a boyfriend. Meeting mates for a drink can help reduce any sense of rejection, inferiority or loneliness but – on a regular persistent basis – can lead to a steady increase in the amount you drink. After all, who's going to have 'just the one' or have 'orange juice'? Even if you've found yourself a man, alcohol – even in small quantities – can reduce the enjoyment of sex. Alcohol can make it difficult to get or maintain an erection – hence the phrase 'brewer's droop'. It can also interfere with your judgment so you may take risks sexually that you wouldn't find acceptable if you were sober. Guys have been assaulted, raped and murdered for less! When we are younger our bodies give us the impression that they can cope with any drink we throw down our neck. The reality, however, is that the body is storing up problems for later life.

Of course, there is always the option not to drink alcohol or to drink low alcohol versions of beer or wines. However, the choice is usually limited and they don't always taste particularly good.

In moderation, drinking can and should be a pleasant experience, helping us to feel that little bit more relaxed, comfortable, and sociable. But despite its acceptability on the gay scene and its normalisation on TV and film, alcohol is still a drug with the potential of being highly addictive. Being selective when using it is vital if we are to enjoy the benefits but not become subject to the harm it causes. Despite protestations that 'I know my limit', there's a fine line between drinking socially and becoming dependent. Anyone who drinks alcohol can become an alcoholic and the more we drink the more we increase the risk of dependency and health problems.

Safer drinking

Alcohol is unlikely to harm your health if you drink only small amounts and avoid drinking every day. Steps to get the best out of drinking and avoid problems include:

- Keeping to the recommended weekly intake.
- Aiming for two or three alcohol-free days a week.
- Drinking slowly instead of gulping.
- Alternating alcoholic drinks with non-alcoholic drinks.
- Experimenting with low alcohol or alcohol-free drinks.
- Not drinking on an empty stomach.
- Not drinking by yourself when you are unhappy or morose.
- Not having 'one for the road.'
- Not drinking to relieve anxiety tension depression or loneliness.
- Not keeping your home stocked with alcohol.

Alcohol dependence

While there does not appear to be a single cause of alcohol dependence, personality, environment and the addictive nature of alcohol contribute to the development of the illness. It is also thought that genetic factors probably play a part in causing dependence, and any person can become alcoholic if he drinks heavily for a prolonged period. Some symptoms can appear over a period of weeks and months, but alcohol dependency usually occurs over a period of years, sometimes decades. Symptoms fall into two categories which can include any combination of the following:

Physical symptoms	Behavioural symptoms
• Bad breath. • Confusion. • Hangovers and headaches. • Flushed appearance or redness in the face. • Forgetfulness and memory lapses. • Incontinence (pissing or shitting yourself). • Nausea. • Shaking in the morning. • Stomach or tummy cramps. • Unsteadiness. • Vomiting. • Weakness, numbness or tingling in the legs and hands. • Severe shakes, hallucinations, and convulsions may occur after the sudden withdrawal of alcohol which can be life threatening.	• Secretive drinking, eg at work • Aggressive, dramatic, or grandiose behaviour. • Neglectful of food. • Neglectful of personal appearance. • Long periods of drunkenness. • Frequent changes of job. • Lying to yourself and others about giving up. • Personality changes such as irritability, jealousy, uncontrolled anger, or selfishness. • Changes in drinking pattern, eg changing from evening to early morning drinking, or changing from beers to spirits.

Do you suffer from alcohol dependency?
Try this simple test

	Yes	No
Do you think you are a 'normal' drinker?	0	1
Do your friends/family think you're a 'normal' drinker?	0	1
Have you ever contacted a help line or support group about your drinking?	2	0
Have you ever lost friends because of your drinking?	1	0
Have you missed work or other important obligations because of your drinking and hangovers?	1	0
Have you ever failed a breathalyser test?	1	0
Have you needed a drink to start off the day?	1	0
Have you woken up next to a complete stranger because of your drinking?	1	0
Have you not been able to remember whether you used condoms because of your drinking?	1	0
Have you ever had to go to hospital because of your drinking?	2	0
Have you ever used alcohol to boost or build up your confidence before going out?	1	0
Have you ever had a drink to get away from worries or problems?	1	0
Have you ever taken a small bottle of something to work?	1	0
Have you need a drink at lunch time?	1	0

If you have scored four points or more, this indicates that you may suffer from a dependence on alcohol at some level. Don't ignore this or feel bad, simply refer back to the section on safer drinking and use this guide to keep within the limits. Alternatively, make the first move to get help, advice and support from your GP, friends, a local group, helpline or agency. There are also useful contacts at the back of this book.

Getting help

Unfortunately, most men who drink too much are either unaware that they have a problem or refuse to admit it. If you or someone close to you is drinking in excess, contact the family doctor or a helpline for advice. It is worth trying to reason with the person when he's sober. Groups such as Alcoholics Anonymous offers advice and guidance for people with a drink problem and provide support for partners. In severe cases it may be necessary to admit an alcoholic to hospital for a period of detoxification with medication prescribed to control the withdrawal symptoms. Even then, long-term treatment to prevent a return to previous drinking habits is invariably required and can include behavioural therapy and psychotherapy. Occasionally the drug known as disulfuram is prescribed, which induces unpleasant side-effects when alcohol is taken.

Alcohol-related conditions

The body adapts to the continual presence of alcohol in the bloodstream so that after a while you have to drink a lot more to notice a change in the way you feel. Just because a heavy drinker no longer appears to be getting drunk doesn't mean that the alcohol isn't causing serious damage to the body.

- Alcohol can have a direct toxic or irritant effect on cells and tissues.
- Many alcoholics eat little or no nutritious food and while the alcohol satisfies the body's calorie requirements, it doesn't provide any protein, vitamins or minerals. Consequently, the body is more susceptible to diseases caused by nutritional deficiency.
- A continual high level of alcohol in the blood and tissues can cause wide-ranging disturbances in body chemistry. These disturbances can lead to hypoglycaemia (reduced glucose in the blood) and hyperlipdaemia (increased fat in the blood) which affects many body organs.

In addition to the many health and social problems that may result from alcohol dependence, people who consume large quantities of a alcohol are susceptible to a wide variety of physical and mental disorders:

- Depression, loss of memory, intellectual deterioration, and eventually dementia.
- Damage to blood vessels near the surface of the skin due to repeated flushing to the face.
- Increased risk of high blood pressure, heart attacks and stroke.
- Cirrhosis (scarring) of the liver, hepatitis, and liver cancer.
- Cancer of the mouth, throat or oesophagus.
- Problems with the digestive system including gastritis and pancreatitis, and peptic ulcers.
- Temporary or permanent numbing, tingling and weakness of nerves.
- Impotence due to hormonal changes and infertility due to sperm damage.
- Neglect of personal hygiene, eg vile breath, dirty sweaty clothes.

That's it then… anyone fancy a drink?!

Further information and contacts

- **AL-ANON** 020 7403 0888 / alanonuk@aol.com / 61 Great Dover Street, London SE1 4YF
- **Alcohol Anonymous** 0845 7697555 / www.alcoholics-anonymous.org.uk
- **Alcohol Concern** 0800 9178282 / www.alcoholconcern.org.uk
- **Alcohol Counselling and Prevention Service** for Lesbians, Gay and Bisexual Men 020 7737 3579 / 34 Electric Lane, London SW9 8JT
- **Drinkline** 0800 9178282

recreationaldrugs

For some, taking recreational (and often illegal) drugs can mean we can better enjoy clubbing, socialising and sex. In recent years, increased accessibility has meant that they continue to play a role in the lives of younger people particularly – straight and gay. However, when we take drugs, our ability to communicate effectively and make informed decisions, our perception of risk, vulnerability and danger can alter immeasurably. If you use drugs, you'll probably say that you know your limits and can handle them. Some people can... maybe you can... but whether you know what you're doing or not, you often increase the risk of HIV/STI transmission, accidents and other injuries. If you are feeling ill, tired, worried or depressed, are on your own or have something important to do in the near future (like go to work) their effects may not be what you want, or expect. Whilst they may make you feel better in the short-term they may also make you feel worse. The effects of any drug can depend on a number of factors:

- The drug itself.
- How much you take.
- Where you do it.
- Who you do it with.
- What you think the drug will do.
- What you've mixed your drugs with.
- How you're feeling at the time.
- What you've eaten that day.
- Any other drugs you've taken (prescription or not).

Party drugs don't create energy, they allow us to borrow it from tomorrow's supply. And then, when tomorrow comes, it's payback time. The key is to minimise the impact of our 'weekend cocktail' on the week. Avoid doing any drugs in

the week, particularly if you're working. A weekend without much sleep, few meals, hours of endless dancing and drugs won't be good for the immune system. Hardly surprising that, come Monday morning, we're feeling a bit trashed. After the highs of Saturday night/Sunday morning, there's nothing like a heavy dose of reality to bring on the midweek blues.

Sleep is vital as it keeps your mind, body and soul in balance. Sleep recharges your batteries so you can do the things you like – so get plenty! Not eating can cause fatigue, cramps and weight loss. It is important to eat properly and regularly – like every day! If you're going out to a club in the evening, eat earlier in the day to avoid stomach cramps. A little extra salt on your food a few days before will also help to retain body fluids, while multi-vitamins through the week can help to keep you fit and healthy.

Top tips for safer drug use

- 'Popular' drugs are illegal and often carry heavy penalties for possession, using, and selling or buying.
- Using any drug involves risks and taking more or mixing drugs increases the risks. Mixing drugs (particularly with alcohol) may make the effects of other drugs seem different or weak, which could lead to you taking too much, and some drug combinations are deadly.
- We quickly develop tolerance to party drugs and our bodies will appreciate the chance of a break to recover. You'll get more out of your drugs if you don't take them every week.
- If you're taking a prescribed medicine, it's only sensible that your drugs don't mess that up. It's important not to miss or change doses set by your doctor, particularly with HIV treatment drugs such as protease inhibitors.
- Eat before you go out. Something high in carbohydrates for energy (eg pasta) and vitamin-packed (such as fresh fruit and veg) will help prepare your body.
- Take a 'disco-nap' before going out.
- Wear lightweight (non-nylon) clothes, don't wear hats or caps, and, if you can, take warmer clothing/change of clothes with you for when you leave.
- Clubs can get very crowded and extremely hot. This can cause you problems like dehydration, serious over-heating, and heat exhaustion – all of which are dangerous. Sweating is how bodies keep cool and stop hypothermia, so drink non-alcoholic sugary drinks to replace lost fluids.
- Don't take more drugs than you need – give them about an hour before taking more.

- Take regular chill-out breaks to help avoid over-heating and dehydration.
- Sip about a pint of water per hour (but don't go mad).
- Try to avoid alcohol which will only dehydrate you more. Drink something sugary (an isotonic drink like Lucozade Sport is ideal) and eat something salty before you finally get some sleep. However much you don't feel like it, eating really helps to start replacing all those lost salts and minerals.
- Whether you're out or at home, if someone gets ill and you have to call an ambulance, don't mess about. Be sure to tell the medics what's been going on. Don't be afraid, it could save a life – maybe yours!

And if you score more than just drugs, remember...

- Drugs and alcohol have a pain-killing effect so you may not be aware of damage being done to your body, particularly your cock and arse.
- Dehydration and raised temperature makes delicate skin more likely to tear and bleed. For fucking, extra lube and strong condoms are a must!
- Though sucking cock is considered very low-risk for HIV transmission, dabbing speed and coke, and chewing gum all night, can cause ulcers and bleeding in your mouth, which may increase the risks of infection.
- Drugs and alcohol can alter your perception of risk and can make you less able to get the sex you want. It can be difficult to be assertive, to say no or to insist on condoms, when you're mashed up.

The law

Drugs and the law is a complicated subject and if you find yourself in trouble you should get legal advice at the earliest opportunity. If the police have reason to suspect that you're carrying an illegal drug they have the right to make you empty your pockets. They can also take you to the police station and search you there. If drugs are found you could be charged with one of two offences: possession which means being caught with an illegal drug for your own use, and possession with intent to supply drugs which means if you had any intention to deal (sell), give away or share drugs.

Shit

Possessing class C drugs such as anabolic steroids, tranquillisers and temazepam (without a legitimate prescription) can get you two years in prison and/or a fine, and supplying them will cost you up to five years prison and/or a fine.

Big shit

Sharing class B drugs like cannabis and speed can put you away for five years. If you supply, you could be facing up to 14 years.

You've drowned

Just taking an E or selling a few to some mates on a Saturday night can get you a heavy spell behind bars. Cocaine, crack, ecstasy, heroin, LSD (acid), magic mushrooms and speed (amphetamines) when prepared for injection are all class A drugs. Also methadone without a prescription is a class A drug. You can get up to seven years in prison and/or a fine, and up to life imprisonment and/or fine for supplying.

And the icing on the cake...

If you have a drugs record, getting a visa to travel to some countries may be difficult and you could even be denied. A record can also affect your job prospects: an employer may check if you have a criminal record or any past convictions.

Ecstasy
E, XTC, pills

What is it?

Ecstasy is usually sold as a tablet or capsule that contains a variety of chemicals. A pure E would be three-quarters Methylenedioxymethamphetamine (or MDMA). Most pills contain other drugs too – MDA or MDEA (both similar to MDMA), amphetamine, ketamine (an anaesthetic) or even LSD. Some pills contain no MDMA at all.

What does it do?

Someone taking ecstasy will experience a loss of inhibitions, excitedness, euphoria, talkativeness and a rush of energy. MDMA encourages people to feel closer, more open and empathic towards the people they are with. Some people call this being 'loved up'. These effects usually start after about half an hour. Someone who hasn't used E before might experience some confusion or anxiety. High doses can initially cause a lack of co-ordination and dizziness. If this happens, it's a good idea to sit down until the rush passes. Ecstasy is a hallucinogenic stimulant. Some pills can cause a distortion of sound and vision. Hallucinations will be caused by pills that contain drugs like LSD or ketamine. The effects usually last for three to four hours, peaking after about two. If someone takes a pill that lasts for longer than this then it probably contains amphetamine (speed). They'd have loads of energy, but wouldn't feel the closeness associated with MDMA.

What does it do to my body?

While someone is on an E their pupils are dilated, their mouth and throat will feel dry, there is a rise in heart rate and blood pressure, their jaw feels tense (often people chew gum to ease this), sweating increases and appetite is suppressed. MDMA interferes with the body's temperature-regulating mechanism, so body temperature can increase to potentially damaging levels. It also prevents your body from excreting urine. Some research suggests that the brain and liver may be damaged by long-term ecstasy use. It's difficult to provide clear information when different pills contain different chemicals. The truth is, no one knows for sure whether E is harmful in the long term.

What are the risks?

The main risks with ecstasy are overheating and dehydrating. Ecstasy is often used at clubs or parties where people are dancing and getting hot and sweaty. Someone using E in this kind of environment needs to drink about a pint of liquid (water and fruit juices, *not* alcohol as this also dehydrates) over the course of each hour to replace the fluid they are losing through sweating. Eating salty snacks will replace the minerals that are also lost. If someone isn't sweating they don't need to take as much fluid on board; drinking too much could actually be very dangerous. Drinking too much water can cause the brain to swell, leading to collapse, coma or even death.

The after-effects of ecstasy use can include insomnia, anxiety, irritability and paranoia. The range and severity of after-effects depends on the amount of ecstasy that is being used, and the regularity of use. Sleeping and eating will help the user to recover. Essential nutrients, particularly vitamin C and calcium, will need to be replaced. If you've been taking E every weekend and are starting to find that the days in between are becoming unbearable it's time to take a break. Some people have developed short-term mental health problems (like anxiety, depression, low self esteem and paranoia) that clear up once they stop using. It needn't be forever. The same applies if you find yourself needing more pills to get the effect you want. Once you're taking more than two pills in an evening the effects are more like speed. If you're going to use E, it's safer to use small amounts, with a long enough gap in between to enable your body to recover.

Legal status

Ecstasy is illegal. A charge of possession of a drug with intent to supply can be brought by the police. This includes giving a substance away for free, and can be for any amount of ecstasy that the court feels is too large to be for personal use only.

Cocaine
Cocaine powder: Coke, Charlie
Smokable cocaine: Crack, Rocks, Wash or Stones

What is it?

Cocaine is a white powder that is refined from the coca plant. This plant grows in South America. The powder can be sniffed or snorted through a straw or rolled-up banknote and is absorbed through the nasal membranes. Cocaine is sometimes mixed with other chemicals to form crack, a smokable form of the same drug. Burning cocaine powder destroys the drug. Burning crack produces a smoke containing cocaine which usually has a purity of 90%. When the smoke is inhaled it passes into the bloodstream through the lungs and quickly reaches the brain.

What does it do?

Cocaine is a short-acting powerful stimulant and is highly addictive. The effects of cocaine powder are similar to amphetamines: talkativeness, confidence, reduced appetite, euphoria and increased energy. These effects last for about 30 minutes. Once the drug starts to wear off, it's common to experience a compulsion to take more coke to avoid coming down. Crack takes people higher (the effects are even more intense), but it is extremely short-acting. Someone using crack will experience peak effects after several minutes and find themselves coming down after ten to 15 minutes. What goes up must come down, and the higher you go, the further there is to fall.

Common after-effects are low energy, hunger and tiredness. Anxiety, irritability and paranoia are also fairly common side-effects. As with all drugs, someone taking large doses or using cocaine regularly will suffer a more extreme comedown than an occasional user. The comedown from crack is far more distressing than the comedown from cocaine powder. Mood swings, irritability, anxiety and paranoia are common. Some people who use crack regularly have developed a dependence to opiates after using heroin to take away the side effects of their crack use.

What are the risks

Regular cocaine use will lead to interrupted sleep patterns, anxiety and paranoia. Someone regularly using cocaine will find themselves feeling unable to cope without the drug They'll get very stressed out and irritable when they're not using. Someone using cocaine every weekend, for example, will soon start to find that the weekdays become something to get through until the next weekend. There is no medically accepted physical dependence associated with cocaine. Someone using it regularly will not become as physically sick as someone withdrawing from heroin. People often experience a compulsion to take more though, and can start to feel unable to have a good time unless they are using cocaine. Cocaine has an image of being a drug for rich people, and unless you're extremely wealthy using cocaine regularly will certainly create a big hole in your bank balance. A cocaine habit can become very expensive, very quickly, especially so for crack. A rock of smokable cocaine can cost £15 – £20, and it's not difficult to get through several hundred pounds' worth of the drug in an evening. Some people use cocaine during sex. Aside from the psychological experience – confidence and euphoria – cocaine is also a local anaesthetic. Rub it on your teeth and gums and they'll go numb – that's why it's been used in dentistry. Cocaine can prolong sex by reducing sensitivity, increasing the time it will take for a man to orgasm and ejaculate. It all depends on where you rub the coke. Prolonged fucking can increase the risk of catching STIs including HIV. Condoms can tear so make sure you have spares, and plenty of water-based lube.

Legal status

Cocaine is a class A drug. If you're found in possession of a class A drug for personal use and sentenced in a magistrate's court, the offence carries a maximum sentence of six months' imprisonment and a fine of £2000. The same maximum sentence applies for supplying the drug if tried at a magistrate's court. If you're found guilty of simple possession of a class A drug and sentenced at crown court, the offence carries a maximum sentence of seven years' imprisonment and an unlimited fine. For supplying or trafficking, the maximum sentence at crown court is life imprisonment and an unlimited fine. A charge of possession of a drug with intent to supply can be brought by the police. This includes giving a substance away for free, and can be for any amount of cocaine that the court feels is too unreasonably large to be for personal use only.

Heroin
Junk, Smack, Brown, Skag, H, Gear

What is it?

Heroin is usually sold as a brown powder. The powder starts life as the milky sap of the opium poppy papaverum somniferum. The sap is collected and dried to form a gum. The gum is washed and becomes opium. Opium contains two painkilling alkaloids, codeine and morphine. Morphine that has been extracted from opium can be further refined to create diamorphine, or heroin. Weight for weight, heroin is about 40 times more powerful than raw opium.

What does it do?

All opiates – drugs that come from the opium poppy – are painkillers, closely imitating your own painkilling body hormones (which is why they are so effective). People who use heroin describe feelings of relaxation, warmth and a sense of wellbeing. Nothing matters. Wrapped up in cotton wool. Initially, most people who use heroin feel nauseous and often vomit. This is followed by a period when the user is conscious but looks like they're falling asleep. Breathing and heart rate decrease. Once this has passed the user is able to interact normally with other people, although to them their experience will have taken on a dream-like quality. Heroin is used in medicine (it's called diamorphine when it's prescribed) as an anaesthetic and powerful analgesic for relief from severe pain. Regular use will cause dependence (see below) and constipation. Female users may have interrupted periods.

What are the risks?

There are two main risks with heroin: overdose and dependence. Heroin depresses the activity of the central nervous system like alcohol, sleeping tablets (temazepam, for example) and tranquillisers (like valium). This is what causes the breathing and heart rate to slow down. Someone who takes more of any depressant drug than their body can cope with (an overdose) will lose consciousness, drift off and will stop breathing. Mixing depressant drugs increases this risk – you can overdose much more easily. Injecting heroin can easily lead to an overdose. If you don't know how strong the heroin is, it's easy to take too much. If somebody is overdosing and starting to lose consciousness don't panic! It is important to call an ambulance and stay with them until help arrives. Try to keep them conscious for as long as possible – talk to them. If they lose consciousness, put them in the recovery position. If they vomit, clear their airway. When the paramedics arrive tell them what drugs have been taken so the right medical attention can be given to the person as soon as possible. If anybody takes an opiate regularly they will develop a physical tolerance to the substance (they need to take more to get the same effect). It doesn't make any difference whether an opiate is being smoked or injected, prescribed or taken without prescription. The body starts to rely on the chemical being present, and without it the user will become physically and mentally sick. It's not that unusual for someone with a heroin habit to find themselves using £25 – £100 worth of the drug each day. Finding the money for this kind of habit can become a problem in itself, often leading to dealing or other criminal activity. Someone withdrawing from an opiate habit (clucking, or going cold turkey) is likely to experience several unpleasant physical symptoms. Hot and cold sweats, nausea, diarrhoea and confusion are accompanied by an intense craving to take more of the drug to make them well again. Heroin withdrawal is not physically dangerous, but will be unpleasant.

Seeking help from a doctor or drug dependence clinic could relieve some of the symptoms. Medication can be given to help someone through withdrawal, and other support will be available. Longer term users may be offered prescriptions for other opiates like methadone. It's usually prescribed as a liquid to drink. It's clean, it lasts for 12-24 hours and it costs a lot less than smack (free if you're on benefits). Just like heroin and other opiates, if you take methadone regularly you'll become dependent. Some people move from smoking heroin to injecting it. Injecting any drug involves extra risks. Overdose becomes more likely. Sharing injecting equipment (intentionally or accidentally) can expose a user to viruses like HIV and Hepatitis B and C (viral infections of the liver).

Legal status

Like cocaine, heroin is a class A drug. The same penalties for possession and supplying apply.

Ketamine
Special K, Ketaset, Ketalar, Vitamin K

What is it?

Developed in the mid 1960's, Ketamine (commercially sold as Ketalar) is a powerful anaesthetic used in the UK mainly by vets on farm animals, although it does have some human medical applications. However, it is also used recreationally and has become increasingly popular in recent years.

How is it taken?

It usually comes as a liquid in its pharmaceutical form (in glass vials), although it is also found as a white powder or pill. A wrap of ketamine powder will cost between £5 - 25. It is usually snorted (up the nose), injected into the muscle or taken orally. Obviously, the table below is only a rough guide.

	Dosage range/mg	Takes effect/min	Lasts/mins
Snorted	15-200	5-15	35-60
Injected	25-125	1-5	30-45
Taken orally	75-300	5-30	60-120

With doses higher than about 50 mg, it is advisable to be lying down.

What happens?

At lower doses, its effects include mild drunkenness, dreamy thinking, stumbling, clumsy or 'robotic' movement, delayed or reduced sensations, vertigo, sometimes erotic feelings, increased sociability and a sense of seeing the world differently. At higher doses, its effects include extreme difficulty moving, nausea, complete dissociation with surroundings, entering other realities, 'near death' experiences, compelling visions and black-outs. Temporary paralysis has been reported in some users, but is rare.

Negative physical effects can include dry mouth, respiratory problems and nervousness/racing heart. Many people also experience nausea and/or vomiting, which can obviously be a problem when taking anaesthetics or sedatives.

Supervision of higher-dose ketamine experiences by a 'sober sitter' can help ensure that an unconscious participant doesn't have problems with vomiting and/or breathing. Two psychological difficulties, which seem to come up for those who use ketamine regularly, are paranoia and egocentrism. There are many reports of regular users starting to see patterns and coincidences in the world around them that seem to indicate that they are somehow more important or integral to the world than others. This same sense of the world focusing on the user can also feed into a sense of paranoia.

Ketamine has the potential to be both physically and psychologically addictive. Tolerance can be quickly built up if it is used regularly. Individuals who use it regularly may find it difficult to stop, and it is not uncommon to hear of users who take it once or more daily.

Legal Status

Ketamine is a prescription-only medicine and so is not covered by the Misuse of Drugs Act. This means that possession of ketamine is not a criminal offence. However, under the Medicines Act, unauthorised supply is illegal.

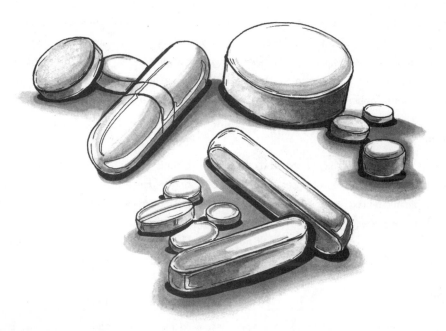

LSD / Acid

Trips, Blotters, Microdot, Tabs, Purple Om, California Sunrise, Blue Star

What is it?

LSD is a synthetic chemical derived from the parasitic fungus ergot, which grows on rye. The full chemical name is lysergic acid diethylamide. LSD is usually sold as a square of blotting paper about a quarter of the size of a postage stamp. The LSD is produced as a crystal, dissolved in alcohol and then dropped onto the acid 'tabs'.

What does it do?

About an hour after someone swallows the trip the effects start. Initially the user will feel disorientated. They may become giggly, confused or anxious. As the trip progresses feelings are enhanced. Colours and sounds seem more vivid. Everything appears to flow. LSD causes perceptual distortions or hallucinations – while someone is tripping they can affect how they perceive their environment. The environment will also dramatically affect how the tripper feels. Change the environment and the nature of the trip will change. Time becomes meaningless. It is impossible to tell whether a moment has lasted a second or a million years. Senses can become confused – you might taste colours or see sounds. It's common for people at the peak of a trip to experience a sense of depersonalisation. They don't feel like an 'I' anymore. They experience themselves as just a part of everything else. If someone doesn't like what they are experienceing and tries to get away from what is happening they are likely to move into a state of extreme fear. They might feel anxious, panicky or paranoid. Tripping on LSD is essentially a trip into your own mind. Trips can last for over 12 hours.

What does it do to my body?

LSD is thought to disrupt the way that seratonin is used by the brain. Seratonin is the chemical in the brain which enables electrical messages to pass through the synapses. The physical changes due to LSD use include a slight rise in temperature and heart rate and dilated pupils. Someone who has taken LSD may appear to be completely normal, although occasionally confused or unexpectedly giggly. The long-term physical effects of LSD use are not known. Concerns about chromosomal damage have not been proven. Some people have suffered from long-term mental health problems after using LSD. It is not known whether LSD caused their mental illness or brought to the surface a problem that was already there.

What are the risks?

Someone using LSD may become less aware of risks from the environment. Busy roads can become impossible to navigate safely. Activities that involve co-ordination like swimming, driving or cycling will be much more dangerous than usual. Even finding your way home can seem an impossible task. When someone trips how they feel will be dramatically affected by the people around them. LSD enhances feelings, so any anxiety or concerns will be amplified. If someone has decided to take LSD, preparing for the trip is a good idea. Are they with friends? Will they feel safe? Will someone know what to do if everything becomes too hectic? Will they be able to get to a telephone? If they want to leave, can they? Are they likely to be interrupted? Do they need to be somewhere else in the next 12 hours? Are they relaxed? Are they depressed?

Even if you feel great and you're with friends you can't guarantee having a good trip. Often trippers re-experience early memories, even pre-birth memories. Bad trips can be triggered by a painful or difficult feeling that the user tries to avoid by resisting the effects of the drug. A bad trip is a bit like a nightmare, and can be extremely frightening. If someone is having a difficult time during their trip it is important to remember how open to suggestion they are. Trying to reassure a paranoid tripper by constantly asking them if they still feel paranoid is really not going to be very helpful. It'll just keep them feeling edgy and anxious. If you're with a friend who's used LSD and is having a bad time you could help by being there to listen to them. Remind them they've used LSD (they might have forgotten), and that they're tripping. Help them to talk if they want to, but without constantly questioning them. If it's possible it might be a good idea to change the environment – go for a walk, change the music. Relaxation is the key. Go with the flow.

Magic Mushrooms
Shrooms, mushies, liberty caps, fly-agaric

How they are taken?

Mushrooms can be eaten raw or cooked, heated with water to make a tea or soup, or added to an omelette or another dish just like non-hallucinogenic mushrooms. Some species have to be cooked first to avoid poisoning. But, before you rush off to the shops, these are not the same mushrooms you'd buy at your local market or supermarket!

What happens?

It can take up to an hour for the mushrooms to take effect. If you have a small amount of the hallucinogenic substances contained in the fungus, you may feel relaxed and a little stoned, a feeling similar to that obtained using cannabis. Higher doses can induce trips similar to LSD. How you feel and who you're with will influence your experience dramatically. A mushroom trip can last for up to 12 hours, with some disorientation the following day.

Physical changes

Compared to the psychological effects these are minor – increased heart rate and blood pressure, and dilated pupils. Sometimes you may experience a mild stomach upset.

Keeping safe

If you are going to pick mushrooms, preferably take someone with you who knows what the mushrooms look like, and where they grow – for example liberty caps grow in open, well manured grassland. If you find something that looks similar growing in a forest it's the wrong mushroom. If you can't take an experienced mushroom harvester, take a good mushroom guide such as Collins' Guide to Mushrooms and Toadstools. Mushroom poisoning can be caused by picking the right species in the wrong condition – it is not safe to eat mushrooms that have been infested by worms or maggots. Older mushrooms should be avoided, as should wet or dirty ones (these tend to go off quickly). If you are going to store the mushrooms at all, remember that they deteriorate and rot quickly if they are damp, closely packed or left in an airtight container. Mushrooms vary widely in the amount of psilocybin they contain – use a small number at first, and increase the dose if necessary. The symptoms of mushroom poisoning can manifest in 20 minutes, but may take up to 40 hours for more slow-acting poisons. Many different poisons can occur in mushrooms; the most common symptoms are vomiting, diarrhoea, cramp, watering eyes, increased saliva flow, jaundice and breathing difficulties. If you are with someone who is ill and has been eating mushrooms, take them to a hospital or doctor immediately – call for an ambulance if you're stoned, don't try to drive. If possible, take some of the mushrooms with you so that any poisons can be quickly identified.

Mushroom tripping isn't something you should do alone, the psychological effects of tripping can lead some people into states of fear and anxiety attacks or 'bad trips'. Being with friends can help you to move through these experiences more quickly and safely. Like any other hallucinogen, mushrooms should not be eaten if you're feeling depressed, anxious or under stress. They won't make your worries go away – generally, hallucinogens tend to amplify how you're feeling at the time. Choose the right environment – somewhere relaxed and safe. Busy roads, rivers, festivals or crowded streets may cause you problems. You should never try to drive if you've eaten magic mushrooms. Mushroom trips can last for eight hours or more.

Legal status

Currently, the possession and consumption of mushrooms is not against the law. Psilocybin is contained in many hallucinogenic mushrooms (including the liberty cap) and is a class A drug. This raises complex legal issues with regard to magic mushrooms; generally, prosecution brought against people for possession of untreated/raw mushrooms alone is likely to fail. Prosecutions have been successfully brought against people for treating or preparing mushrooms (drying, crushing or making a tea for example) with the intent to consume them and the controlled drug contained within them.

Benzodiazepines Temazepam, Valium, and Rohypnol
Tems, Temazzies, Eggs, Green Eggs, Jellies, Norries, Rugby balls

How it is taken?

Benzodiazepines are a group of prescribed drugs with sedative and relaxant properties. They are normally prescribed to people who have difficulty sleeping, or occasionally to reduce anxiety. They are usually taken orally as tablets or gel-filled capsules (temazepam) and occasionally as a liquid for injection (valium).

What happens?

If you have a normal dose of any benzodiazepine you may feel less anxious and start to feel relaxed and sleepy. At higher doses the effects are similar to alcohol – you may feel less inhibited towards other people. Your behaviour may be exaggerated (people who are using them are often very talkative or over-excited, sometimes even hostile or aggressive) and judgement is impaired. You may have a false sense of confidence, or even believe you are invincible or invisible.

Physical changes

Benzodiazepines are usually prescribed to help people sleep or relax, and the main physical effects of the drug are as a muscle relaxant. The other effects described above are experienced if you take the drug and stay awake. If you use benzodiazepines regularly you can become dependent – withdrawal symptoms include anxiety, sleeplessness, panic attacks, loss of appetite, nausea, tremors and sometimes even hallucinations. These symptoms can persist for weeks after stopping use of the drug. Abrupt withdrawal from high doses can cause convulsions and fits, and should never be attempted without medical supervision.

Keeping safe

The effects of downers like temazepam make it more difficult to judge and assess situations than normal. Because of this, if you use the drug you are more vulnerable to accidents (for example when crossing a busy road). You can overdose on temazepam (causing loss of consciousness), especially if you are using another depressant drug like alcohol or heroin. If you vomit while you are unconscious, you may choke – avoid using this drug on your own if you can. As with any drug that reduces inhibitions, benzodiazepines may make you more likely to have unprotected sex, exposing yourself to STIs. Temazepam is a drug that should not be injected – the gel in the capsules can resolidify after injection, leading to thrombosis (a blood clot) and collapsed veins; if you hit an artery by mistake, the blockage can cause gangrene, possibly leading to amputation of a hand, a foot, even an arm or a leg. If you do inject and are with other people, the effects of the drug could make you careless or forgetful – mixing used and clean needles and syringes increases the risk of exposing yourself to infections like Hepatitis B or C, or HIV.

Cannabis
Spliff, Grass, Weed, Marijuana, Dope, Ganja, Hash(ish), Smoke, Joint, Pot, Puff, Blow

Cannabis has been used for many years as an aid to relaxation, and was first introduced to this country in the middle of the 19th century as a medical aid for delirium tremens, period pains, insomnia and headaches. Before prohibition in 1925, products derived from the plant cannabis sativa or hemp were widely used in industry. Seeds were used in bird food, cannabis oil was used in paints and varnishes, and hemp fibres were used instead of cotton for making rope and coarse cloth. The plant from which the leaves, buds and resin are collected originated in Asia, but has now been introduced throughout Europe and America as it grows well in any temperate climate. The main psychoactive ingredient of cannabis in any form is delta 9 tetrahydrocannabinol, shortened to THC. Modern drug companies produce drugs derived from THC or using synthesised THC, which isolate wanted effects whilst trying to keep the high which cannabis users seek to a minimum. Such drugs are Nabilone, Levonantradol and Dronabinol (synthetic).

How it is taken?

Cannabis can be smoked (on its own or with tobacco) or eaten. Cannabis oil is sometimes spread on a normal cigarette, but by far the most common form of cannabis used is resin. This comes in a variety of forms (for example a flat press) and is usually chocolate brown in colour with a hard consistency. The resin is heated (to soften it) and then a small amount is mixed with tobacco and rolled into a cigarette. If the dried leaves and buds (grass) are used then this is often smoked on its own, without using tobacco. Cannabis can also be smoked through a pipe or a bong (a pipe in which the smoke is pulled through water first to cool it down). Pipes are often home-made, using whatever equipment is available.

If cannabis is eaten the effects can often be confusing – it is usually between five to ten minutes before the effects of the drug can be felt when smoking, but up to an hour or more when eaten. Sometimes the user can suddenly find themselves more 'stoned' than they had expected, and may panic. Once eaten, the amount of cannabis consumed cannot be regulated as it can when smoking.

What happens?

A lot depends upon the user's mental state before smoking, the environment and the user's expectations. Cannabis causes perceptual changes which make the user more aware of other people's feelings, enhance the enjoyment of music and give a general feeling of euphoria. It can also make the user feel agitated if they are in a situation which is not pleasant – if they are with strangers or trying to hide the fact that they are using – which is often referred to as paranoia. In extreme moments, the user can feel that everything said around them is directed at them in a malicious and hurtful way. Using cannabis with other drugs such as alcohol can make the user feel dizzy and disoriented. A change of environment – turning the music off, having a glass of water, turning a light on or having a breath of fresh air – will often make you feel better quickly. If you're feeling low, using cannabis will not make you feel better. It is more likely that you will sit and think about what is going on than forget about it.

Physical changes

Cannabis causes a number of physical changes – these are the things that any commercial drug based around THC is trying to isolate. It can produce an increased pulse rate, a decrease in blood pressure, the alleviation of excess pressure in the eye, an opening of the airway leading to the lungs and suppression of the vomit reflex. It can also produce blood-shot eyes, dry mouth, dizziness and an increased appetite. Sometimes short-term memory loss (ie the last couple of minutes) can occur, although this passes as the effects of the drug wear off. To fatally overdose on cannabis it is estimated that you would need to eat about one and a half pounds of resin in one sitting. Cannabis is not physically addictive.

Keeping safe

Whether cannabis use leads to long term health problems is not known. There has been little research in this country, and research undertaken in other countries is clearly affected by other environmental factors, hence inconclusive. If cannabis is smoked regularly, then respiratory complaints similar to those linked with cigarette smoking are likely to occur. If a cannabis user does have an unpleasant experience when using the drug it is often the result of a high dose coupled with inexperience – perhaps after eating a large amount (ie more than a sixteenth of an ounce) and then panicking when the drug takes effect, or when cannabis is used with another drug such as alcohol. Cannabis is fat soluble, and so someone who regularly uses a large amount of the drug may store some of it in their body. It can take up to 30 days for this to be fully metabolised and for the body to be clear of the drug. Cannabis is a hallucinogen. Hallucinogens have been linked to mental health problems – the hallucinogenic experience may trigger a psychotic episode for someone with a pre-existing mental health condition (which they may or may not know about). There has been a lot of discussion about the potentially beneficial medical uses of this substance, and its place in modern medicine. However, there is still little research into new cannabis-based products because of the difficulties in obtaining research licences and the political issues around the legalisation of cannabis.

Legal status

Cannabis is illegal. Cannabis plants and resin are class B drugs in the Misuse of Drugs Act, 1971, whilst cannabis oil is a class A drug. An ounce of cannabis in eight separate blocks may be seen by a court as intent to supply, as if it were for personal use there would be no need to cut it up. Dealing in larger amounts of cannabis can lead to a charge of trafficking. At crown court a maximum sentence of 14 years' imprisonment and an unlimited fine could be imposed for this offence.

Amphetamines
Speed, Billy Whizz, Pink champagne

Amphetamines are powerful central nervous stimulants. Most street speed contains amphetamine sulphate. Other amphetamines include dexamphetamine and methamphetamine, both less common and more powerful stimulants. Speed is usually sold as a white-ish powder.

What does it do?

Most people experience increased confidence, talkativeness and sociability, euphoria, increased energy, loss of appetite and insomnia. these effects last for four to six hours. As the drug wears off and the person comes down from the effects, these feelings are replaced by a low roughly opposite to the high given by the drug.

Common after-effects are low energy, hunger and tiredness. If someone uses amphetamine regularly or takes a high dose they are likely to feel anxious, irritable and sometimes paranoid. Large doses of amphetamine are known to cause amphetamine psychosis. This is clinically very similar to other psychoses like paranoid schizophrenia. People suffering from amphetamine psychosis often feel that there's a conspiracy, people are out to get them, they've done something wrong and that everyone else knows all about it. This can be extremely frightening, but will usually wear off as the speed wears off.

What does it do to my body?

Amphetamines stimulate the central nervous system. Common reactions include dilated pupils, dry mouth, loss of appetite, an increase in body temperature and insomnia. Higher doses can cause stomach upset, sweating, jaw tension, a disturbed heart rhythm, flushing and cold hands and feet. Less common are increased blood pressure, palpitations and tremors.

What are the risks?

Regular use of amphetamines will interrupt sleep patterns and eating habits, and can lead to extreme paranoid delusions. Someone who feels upset or anxious and uses speed will find that their feelings are intensified as they come down from the effects of the drug. Someone who is speeding and drinking alcohol will not feel the full effects of the alcohol until the speed starts to wear off. They will still get drunk, but they'll be wide awake and drunk. They'll still find it more difficult to make rational decisions than normal.

Illegal amphetamines are cut or adulterated with other substances. Some speed has been confiscated by the police with a purity as low as 2%. Most speed will be 5% to 10% pure. Someone paying £10 for a wrap of speed is spending 50 pence on speed and £9.50 on everything else that's in it. Amphetamines increase metabolic rate, and will use up stores of nutrients in the body. Someone using speed will recover more quickly afterwards if they replace essential nutrients like vitamin C and calcium, and rest properly. Using speed causes an increase in heart rate, blood pressure and body temperature. At high doses it is possible for your heart to go into arrythmia – it starts jumping about all over the place. Body temperature can soar, causing overheating. Taking speed with other stimulants like E increases these risks.

Amphetamine use can affect sexual behaviour. Libido may increase or decrease. Orgasm and ejaculation are inhibited. Sex can last for a long time. Make sure that you have plenty of condoms, just in case. Most people who suffer from amphetamine psychosis find that it wears off as the drug does. As they come down, they can distinguish between their delusions and what's really happening. Regular use can cause long-term or even permanent psychological problems. Whilst tolerance develops quickly to amphetamine use it doesn't cause a medically accepted physical dependence, although there is a strong risk of psychological dependence. Chopping out a line on Monday to 'sort your head out' after a heavy weekend will only make Tuesday even more difficult to cope with.

GHB
GBH, Liquid E, Liquid X

Gamma Hydroxybutyrate (GHB) was originally developed as an anaesthetic, but withdrawn due to unwanted side-effects. Other uses have been for the treatment of narcolepsy, for the relief of symptoms when withdrawing from dependent alcohol use and more recently as a growth hormone stimulant used by body builders. The substance is currently circulating in clubs as an alternative to ecstasy or speed.

How it is taken?

GHB is usually available as an odourless, colourless liquid which you drink (it tastes slightly salty). Sometimes the substance is available as a powder, or in a capsule. In its liquid form, GHB is sold in small (30ml) bottles; this would normally be enough for three doses. It is difficult to give a clear safe dose, as the concentration of the liquid will vary.

What happens?

You can usually feel the effects of the drug ten or 15 minutes after you have taken it, although it may take up to an hour. In small doses, GHB encourages a reduction of social inhibitions, similar to alcohol, and an increased libido. At higher doses, this euphoria gives way to feelings of sedation. Some users have likened the experience to taking mandrax, a sedative that was popular on the illegal market in the 70s.

Physical changes?

As an anaesthetic, GHB works as a sedative rather than a painkiller. Most reported physical side effects are actually connected with taking more GHB than a normal recreational dose, when the drug starts to work as an anaesthetic. Common unpleasant reactions are nausea, drowsiness, amnesia, vomiting, loss of muscle control, respiratory problems and occasionally loss of consciousness. After excessive use, some users have experienced seizures and coma.

Keeping safe

The amount of GHB you need to take to feel the effects is very close to the amount needed for anaesthesia, and this is very close to the amount that can cause seizures or coma. If you decide to use GHB, start by using a couple of capfuls and see how you go. Many of the people who have collapsed whilst using this drug don't remember being ill, but actually think they have been dancing around and having a great time – you will be safer if you are with friends who can help if you get into difficulties. If you are with someone who is using GHB and they become ill, call an ambulance and take them to hospital. Let the paramedics or doctor know what they have taken so that help can be given quickly. The people who have been hospitalised after this sort of reaction have made a full recovery – in this country there have been no confirmed deaths from taking GHB. There is far more likelihood of serious illness or overdose if other sedative or depressant drugs are used – if you do use GHB, do not drink alcohol. Drinking alcohol on top is far more likely to lead to a distressing reaction such as respiratory collapse or coma. GHB is easily made from chemicals that you do not need a licence to obtain. Because of this, it is often made in underground laboratories (usually someone's kitchen) and the concentration is consequently variable. 'Safe' doses vary, depending on the source, and the physiology of the user – their weight, sex and general state of health.

Legal status

GHB is not listed as a controlled drug in this country, so possession or use of the substance is not currently illegal. It is classed as a medicine, and manufacture is regulated by the Medicines Act. A conviction under this Act carries a maximum sentence of two years' imprisonment and a fine of £2000. This law does allow the drug to be imported for personal use only.

Butyl/amyl nitrite(nitrate)
Poppers

Known collectively as alkyl nitrites, amyl, butyl and isobutyl nitrites are yellowy-clear liquids inhaled for their intoxicating effects. These are commonly referred to as nitrates although this is technically incorrect. Amyl nitrite was first produced in 1857 and originally used from the mid-1860s as a treatment for angina (chest pains). Although other forms of treatment are more usual, its only remaining medical use is as an antidote for cyanide poisoning. The name 'poppers' comes from the way the substance used to be packaged - in small glass capsules, which were cracked open to release the vapour (the capsules 'popped' when they were opened). Nitrites are now sold in small bottles, and are usually butyl nitrite, a substance similar to amyl nitrite but less potent. It is a highly volatile flammable liquid, which evaporates at room temperature. Butyl nitrite has no medical uses and was originally sold in America as an a room odoriser and aphrodisiac. The drug became popular in the UK first on the gay scene of the 1970s and have continued to be popular in rave, dance and club culture.

How it is taken

Once opened, the amyl or butyl nitrite evaporates and the vapour is inhaled. These products are usually described by the manufacturers as 'room odourisers' with an implicit suggestion that the bottle should be opened, and the vapour allowed to fill a room.

What happens?

The effects of this drug can be felt around 15 seconds after you have inhaled. Most people experience a rush of light-headedness and some dizziness, followed by relaxation and a general feeling of well-being. Sometimes you may feel flushed, or may lose some control of your body function – as well as feeling dizzy, you may actually fall over. The effects are very short lived, usually lasting for up to three minutes.

Physical changes?

These nitrites cause blood vessels to enlarge, lowering blood pressure and increasing the rate at which your heart pumps. The other main effect is as a muscle relaxant; poppers have been popular within the gay scene for a number of years because they make it easier to get fucked.

Keeping safe

Anybody who suffers from circulatory problems or from low blood pressure should be particularly wary of this substance, which acts as a stimulant to the system. Nitrites are known to be potent inhibitors of the human immune system, and there is currently some debate about the role these substances have with regard to HIV. Researchers based at the US National Institute on Drug Abuse have been studying the physiological effects of nitrites, and their research suggest that use of this drug can cause 'sustained alterations to the human immune system', and may be connected to the development of cancers such as Karposi's Sarcoma.

Legal status

It has always been illegal to sell poppers if they are to be inhaled. This is because they are classed as a medicine and you would need to be a chemist to sell them. If you did break the law in this regard then you would be committing a civil offence and would be prosecuted by the Medicines Control Agency, part of the Department of Health. However, poppers are not illegal if they are used as 'room odourisors' There are currently moves afoot to close this loophole and a distinct possibility that they will no longer be available through shops, pubs, clubs and mail order where they are freely available at the moment.

Interactions between HIV treatments and recreational drugs

The much-publicised death of an HIV-positive clubber on London's gay scene threw the spotlight on the possible interactions between treatments prescribed for HIV infection and recreational drugs. This section aims to set out helpful up-to-date information. Any drugs which inhibit the liver enzymes needed to break down other drugs. Chiefly these are protease inhibitors (PIs), drugs used in the treatment of HIV-related illnesses such as ketoconazole and itraconazole (anti-fungal drugs) and a new anti-HIV drug called non-nucleoside reverse transcriptase inhibitors such as neviropine and delaviridine. It's important to stress that any interaction is possible but by no means a certainty. Most of the press speculation centred on the PI ritonavir. The information here is derived from interactions with ritonavir. It may be true of other liver enzyme inhibiting drugs, but to a lesser extent.

So what's the score?

It's difficult to predict an interaction between a pharmaceutical drug and an illicitly-manufactured one because:

- The chemicals in street drugs are not consistent in terms of strength or content (how often does an 'E' actually have MDMA in it?)
- We all have different reactions and sensitivities to drugs. Some have overdosed on relatively small doses. Others have survived massive overdoses.
- No actual experiments have taken place into the interactions.

What is the interaction?

Because PIs have the potential to inhibit liver enzymes, they can slow the rate at which our bodies excrete other drugs. It's rather like rush hour at the tube station! If all the barriers are open, everyone can get through easily. If half the barriers are closed, more people are competing for fewer gates, and a build-up begins. The level of the illicit drug and any breakdown products in your bloodstream can rise to higher than normal levels, which may cause you serious problems.

Can this happen with all recreational drugs?

No. The drugs with which they may interact badly are:

- MDMA (ecstasy).
- Speed (amphetamine sulphate).
- Anabolic steroids.
- Ketamine.
- Benzodiazepines (eg valium, temezepam, rohypnol)
- Lustral and Prozac (anti-depressants).
- Opiates, eg heroin, morphine and methadone.

With all of these, there is likely to be a minimum twofold increase in blood levels. With ecstasy and valium this is potentially much higher (up to ten times). Whether you are sensitive to these drugs at such levels will depend on your individual metabolism and whether your liver enzymes have been inhibited. Drugs such as cocaine, crack, alcohol, GHB, poppers, cannabis and LSD are currently thought not to interact seriously.

Reducing the harm

During the first six weeks of treatment with PIs, blood levels of these drugs are at their highest, while your body gets used to the chemicals. The risks of a bad interaction are probably greater during this time. It's best to avoid taking the recreational drugs listed above during that time. After six weeks, if you choose to use the drugs affected by PI's, the table below gives an example of advice you are likely to receive.

Esctasy
Divide dose. Take a tablet and wait and see what effects you feel.
Avoid ecstasy use within first six weeks of commencing PI treatment.

Speed
Don't be greedy! Dab little bits rather than bomb the lot and see what effect it has.
Remember that if you're snorting or injecting you'll need to be extra careful.

Heroin
Take normal dose initially and increase it if you experience withdrawal effects.

Methadone
Consult your drug dependency unit (DDU). Only take as much as you need: if you normally take 90mls a day, try just 30mls and see what effect that has. Only take more if you start to withdraw or you may get tolerance and increased dependence.

Valium
Increases in your blood 2-10 fold. It's best not to use this recreationally. Consult your doctor if you use it on prescription.

Temazpam
If it's on a prescription, consult your doctor. Reduce your usual
dose and only increase it if you're not getting your usual effect.

Rohypnol
Start by halving the dose. Give it chance to work. Increase only if necessary.

Steroids
Talk to your HIV doctor before starting PIs or steroids together. Start with half of
the dose you usually use and see what happens. Only increase if necessary.

Ketamine
Start off with a smaller dose (say, one third of your usual dose). Wait for effects before taking more.
Only take more if you feel you need to. Don't forget the effect is sometimes delayed.

Further information and contacts

- **National Drugs Helpline** 0800 776600 (24hrs)
- **Release** Information, advice and legal help 020 7729 9904 (10am-6pm, Mon-Fri) 7603 8654 (24hrs) www.release.org.uk / 388 Old Street, London EC1V 9LT
- **DrugScope** 020 7928 1211 / www.drugscope.org.uk / Waterbridge House, 32-36 Loman Street, London SE1 0EE

DIY check-ups & personal hygiene

Two key aspects of staying physically healthy are caring about your personal appearance and 'do it yourself' body checks. If you look good you're likely to feel better about yourself. A balanced diet and plenty of water during the day will help keep your skin, nails and hair in good condition, but it's important not to neglect other parts of your body through inadequate personal care or other unhealthy habits.

Testicular cancer

Cancer is abnormal cell growth and may develop for a wide variety of reasons, some of which are known and others that aren't. Normal cells have certain limits to their growth, cancerous cells continue to grow without controls, eventually causing serious and life-threatening damage. You can't 'catch' cancer and it is not a sexually transmitted infection. Testicular cancer is on the increase, mostly affecting younger men in their 20s to 40s. It's easy to deal with when treated quickly so, in addition to regular sexual health check-ups, DIY ball checks can pick up early warning signs that something may be wrong.

DIY ball check-up

Check your balls monthly in (or just after) a shower or bath when your ball sack is relaxed and stretchy:

- Rest your ball sack in your hand, feel its weight and use your fingers and thumb to feel each ball. It is normal for one ball to be slightly larger and/or lower than the other.
- Gently roll each ball between your fingers and thumb. At the top you will feel the tube which it is attached to, and the firm, bumpy area where it joins on. The rest should be smooth without lumps or swelling.

- If you feel anything that seems unusual or that concerns you, go to a clinic or to your GP.
- Over time you'll get used to how your balls look and feel. This way you will notice any differences and problems quickly. Though most lumps and bumps turn out to be harmless, you should get them checked.
- Remember, the earlier testicular cancer is found, the easier it is to treat.

Prostate problems

Situated just below the bladder, the prostate gland is 'hooked-up' to the plumbing along which your spunk travels. It is responsible for producing the fluid in which sperm swim and a secretion which keeps the urethra moist.

- It gets bigger as we get older and can sometimes begin to squash the tube that takes piss out of the body.
- It can become infected or inflamed, most common between 25-45yrs.
- It can get enlargedto the size of a small grape fruit if untreated.
- Prostate cancer usually occurs to the over 50s but can happen earlier.

Signs and symptoms that something is wrong include:

- Needing to piss often and getting little warning that you need to go.
- Finding it hard to start or stop pissing.
- Lots of dribbling at the end of a piss.
- Finding it a strain to empty your bladder properly.
- Leaking or dribbling piss.

Prostate cancer

Early prostate cancer rarely causes any symptoms, these only occur at a later stage of the disease. The prostate-specific antigen (PSA) test may help to detect early prostate cancer but because many small prostate cancers are not dangerous, it is not yet known whether early detection and screening is worthwhile for prostate cancer. Studies are underway to find out, but until the results are known, screening for prostate cancer is not be routinely offered in the UK. There are treatments for men with an enlarged prostate gland: contact your GP a sexual health clinic. Prostate cancer tends to affect men in their 40s onwards but can be treated effectively if found early. The symptoms above may point to prostate problems and are sometimes felt by men with prostate cancer, but not always. If you are aged 50 or over, you should have yearly checks which can be performed simply by a doctor or at a sexual health clinic.

Skin

Covering the surface of the body and weighing over 4kg (9lbs), skin is the largest body organ. Made from keratin, a hard protein, it provides a barrier against the environment, bacteria and other foreign organisms and keeps many organs from falling through the skeleton. Just as well then. Self-repairing and self-regenerating when damaged, unbroken skin is waterproof and protects the body from exposure to the sun's harmful rays by producing melanin, a dark pigment, which forms a layer to absorb ultraviolet light; this is why we tan in the sun. Skin also plays a key role in controlling body temperature and water balance. For example, body hairs become erect in the cold trapping warm hair close to the skin, and sweat glands secrete sweat to cool the body when it's too hot. Full of nerve endings, skin also helps us understand our surroundings as it constantly transmits information about touch, pressure, pain and temperature to the brain to interpret. So, in short: don't leave home without it.

Skin is attached to deeper body tissues with elastic fibres called collagen which allows the body to grow and stretch. As we get older, those parts of the body which have been exposed to the ageing effects of sunlight (the face, neck and hands, for example) lose elasticity as the collagen fibres break down. This is what causes bagginess and wrinkles and turns some of us into prunes.

Since the purpose of skin is to protect us from the environment, it's not surprising that – from time to time – it breaks down. While many skin problems are rarely life-threatening and are relatively easy to treat, their effects can be devastating particularly if you suffer from recurrent episodes. That 'hot date' suddenly becomes a nightmare as you explode with spots or an unexplained body rash. Common skin problems include:

- **Acne** (spots) – skin follicles blocked with excess sebum (which lubricates the skin) and infected with bacteria. Also known as white/black heads which usually affect men during puberty but can affect us later on in life as well.
- **Eczema or dermatitis** – inflamed, irritable, flaky, dry skin sometimes caused by allergies, although in many cases the cause is unknown. However, skin tests can sometimes determine the cause.
- **Athlete's foot** – a fungal or bacterial infection causing itchy and sore skin between the toes usually associated with wearing shoes and sweaty feet.
- **Dandruff** – see 'Hair'

DIY help

Unless you know the cause of your skin condition (and any appropriate treatment) seek professional help – probably your GP in the first instance.

- If you are an acne sufferer – avoid greasy skin and hair preparations that clog up the pores making it more difficult for your skin to breathe properly. A chemist should be able to suggest acne prepara tions which can be helpful in mild cases.
- If you suffer from eczema or dermatitis an inexpensive moisturiser can help ensure your skin doesn't dry out.
- Changes in your diet can reduce the problem; for example, some eczema sufferers find that reducing dairy products can help.
- Stress can trigger or exacerbate skin complaints – consider learning a relaxation technique. Many skin conditions can be helped by some exposure to sunlight – but we're not talking suntanning or burning!
- If you suffer from athlete's foot, a range of over-the-counter creams, sprays and powders are available. Simply ask your chemist.

DIY skin cancer check-up

A regular check-up can help detect skin cancer. As with testicular cancer, the sooner skin cancer is discovered and treated, the more likely you are to achieve a complete cure. Warning signs to look out for include:

- A slowly growing lump or bump.
- A change in skin colour or texture.
- A mole or blemish that has changed in shape, size or colour or has started to itch, bleed or become sore.
- The sudden appearance of a new mole.
- A sore or ulcer that hasn't healed with three weeks.

Don't become paranoid! You also need to bear in mind that your body's appearance changes as you get older.

Skin care tips

- Make sure your diet contains plenty of fresh fruit and vegetables.
- Drink at least eight glasses of non-carbonated water every day; drinks containing caffeine, eg tea, coffee, and soft drinks don't count.

- Give up smoking which can cause premature wrinkling.
- Wash regularly with a mild soap and water to remove dirt and dead skin, rinsing off all soap thoroughly.
- Don't spend too long in the bath or shower and make sure the water is not too hot.
- Use a moisturiser compatible with your skin type.
- Dry carefully but thoroughly between your toes and fingers.
- When you're out in the sun, put on a sunscreen (with an appropriate factor) on exposed skin, wear sunglasses to protect your eyes and a cap to protect your head and the back of your neck.
- Wrap up well in cold and windy weather.
- Avoid direct contact with hazardous irritant substances such as household bleach and paint stripper.

Tattoos

The word, tattoo comes from the Tahitian word tattau, which means to mark, and was first mentioned in explorer James Cook's records from his 1769 expedition to the South Pacific. Some scientists have said that certain marks on the skin of a mummified human body dating from about 3300BC are tattoos. If that's true, these markings represent the earliest known evidence of the practice. More widely recognised are tattoos found on Egyptian and Nubian mummies dating from about 2000BC.

Today, tattoos are created by injecting ink into the skin. The tattoo machine as we know it today has remained relatively unchanged since it was invented in the late 1800s and carries ink into your skin through a needle that moves up and down like a sewing machine. Today's machines puncture the skin at the rate of 50 to 3,000 times a minute. The sterilized needles are dipped in ink, which is sucked up through the machine's tube system. Using an up-and-down motion to puncture the top layer of the skin they drive the ink into the skin, to about one-eighth of an inch deep. What you see when you look at a tattoo is the ink that's left in the skin after the tattooing. At this depth, cells of the dermis are remarkably stable so the tattoo's ink will last, with minor fading and dispersion, for your entire life.

The size and type of your tattoo and the skill of the artist help determine the amount of pain involved. Pain also depends on the location of your tattoo: the lower back and ankle are popular places for tattoos but it's much less painful to get one on your chest or upper arm. This is because skin right above your bones tends to be more sensitive to needles while there's extra body mass in the upper arm or chest to cushion the bones.

You should think carefully before getting a tattoo and the following points may be helpful in coming to a decision. A tattoo is to all intents and purposes permanent, and what you want when you are younger usually changes as you get older. Tattoo removal is considerably more painful and expensive than tattooing. The process usually takes several sessions and offers varying results. Highly visible tattoos have been know to hinder career interests and plans. Speak to a friend who has a tattoo and ask him about his experience.

Check list

- Ask your GP if there are any reasons why you shouldn't have a tattoo (other than his/her personal thoughts on the matter).
- If you need more than one visit to choose what you want, check over the clinic and discuss your needs with the studio – do so.
- Believe it or not there is no uniform standard in the UK. However, studios have to be registered in London with their London Borough, elsewhere they are usually registered with the local council (where they have to have a licence) or the health authority.
- Set sufficient time aside, it's not a particularly intelligent idea to have a tattoo or piercing on your way to work!
- Make sure the studio is covered by the appropriate health certification.
- The studio should be scrupulously clean with separate waiting, tattooing/piercing and sterilisation areas.
- Ask the studio to explain in advance the procedures involved, and answer any questions that you may have.
- After the tattoo/piercing, the studio should provide you with a written aftercare sheet.
- If you have any doubts – follow you gut instinct – and leave.

Tattoo aftercare

- Remove any dressing after two hours.
- Wash with warm soap and water and pat dry with a clean towel.
- Do not recover the tattoo.
- Do not get the tattoo contaminated with grease, dirt, paint etc.
- Do not expose the tattoo to the sun.
- Apply small amounts of Savlon cream to the tattoo for the first two days.
- Do not pick or scratch the tattoo.
- Wash the tattoo twice daily.

Piercings

These days, nipple, ear, navel and eyebrow piercings are relatively common. Nipple piercing goes back thousands of years, and is believed at one time to have been a sign of allegiance and manhood within Caesar's Pretorian Guard. Many Roman statues are thought to show pierced nipples but they could be representing a lorica or breastplate. There are even suggestions that cloaks were fastened to them. If true, they would have been very lightweight particularly when in battle – for obvious reasons!

Genital piercings (through the cock and balls) also have a long history. The ampalang (a barbell placed horizontally through the glans) comes from Borneo, where the women of certain tribes will not marry a man who does not have one. This and other piercings like the hafada (a ring through the ball sac) were considered rites of passage by some cultures, to mark the passage of a boy to a man. The Prince Albert (a ring passing in through the urethra and exiting at the back of the glans, underneath and to one side or other of the frenum) has a more intriguing origin. During the Victorian era, the bulge of a cock in a man's trouser was considered unsightly. This piercing could be used to strap the penis in place which is where the saying '…on which side does Sir dress' is thought to originate. It is also rumoured that Prince Albert wore one, hence the piercing's name. While genital piercings have become popular with some gay men, they are still a relatively small group, even though in some 'specialist clubs' you could be forgiven for thinking that you'd walked into an armoury.

Part of the pleasure of piercings has to do with the subtle sensations of wearing them, and there is no doubt that these types of piercing can be strikingly visual and a real turn-on both for those exhibiting them and those admiring them. What you can have pierced will depend on your personal anatomy. A good body piercer should be able to advise you as to what will suit and the types of jewellery that will be most comfortable or visually striking.

Choosing your piercing

The barbell, the ball closure ring and banana bell (with equal sized balls) are not unusual. Normally a barbell in any body piercing will heal quicker than a ring, as there is nothing sticking out to catch or rub on clothes. Only jewellery made from highest grade surgical stainless steel or solid gold should be worn in a piercing. Silver and other metals which can tarnish should never be used. The important thing is to discuss what you want with the piercer who – if they're good – will encourage you to do so. It may also be helpful to discuss it with friends who have piercings. For men the experience of the piercing can be quite intense and can lead to an endorphin rush and can be a essential part of the ritual. For others, it's a sharp intense feeling, but like with a tattoo, you only really feel it as the needle goes through.

Check list

- Ask your GP if there are any reasons why you shouldn't have a piercing (other than his/her personal thoughts on the matter).
- If you need more than one visit to choose what be want, check over the clinic and discuss your needs with the studio – do so.
- Believe it or not there is no uniform standard in the UK. However, studios have to be registered in London with their London Borough and, elsewhere, they are usually registered with the local council (where they have to have a licence) or the health authority.
- Set sufficient time aside, eg it's not a particularly intelligent idea to have a tattoo or piercing on your way to work!
- Make sure the studio is covered by the appropriate health certification.
- The studio should be scrupulously clean with separate waiting, tattooing/piercing and sterilisation areas.
- Get the studio explain in advance the procedures involved and answer any questions.
- After the tattoo/piercing, the studio should provide you with a written aftercare sheet.
- If you have any doubts – follow your gut instinct and leave... you can always go back or find another studio.

Piercing aftercare

- Remove dressing after four hours.
- Clean with TCP antiseptic for two days only.
- Continue to clean with pre-boiled water and salt.
- Do not pull or tug jewellery.
- Ensure that your hands are pre cleaned using an anti-bacterial soap prior to touching your new piercing.
- If you have any problems then contact your piercer for advice, this can usually eliminate a trip to your local GP.

Teeth

Adults have 28 to 32 teeth depending whether the person finally grows their wisdom teeth, which do not appear in everyone. In many cases, wisdom teeth don't emerge fully from the gum because of over-crowding. Your dentist will determine whether they are best left alone or taken out. Teeth are largely made up of dentin on the outside and a pulp on the inside where blood vessels and nerve endings are situated. The crown, or visible part of a tooth, is covered with about 2mm of enamel. Below the gum line, the root of the tooth is made from cementum. Both dentin and cementum are tough bony substances. Teeth are 'glued' by a special membrane that anchors them to the surrounding socket. Poor oral hygiene or the failure to clean and floss your teeth regularly weakens the mouth's ability to fight off infections and the membrane that fixes your teeth to the sockets. Consequently, despite the best efforts of saliva, which is you body's natural answer to bleach, you are more inclined to get mouth ulcers and bleeding gums – obvious gateways for bacterial infections like gingivitis and viral infections like hepatitis and HIV.

Bad breath

Bad breath is caused by bacteria, tooth decay, smoking or rich and spicy food. It can seem particularly unpleasant when you wake up in the morning after you've been drinking the night before. During the night your body produces less saliva (a natural mouthwash) and a thin creamy coating forms over your teeth, tongue and gums. Healthy bacteria break it down producing mild toxins which smell and taste horrid. However, in some cases bad breath can be caused by medication and stomach ulcers.

Plaque

Plaque is a sticky coating on the teeth made up of saliva, bacteria and particles of food. It is the main cause of tooth decay and gingivitis (an infection of the gums). If allowed to accumulate it will become hard and increasingly difficult to remove. Plaque begins to form within hours of cleaning and is responsible for the furry feeling of un-brushed teeth. If the gums are unhealthy the plaque tends to spread more quickly. The bacteria can also rapidly erode teeth enamel and voilà... a cavity! Or voilà, voilà, voilà... lots of cavities. Plaque should be removed at least twice times a day using a toothbrush and dental floss.

Gingivitis

Gingivitis is usually caused by a build-up of plaque. It is thought that the toxins produced by bacteria within the plaque irritate the gums causing them to become infected, tender and swollen. Gingivitis can also result from injury to the gums usually from rough brushing of teeth or flossing as if you're lassoing a steer. Healthy gums are pink or brown and firm. Poorly gums become a reddish-purple, mushy, shiny and swollen. The gums bleed easily during brushing and are often tender. Good oral hygiene is the main means of preventing and treating gingivitis – and not letting the plaque form in the first place. In some cases, a special mouthwash will ease the symptoms.

Tips for teeth

- You should visit a dentist every six months. If not, or if you leave it until pain and discomfort occurs you are storing up potentially horrific problems for later on.
- Clean your teeth at least twice a day, ideally after each meal. This should take no less than 3-4 minutes.

- Renew your toothbrush or electric toothbrush head every couple of months, or per instructions.
- Electric toothbrushes are recommended, especially for removing plaque.
- Floss your teeth at least once a day to help prevent your gums from receding (a major cause of tooth loss).
- After meals use a tooth pick to dislodge food from between your teeth.
- Chewing gum produces saliva which breaks down bacteria. Choose a sugar-free variety.
- Sugar rots teeth so choose foods, sweets and drinks with reduced or no sugar.
- Mouthwashes and freshener sprays mask bad breath, they don't sort it out.
- Teeth whiteners which use bleach can produce results but can damage the enamel. Check with your dentist first.

Nails

Like skin, nails are made from keratin and protect our fingers and toes from wear and damage. They also help us pick up objects and allows us to scratch the little bastard's eyes out when he cheats on us. Fingernails usually take five or six months to grow from base to tip (just under a millimetre a week). Toe nails take twice as long to grow which is why we don't have to cut them so often(some of us seem to forget about them altogether).

Damage and indicators

Nails are susceptible to damage through injury, pressure or crushing (in a door, for example) but more usually through bacterial or fungal infections and general illnesses. Brittle or ridged nails, black splinter marks beneath the nail itself, blue and green discolouration may be signs of vitamin deficiency and generalised disease.

Nail biting

Nail biting is a nervous is nervous habit. A badly-bitten nail is more susceptible to infections, pain and bleeding. The usual treatment is to paint the nails with a clear solution which tastes horrible, but this has obvious limitations. Examining why you bite your nails can be helpful in devising a strategy to break the habit. Perhaps the best reason for quitting is being able to see a full set of neatly trimmed nails – it will only take a month to see significant improvements.

Nail care tips

- Clean your nails carefully by prising out dirt beneath them. (A nail brush may be helpful).
- Soften your nails in warm water before cutting them.
- Don't cut your nails too short.
- Cut your toenails straight across to stop them in-growing.
- Don't bite your nails. It doesn't just look tacky, it really shows you up when you're holding a glass, shaking hands or he's trying to suck your fingers romantically. (He may as well nibble them for you).
- To protect against nail infection, wear rubber gloves when your hands are being continually immersed in water.
- See a doctor if your nails become discoloured or brittle as this could be due to a fungal infection or vitamin deficiency (which are usually easily treated).

Feet and toenail tips

- If you shower (rather than bath) don't forget to clean your feet, toes and toenails everyday making sure your dry them properly, particularly between the toes.

- If you are prone to bacterial or fungal infections a range of creams, powders and sprays from your chemist can help combat this. Keep a separate foot towel (which you don't use on your face).
- Change socks daily to prevent foot odour.
- Use a pumice stone to gently remove dead skin from the heels and balls of your feet.
- Discard shoes that are worn beyond repair, or no longer fit properly.
- Wear natural materials, such as cotton socks and leather shoes to reduce sweating. If you suffer from smelly feet, wear insoles made of activated charcoal, which absorbs sweat and odour particles.
- If you develop a foot problem, such as a callous, bunion or verruca, see your doctor or chiropodist.

Hair

Like skin and nails, hair is made from keratin. Hair acts as a protective barrier. For example, eyelashes protect the eyes, hairs in the nostrils and ears trap and prevent the entry of foreign bodies and eyebrows prevent sweat dripping into the eyes. Attached to the base of each hair is a minute strip of muscle which is stimulated by cold or emotional stress. When the muscle tightens, the hair stands up trapping air and conserving heat. Each hair grows for up to five years before entering a 'resting' phase. As the growth stops, the hair falls out and after about three months a new hair begins to grow to take its place. Obviously, the number of hairs varies between individuals but, on average there are about 100,000 hairs on your head and you might lose anything between 40-120 hairs a day. Colour is determined by how much pigment hair contains. As we get older, we tend to produce less pigment which is why hair goes grey.

Hair loss

The reasons for hair loss are various including physical ailments, skin conditions, allergic reactions, and mental stress. The most common type of hair loss is baldness which is caused by hormonal change in the body as we get older. Unless you intend to stick the bum of a Canadian beaver to the top of your head – get used to it, it's a fact of life! Shorter hair – properly groomed – can be dead sexy in a man of any age. For some men, however, hair loss is a major upset particularly when their young. If hair loss causes you stress, depression or makes you feel inadequate talk to your GP before spending money on potions or transplants.

RRRRRRK

Dandruff

Dandruff is a common but relatively harmless condition where dead skin cells are shed from the scalp. This produces white flakes which are best noticed on dark suits. The usual cause is a scaly rash called seborrhoeic dermatitis that can also affect the chest, face and back. Treatment involves regular use of a medicated anti-dandruff shampoo from your chemist although a cortico-steroid or anti-fungal drug are sometimes required (through your GP).

Hair care tips

- Shampoo your hair regularly to remove any build up of dirt and grease.
- Beware of harsh anti-dandruff shampoos – ask your hairdresser, chemist or perhaps barber for advice.
- When washing your hair massage your scalp to stimulate blood flow and to release tension.
- Rinse your hair thoroughly (under a shower stream if possible).
- Use a conditioner to smooth the outer surface of the hairs.
- Keep hairdryers at least 15 centimetres away from the head to avoid heat damage.
- Don't brush your hair when it is wet, as it is at its weakest then.
- Avoid over-vigorous rubbing of wet hair, which can cause split ends and tangling.
- If you cut your own hair with electric clippers make sure you choose the correct setting. (Once it's cut – it can't be undone!) Make sure that you cut evenly; uneven patches or tufts of hair which have not been trimmed look truly dreadful.
- Ear and nose hairs can get long and straggly but can be kept short with a trimmer, or plucked out (which does a better job).
- Stray eyebrows can be plucked.

Hearing

Our ears are designed to pick up sound and convert it into electrical signals which can be understood by the brain. The outer ear catches sound waves and channels them along a passage to the ear drum, causing it to vibrate. Wax is produced naturally and, along with the hairs which grow at the entrance of the ear, traps dirt and dust particles. On the other side of the drum is the middle ear in which three tiny bones transmit the vibration across a small air filled cavity to the inner ear. The middle ear is connected to the back of the nose by the eustachian tube which acts as a drainage passage and regulates air pressure. It opens during swallowing and yawning allowing air to flow up to the middle ear and equalising air pressure on both sides of the ear drum. Without this, the ear drum cannot vibrate properly which is why our hearing can become dull or muffled when we have a blocked nose or experience a change of air pressure when flying, for example. The inner ear is made up of the cochlea, a small snail shaped organ filled with fluid, through which sound waves vibrate. Minute hairs are stimulated by sound and converted into electrical impulses which are sent to the brain. Attached to the cochlea are three fluid-filled semi-circular canals at rightangles to each other that help maintain balance by detecting even the slightest body movement.

The human ear is able to hear different ranges of sound from around 20Hz (hertz) to 30,000Hz. The top note on a piano, for example is around 4,000Hz. Comparative noise levels are measured in Decibels (Db) and the chart below shows a range of noises. Risk of injury starts at 90Db and probable permanent injury from 120Db.

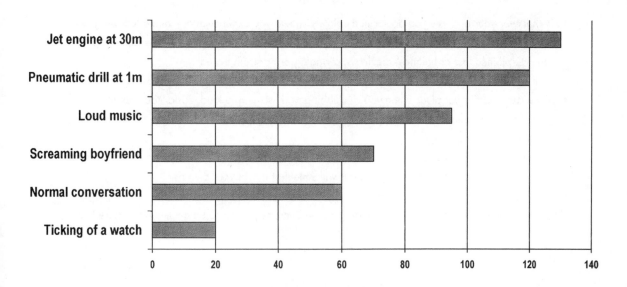

Damage to hearing

Hearing may be damaged by exposure very loud noises for a short period (such as an explosion at close range) or by prolonged exposure to low levels of noise (such as might occur in a machine room). The most likely risk to gay men is loud music in a club or through headphones. Muscles in the middle ear normally respond to loud noise by altering the stiffness of the bones that pass the vibrations to the inner ear. This reduces their efficiency and dampens the intensity of the noise. When a loud noise occurs without warning these protective reflexes don't have time to respond and the full force of the vibration is carried into the inner ear causing severe damage to delicate hairs in the cochlea. Occasionally, loud noises actually rupture the ear drum. More commonly though, damage from loud noises occurs over a period of time, with a gradual destruction of the hairs causing permanent hearing loss. Sound at 90Db+ may cause pain and temporary deafness lasting for minutes or hours. This is a warning that hearing may be damaged. Tinnitus (ringing or buzzing in the ears) occurs after the noise has stopped and is an indication that some damage has probably been done. Prolonged exposure to loud noise leads to a loss of ability to hear certain high tones. Later on, deafness extends to all high frequencies and just listening to somebody talking becomes increasingly difficult. Eventually, lower tones are also affected.

Protecting your hearing

- What ever your age, see you doctor immediately should you experience any of the following symptoms: difficulty hearing someone talk, regular use of TV subtitles, persistent earache or pain, an unexplained loss of balance, dizziness, a ringing or noises in the ear.
- Ear protectors should be worn in noisy environments over 80Db, this includes clubs.
- Consider wearing ear plugs when you're clubbing and listening to loud music. You may like to ask a club the maximum level at which music is played (but they probably won't have the faintest idea what you're talking about).
- Many personal players (cassette, mini-disc, and CD) have limits on the volume control. While these can often be over-ridden, the manufacturer will state that it is at your own risk.
- Ears usually are very good at cleaning themselves. If wax builds up – see your doctor before you start poking around. If you're used to using cotton buds, remember to be gentle! A punctured ear drum can cause permanent deafness.

Eyes

The eye is a fluid filled ball held inside the eye socket by delicate muscles, which control eye movement up, down, left and right. At the front of the eye is the cornea which helps you focus. (People who wear contact lenses place them on this part of the eye.) Behind this is the iris which controls the amount of light entering the eye. In its centre, a small aperture (the pupil) widens to let more light in when it's dark and narrows when there is bright light. A circular ring of muscle surrounding the iris relaxes and contracts changing its shape to provide additional focus. Light then passes through the fluid in the eye ball to the retina at the back where millions of sensitive cells convert light into nerve impulses. These are sent to the brain where images – including the words you're reading now – are assembled into stuff you can understand.

Tears

Tears keep the cornea and conjunctiva (which covers he white of the eye and the inside of the eyelids) constantly moist. Blinking sweeps a film of tears across the eye, keeping the surface well lubricated and washing away dust and dirt. In addition to salty water, tears contain a natural antiseptic. Tears drain away through a single hole near the inner end of each eyelid into small tear sacs and then down through the nose which is why your nose runs when you cry.

Short and long sightedness

Short sightedness is when near objects can be seen clearly while objects further away (even by as little as a foot) can appear blurred or indistinct. Short sightedness is usually caused by the eye being too long front to back (horizontally) and, as a result, images of distant objects focus just in front of the front of the retina. Conversely, long sightedness is when the eye is too short affecting your long distance vision. These conditions are usually treated with glasses or contact lenses and regular check-ups for this and other sight conditions is essential – even if you think you have 20/20 vision.

Contact lenses

Contact lenses have been around for just over 100 years although Leonardo da Vinci was the first to describe the possibility of using them over 500 years ago. While there are different types of lenses, soft lenses tend to be the most popular because they are easy to wear from the start, but an optician will be able to recommend a lens best suited to your needs. The high water content in soft lenses (40-80%) allows more oxygen to reach the eye covered by the lenses and so they can be worn for longer periods. However, despite their obvious success, problems can occur such as:

- Eye infections through a failure to keep lens maintenance equipment clean, wash hands thoroughly before putting in/taking out lenses.and keep lenses properly disinfected.
- Sensitivity to the lens or maintenance solutions.
- Using lenses for extended periods of time.

- Hard lenses that scratch the eye if they're put in roughly or are worn for too long.
- Problems with tear production.
- Sleeping in lenses particularly after a long night out when you may be dehydrated. You sometimes have to peel the lens off the eye. This is not good.

Symptoms include:

- Redness, stinging and a sensation of heat in the eye.
- Pain or prickliness in the eye.
- Lenses jumping around the eye.
- Increased mucus leading to cloudy or foggy vision.

If you experience any of the above, stop wearing your lenses immediately and head straight for your optician or GP.

Conjunctivitis

Conjunctivitis is an inflammation of the eye causing a range of symptoms including redness, discomfort, discharge and a sensitivity to light. Most cases are caused by bacteria which are spread from hand-to-eye contact or by viruses (eg cold or sore throat). However, an allergic response can also be caused by contact lenses and associated cleaning solutions, pollen and cosmetics.

While warm water will wash away the discharge and remove any crusts on the eyelids, the infection itself usually requires treatment with eye-drops or an ointment containing an antibiotic, antihistamine or cortico-steroid drug. The important thing to remember is to see your optician or GP as soon as you think you have a problem. (This doesn't mean making an appointment in a weeks time.)

Eye care tips

- Whatever your age, get your eyes tested at least once a year – or sooner if you notice any change.
- Depending on how long you use a computer at work, you employer has a legal responsibility to provide you with an eye test.
- TVs are brighter than you might think, sit at least five feet away from the screen.
- When using a computer, rest your eyes every 15 minutes by focusing on something else. Every hour you should have a few minutes break away from the screen. This will help prevent eye strain.

"I think you **look** really horny!"

- If you're using artificial light to read, ideally the light should shine on to the page from behind you.
- Wear sunglasses in bright sunlight; never look directly into the sun.
- Swimming pools are usually highly chlorinated – consider wearing goggles.
- Protective goggles should be worn when welding, handling dangerous chemicals or working high-speed machinery.
- When you'er doing DIY, always wear protection. It may seem like overkill but splinters, glass fragments, dust, metal fragments, plaster, paints etc can also seriously damage your eyesight.
- Avoid rubbing your eyes as this a common way of picking up infections.
- Moisturisers, soaps and other beauty products can badly irritate the eyes even if they are low allergy.
- Last but by no means least – a surprising number of everyday substances will sting badly if you get them into the eye, eg poppers, cum, and sweat.

If you get anything into your eye(s) wash out with plenty of water and if you have any worries seek medical advice immediately.

Further information and contacts

- **Acne Support Group** 020 8561 6868 / www.n2w3.com / P.O.Box 230, Hayes, Middlesex UB4 0UT
- **Acne Support Group** 020 8743 2030 / 16 Dufour's Place, Broadwick Street, London W1V 1FE
- **British Chiropody Association** 01628 621100 / Smae_institute@compuserve.com / The SAME Institute, 149 Bath Street, Maidenhead, Berkshire SL6 4LA
- **British Deaf News** fax: 01527 592083 / text: 01527 592044 / voice: 01527 592034 / video 01527 595318 / www.britishdeafnews.com / 7, Empire Court, Albert Street, Redditch, Worcestershire B97 4DA
- **British Dental Association** 020 7935 0875/3963 / www.bda-dentistry.org.uk / 64 Wimpole Street, London W1
- **British Dental Health Foundation** 01788 546365 / www.dentalhealth.org.uk / Eastlands Court St Peter's Road, Rugby, Warwickshire CV21 3QP
- **Cancer Index** Comprehensive internet guide to for cancer www.cancerindex.org

- **CancerBACUP** Comprehensive information, news and events 0808 8001234/020 7613 2121 (9am-7pm Mon-Fri) www.cancerbacup.org / 3 Bath Place, Rivington Street, London EC2A 3JR
- **Hairline International/The Alopecia Society** 01564 775281 / Lyon's Court, 1668 High Street, Knowle, Solihull, West Midlands B93 0LY
- **Institute of Cancer Research** 0800 7319 468 / www.icr.ac.uk Freepost LON 922, London SW7 3YY
- **International Glaucoma Association** 020 7737 3265 www.ita.org.uk/iga/ Kings College Hospital, Denmark Hill, London SE5 9RS
- **National Association for Deafened People** 01494 724830 / Ashby Place, 26 Stubbs Woods, Chesham Bois, Buckinghamshire HP6 6EY
- **National Eczema Society** 0870 2413601 (Mon-Fri 1pm-4pm) / www.eczema.org / Hill House, Highgate Hill, London N19 5NA
- **Prostate Cancer Charity** 0845 300 8383 (9am-5pm Sat-Mon) / www.prostate-cancer.org.uk / 3 Angel Walk, London W6 9HX
- **Prostate Help Association** www.ishop.co.uk / Langworth, Lincoln LN3 5DF
- **Royal National Institute for Deaf People (RNID)** 0870 6050123 / textline: 0870 6033007 / www.rnid.org.uk / 19-23 Featherstone Street, London EC1Y 8SL
- **Royal National Institute for the Blind (RNIB)** 0345 669999 / www.rnib.org.uk / 224 Great Portland Street, London W1N 6AA
- **General Optical Council** 020 7580 3898 / 41 Harley Street, London W1N 2DJ
- **Society of Chiropodists** 020 7486 3381 / 52 Wellbeck Street, London W1M 7HE

sexually transmitted infections (STIs)

If you've ever thought that you were the first or only person to have had a sexually transmitted infection (STI) – think again; they have been around for thousands of years. Gonorrhoea was first mentioned in the Bible and the name of the disease was given by the second century Greek physician Galen. The origin of syphilis is less clear but by the 16th Century it was making its way across Europe. More recently , HIV has affected the lives of gay and bisexual men everywhere and has changed the way we think about sexual health. Not only do we have a better understanding of our health needs but many genito-urinary medicine (GUM) and sexual health services have responded to the need for improvement. None of us really want to dwell on STIs, but being aware on what's going on leaves you free to concentrate on having a good time. Anybody can get a STI from someone who already has one. The trouble is that STIs are usually passed on by someone who doesn't know that they have an infection and so just asking your partner won't protect you.

The majority of STIs enter the body through tiny abrasions, sores or cuts in the body, many of which can be invisible to the eye. A few STIs only itch, some are painful, some are permanent and many can be serious if left untreated. Effective prevention, protection and treatment will significantly reduce the likelihood of getting STIs or if you do get them, will reduce or eliminate the harm they can cause.

Reducing the risks of infection

Being sexually healthy is not only about dealing with sexual problems as they arise, it's also about avoiding problems in the first place. Most sexual activity carries some kind of risk of getting an STI and, while never pleasant, many gay men see them as an occupational hazard. You can significantly reduce the risk of getting or passing on STIs by:

- Vaccination against hepatitis A and B.
- Using condoms when fucking
- Routine clinic check-ups every four to six months.
- A prompt visit to a sexual health clinic if you think you have an STI.

Causes and common symptoms

Sexually transmitted infections are caused by:

- Bacteria which generally live and multiply in the warm and moist parts of your body like your throat, inside your penis and in your anus and rectum.
- Viruses which generally need to get into the blood stream before they can do harm.
- Parasites which live on your body in areas like your groin and armpits.

While some STIs have no symptoms, most do and can include:

- Itching in or around the penis, testicles or anus.
- Burning or itching when you urinate or shit.
- Needing to urinate or shit and then not being able to go, or only going a little.
- Spots, scabs or rashes on the penis, testicles, or anus.
- Pus from the end of the penis or from the anus.
- Unusual lumps or bumps.

If you have any of these symptoms, even if you have not had sex recently, you should be checked by a doctor. STIs don't clear up on their own and can be serious if left untreated. It is worth examining yourself about once a month to make sure you haven't picked anything up – apart from the man you always wanted. However, some STIs *don't* have symptoms. You are recommended to go for a check-up at least twice a year at a sexual health clinic, someof which have specific services for gay men.

HIV and STIs

Having HIV already and getting an STI can put extra strain on the immune system and increase your viral load (the amount of virus present in the blood). This, in turn, can make you more infectious (in terms of HIV) to others. If you get infected with another strain of HIV, this could do more harm than the one you already have and increase the likelihood of disease progression. If you get infected with a drug-resistant strain of HIV, drug treatment will be less effective.

It's therefore essential that you have regular sexual health check-ups to make sure that you haven't picked anything up, particularly STIs which show few or no symptoms. Since most men find out that they have HIV at a clinic, you may already have a doctor who manages your sexual health. If you have any concerns or problems – don't hesitate to pick up the phone or visit.

Sorting out symptoms and what they may mean

If you think you have an STI, you might wonder what kind of STI it is. The symptom chart opposite matches a range of symptoms commonly associated with sexually transmitted infections. By relating your symptoms with the chart, you should get an indication which STI you could have. Some symptoms can indicate other illnesses or medical problems. All the more reason to see someone as soon as possible. The chart is for guidance only and you should not attempt to diagnose or treat yourself. Always consult a doctor. Almost all STIs require a test at a sexual health clinic to determine whether or not you have a STI.

		Chlamydia	Warts (Genital)	Gonorrhoea	Hepatitis	Herpes	HIV	NSU	Crabs	Scabies	Syphilis
Body	- rash									●	●
	- itching (in hairy parts)								●		
Cock	- blisters					●					
	- rash or sores		●			●					●
	- discharge of pus	●		●		●		●			
	- inflamed entrance	●		●							
	- discomfort inside	●		●							
	- sores just inside entrance		●			●					●
Cock and balls	- cauliflower shaped sores		●								
	- inflamed	●				●		●			
	- blisters					●					
	- itching					●			●	●	
Arse (hole)	- itching		●			●					
	- pus discharge			●							
	- lumps /bumps		●			●					
	- discomfort / pain		●			●					
Groin	- soreness and / or swelling						●				
Mouth	- sores					●					●
Eyes	- yellowy				●						
Skin	- yellowy				●						
Pain	- during sex	●	●	●		●		●			
Pissing	- discomfort or pain	●		●		●		●			
	- need to piss more			●				●			
Throat	- sore	●		●							●
Urine	- darker in colour										
No symptoms	- some STIs have none	●	●	●	●	●	●	●	●	●	●
Flu-like symptoms	- inc. shivers and aches				●	●	●	●			●
Tiredness	- without energy, feeling weak				●		●				

Chlamydia

Chlamydia is a bacterial infection which you get from unprotected fucking, fingering, rimming, deep kissing and oral sex. Symptoms show themselves one to three weeks after infection. It affects the penis, anus and the throat but can also spread to the bladder and the prostate gland. The body develops an allergic reaction to untreated chalamydia causing an acute form of athrirtis in the joints where it cause permanent damage. It is easily treated with antibiotics although you should go back to the clinic to check that it has cleared up.

Crabs Pubic lice

Pubic lice are small insects no more than 3mm across and under the microscope look very much like crabs, hence the nickname. They can be seen with the naked eye particularly when they've eaten your blood and are bloated. Crabs have a long sharp hollow nose which they use to pierce the skin and draw up a tasty meal . They live in hair anywhere on the body but you will usually find them first in the groin and chest areas. They move around like Tarzan, holding tightly onto a hair with their claws and swinging to the next. They can easily be passed on though close physical contact including shared bedding, towels and clothing. You don't only get crabs through sex, so be careful before you point that finger! They are sometimes passed on through day-to-day social contact with friends, flatmates or anyone with whom you share your home. Crabs are easily treated with a special lotion, available from any chemist, or free, from a clinic. Even after effective treatment you can still feel itchy for a few days and – believing the crabs still there – some people re-treat themselves which can cause skin irritation. All bedding and clothes that have come into contact with you should be washed at no less than a 60° c wash.

Gonorrhoea

Gonorrhoea is a highly infectious bacterial infection which you get from unprotected fucking, fingering, rimming, deep kissing, and oral sex. Left untreated the infection can spread to the prostate gland, bladder, the balls and joints and cause permanent damage. Blindness has be known and in some cases, death. A course of antibiotics is usually prescribed.

Hepatitis

Hepatitis is caused by a family of viruses – such as A, B and C – that affect the liver and reduce its ability to function. One of the largest and most important body organs, the liver makes and regulates many of the body's chemicals and helps break down and eliminate drugs, toxins and others poisonous substances from the blood. When it's infected, it becomes swollen, painful and doesn't work properly which means that poisons – which would otherwise be processed by the liver – build up in the bloodstream. Recovery can take many months and the consequences of hepatitis can be serious, cause long-term damage and in some cases liver failure. (Hepatitis can also be caused by the side-effects of some medical drugs, overdosing on some drugs eg paracetamol, and long-term alcohol abuse – which put the liver under great strain).

Vaccination

Unlike the majority of STIs, Hepatitis A and B are preventable through vaccination. So with few exceptions you can virtually eliminate getting it in the first place, and it's difficult to understand why so many gay men who know about it don't bother. If you're gay and sexually active, it's essential!

How you get it and symptoms

Hepatitis A

Hepatitis A is most commonly associated with poor toilet hygiene and contaminated food and wate,r although you get it from rimming, scat, and kissing. While some people don't get any symptoms at all, they usually occur two to eight weeks after infection and include diarrhoea, loss of appetite, aches and pains, pale slimy shits, dark coloured piss and a yellowing or jaundice of the skin and eyes. Although very unpleasant, hepatitis A is rarely serious and the body usually fights off the infection within a few weeks, though some symptoms may persist for up to six months.

Hepatitis B

Hepatitis B is much more serious than hepatitis A and can cause long-term liver damage. In a minority of cases, this can cause chronic liver damage leading to death. You can get hepatitis B from unprotected fucking and shared dildos, oral sex, watersports (if the piss gets into the eyes and mouth) and rimming. In fact, it's a bit of an all rounder which is why vaccination is essential! Most people experience no symptoms but have a period of illness up to six months after infection. These include tiredness, jaundice, dark coloured piss, pale slimy shits, stomach pains and itching. The majority of people recover fully although a small percentage remain carriers of the virus and can pass it on to others and run the risk of problems later on.

Hepatitis C

Hepatitis C is on the increase. Identified just over a decade ago, it is more serious than either A or B and like hepatitis B can cause liver disease and death in the longer term. Hepatitis C is much harder to transmit than A, B, or HIV and most infected people are injecting drug users, recipients of blood transfusions, or have fucked, sucked or rimmed without protection. However, unlike HIV, hepatitis C has a tough outer coating and can remain active for several weeks on shared personal items like toothbrushes and razors.

Treatment and recovery

There is no treatment for hepatitis A and B and so the key to recovery is resting sufficiently to allow the body to overcome the virus and get the liver working properly again. This can take several weeks, in some cases months. Your recovery plan should include:

- Plenty of rest.
- No alcohol.
- No fatty, rich or spicy foods.
- No recreational drugs including dope and tobacco.

This may seem strict but if you don't stick to it the liver won't get the rest it needs to recover and you are likely to get sick again. Treatment for hepatitis C is more complicated and in addition to the above, a drug called interferon alfa is sometimes given which can reduce the amount of the virus and halt or slow down damage to the liver.

Herpes

Herpes viruses cause small fluid-filled blisters on the skin. There are different types of the herpes virus. Type I causes cold sores around the nose and mouth while Type II affects the cock, balls and arsehole. Herpes can also affect the eyes and the passage between the mouth and the stomach (oesophagus), particularly in those with weakened immune systems. Herpes is passed on through unprotected fucking, oral sex, kissing or physical contact with the affected areas, particularly when someone has an attack of herpes at the time and the blisters are open and weeping. Symptoms include tingling or burning on the skin (prior to the blisters appearing), discomfort or pain when urinating or shitting and flu-like symptoms. These are often called 'attacks' or 'episodes'. During an attack the virus moves from the root of the nerve to the surface of the skin where the blisters occur. They are often very painful and take several weeks to heal, forming dry flaky scabs that eventually disappear. When the attack is over the virus travels back to the nerve root where it 'rests' until the next time. As far as we know, you will remain infected for life and, from time to time, the virus will travel back along the nerve reactivating the sores on the skin surface.

You are more prone to attacks if you are ill, stressed, or feeling run-down. Regular rest and relaxation, and de-stressing techniques combined with a healthy diet will reduce the likelihood of attacks. Acyclovir is thought by many to help prevent attacks in the first place or shorten attacks when they happen However, it's expensive and some clinics don't like giving it out or will make you jump through hoops before they give it to you. For example, you have to prove you have regular attacks and that they are bad. (Well, you can't get more subjective than that.) Bathing sores can relieve symptoms and shorten episodes, and staying out of bright sunlight (which aggravates them) can help. For some guys, herpes is particularly depressing and debilitating and clinics can fail to take this into account when providing treatment.

If you choose to have sex while having a herpes attack make sure that neither of you comes into contact with a sore. You should also wash your hands after touching a sore to prevent spreading it. There is also a low risk of the virus being transmitted by sharing towels or face flannels. To stop the virus being spread from mouth to the genital area, you should not have oral sex if you've got cold sores. Also be careful of transferring the virus from one area to another (fiddling with herpes sores or aggravating scabs while wanking for instance). Always wash your hands after coming into contact with them.

HIV and AIDS

What it does

HIV stands for Human Immunodeficiency Virus. Isolated in 1983, it belongs to a family of viruses known as retroviruses. Although the syndrome of illnesses associated with HIV infection was only recognised in the early 80s, analysis of stored blood samples reveals it was present as long ago as 1959. A virus is a very simple organism, consisting of an outer coating enclosing genetic material. When a person becomes infected with HIV, the virus enters the cell and the viral genetic material is copied into the gene of the infected cell. These cells will remain infected for the rest of their lives, as HIV uses them as factories to produce more copies, which can then go on to infect more cells. Although many different cells within the body are infected with HIV, it particularly damages cells which are part of the body's defences against infection (the immune system). This is why people with advanced HIV infection are much more susceptible to certain infections (and types of cancer) since the function of the immune system is progressively weakened by the damage done by HIV. AIDS (Acquired Immune Deficiency Syndrome) is the name given to the collection of illnesses (or syndrome) which someone can get if their immune system has been severely damaged by HIV.

How you get it

Fucking without condoms and sharing needles to inject drugs are the two main ways HIV is transmitted. While there is some risk with other sexual practices such as cocksucking, rimming, finger fucking and fisting, the risks are negligible compared to unprotected fucking, which accounts for a significant number of HIV transmission cases between men. The most effective way to prevent HIV transmission – and protect yourself against many other STIs – is to fuck with condoms or not to fuck at all. That said, if you are determined to fuck without condoms and you aren't sure if you might get HIV or pass it on, there are things you could do that would make it less likely.

Treatment

While there is no cure or vaccine, there is a range of treatments which have improved significantly in recent years. Treatments to fight HIV work in different ways but many aim to make it more difficult for HIV to copy itself, so reducing the amount of virus in the blood. This in turn means that HIV does less damage and reduces the likelihood of an AIDS-related illness. While there have been major advancements in the way we combat HIV, there is neither a cure nor a vaccine and both are unlikely in the near future.

Testing for HIV

Once someone is infected, the body will produce antibodies or markers in the blood and these can be detected, usually, after 8-12 weeks of infection, with a blood test. Symptoms associated with HIV are also common to many other medical conditions. A proper check-up and an HIV antibody test will only determine whether you have HIV, the common 'flu or something else. If you are concerned, go to clinic.

The HIV test detects HIV antibodies, not the virus itself. Antibodies are produced after someone has been infected with the virus. HIV antibodies do not effectively remove the virus from your system and so do not make you immune. It can take up to three months after infection for the test to detect antibodies. This means that if you have become infected within the last three months, a test will not necessarily be positive. If you decide to have an HIV test you should think carefully about the possible results. Positive means antibodies are present, negative meansthey are not. Some people are convinced they are negative but test positive and vice versa. It's natural to speculate but you could be wrong.

A negative test result will mean that you have not got HIV (provided you have not put yourself at risk within the last three months) and that you cannot pass HIV on to anyone else. Recently there have been reports about certain people being immune to HIV. These cases are extremely rare, there are estimated to be only a handful of people in this country. For the majority of gay men, a negative result does not mean they are immune. If you've fucked without a condom in the last 15 years with someone you could not be 100% sure was HIV negative, then you're probably lucky, not immune. A positive test result means you are infected with HIV and can pass it on to someone else. It does not, on its own, necessarily mean that you have AIDS, nor does it tell you if or when you will develop an AIDS-related condition.

If you go for a test at a GUM/sexual health clinic you should be offered the opportunity to talk to a counsellor, a health adviser or a doctor beforehand. Staff are there to ensure that you fully understand what the test involves. They are not there to tell you whether you should have a test or to pressure you into making a decision either way. There may be advantages and disadvantages to taking an HIV test. These will depend on you as an individual and what you think your test result might be. There can be no overall recommendation about testing, it is up to you. If you decide to have an HIV test, think about who you tell that you are having one. If someone knows you are going for a test, they might want to know the result. Would you really want them to know? If you or your partner are thinking about testing, don't put pressure on each other to make a quick decision. Respect each other's choices.

After an HIV positive diagnosis

Everyone's experience of living with HIV is different. As the news sinks in and you start to come terms with what it means, you may feel like being by yourself or with your partner, chatting with a close friend or someone at the clinic where you received your diagnosis. There are also groups where you can share your experiences with other newly diagnosed gay men, although you won't necessarily ask the same questions or all go through the same feelings and emotions. 'I feel so lonely…', 'I'm so relieved…', and 'there's just so much to think about…' are not unusual responses. And, '…am I going to die?'… 'who gave me it to me?'… 'what am I going to do now?' and '…who should I tell?' are commonly asked questions. The quick answers are 'yes'… 'why does it matter?'…'take your time' and 'no one until you are ready.' But you will also learn that the answers to these and other questions are not necessary black or white, right or wrong, or good or bad.

Take things at your own pace. Don't rush into taking decisions or allow yourself to be coerced or bullied into doing things you may later regret. Most things can wait for a while, this includes talking to you family or partner, seeking proper advice before telling your employer (though as a rule you're encouraged not to) or leaving your job and becoming destitute. For some HIV positive gay men, telling others about their status can be as traumatic as coming out as gay. It is important to think carefully about who you want to tell and why. Once you have told someone about being HIV positive, you cannot take the information back. Coming out is a very personal process and should be your choice. Obviously, it can feel very natural to want to tell your partner and/or your family immediately but the response may not be what you expect. It certainly doesn't help to be dealing with other people's crap while still sorting out your own. If, however, you have decided to come out, the following may be helpful:

- Be aware that telling people may affect you more than you think and they may not react in the way you expect.
- Don't ell people if you don't want them to tell others.
- Try and prepare yourself for the questions they may ask or the issues they may bring up.
- Try and choose the right time and place.

People have different reasons for coming out. For some it may be to get support or health care whilst others might want their sexual partner(s) to know. Not telling someone about your diagnosis might prevent you getting the support, advice and services that are appropriate to your needs. Whatever reaction you get to coming out, being positive is nothing to be ashamed of.

Step by step

After your HIV diagnosis, several things are likely to happen:

- You will subjected to a flurry of medical tests to establish your state of health and to what extent virus is affecting your immune system.
- If appropriate, you may be offered treatments to reduce or stabilise the level of HIV in your body or treatments to help prevent the development of opportunistic infections.

- Depending on your needs, state of health and circumstances you will be helped to apply for benefits or put in touch with a social worker or home care support team.

There is sometimes an assumption by professionals that because you are gay you know what to do and where to go. This is, of course, not likely to be true where your new HIV diagnosis is concerned. Of course it may be difficult to gauge whether you're getting the information you need and want, but if you have any doubts ask – or get a second opinion from a helpline or other organisation. This can be overwhelming particularly at a time when there is likely to be a lot on your mind and you may be feeling very stressed and emotional. Spare some thought for how you are feeling. Being HIV positive can play havoc with your emotions. Whether you chat regularly with a mate, attend a group, phone a helpline or seek professional help – don't ignore your feelings. Some find it difficult to ask for help or accept it, but there's nothing wrong with getting it or for asking for it. We all need help once in a while – it doesn't mean that we are weak or incapable. Equally, saying 'no' doesn't necessarily mean you are being awkward – so don't feel guilty or afraid about saying it. The following tips are designed to make getting help and support easier, and so you make decisions which suit *you* and meet *your* needs.

- Try to deal with one thing at a time.
- Find a doctor or clinic you like. If you don't like them, change them.
- Make decisions in your own time.
- Take at least some time to learn more about HIV and how it could affect you. But you don't have to become an expert or know everything at once. Knowing more will help you feel more in control.
- Consider how you could make your lifestyle healthier. It may include, for example, changes to your diet, having more fun or doing relaxation exercises. Even if you think you're a sceptic give it a chance; you can always go back to clubs, drugs, and ready-made-meals – they ain't going nowhere!
- Listen to your body, it's usually pretty good at telling you what it likes and doesn't like. You may take it for granted but it is your friend, get to know and understand it better.
- If there are changes to be made to your life, they are rarely drastic or wholesale and you don't have to make them all at once. You have time.
- If you're attending an appointment, there's nothing to stop you taking someone with you. A little moral support and another pair of ears can be very helpful.

When you are speaking about your HIV, particularly in relation to HIV services, you may come across people whom you don't know, don't like or who don't seem to understand what your needs are. Here are some tips to get you through:

- Be honest and direct – say what's on your mind.
- Consider taking notes and preparing some questions beforehand. This way you can take the

information away and understand it better in your own time.

- Listen to what is being said and think what you want to say next before opening your gob. I

- If you're getting irritable or angry say so, then take some deep breaths, take a break, or go to the toilet. If you really can't handle it, leave. You can always go back when you're ready.

- If you're told something which you don't understand, repeat what's been said in your own words and ask if you've understood correctly.

HIV treatments

Over the past 5 years, the development of HIV treatments has revolutionised the way HIV is managed. A new generation of drugs work principally by slowing down the rate at which HIV reproduces in the body. This allows the immune system to regroup and strengthen which means that the body can fight off infections more easily. Death rates have been significantly lowered and people with HIV are staying healthier for longer. Although there are many benefits from taking these drugs, there is still a lot which isn't known about them – for example, doctors don't know how long the drugs will be effective. Some people experience side effects with these drugs. Often these will be mild, or will only last for a few days or weeks after starting the drug, but in a small number of people these side effects may be more severe, causing them to change drugs.

It's vital to take these drugs exactly as prescribed. This is called being 'compliant' or 'adherent'. For some of the drugs this means taking a specific dose at specific times during the day, and changing diet in order to increase the effect which the drugs have on the body. This can have an impact on people's lifestyles, for example getting up early or staying up late to take a drug. However, if these guidelines aren't complied with, there is a significant risk that some of the drugs will not be effective and you could develop drug-resistant virus. Resistance means that the virus has changed so that the drug will no longer affect it. Resistance may happen even if drugs are taken exactly as prescribed. Reinfection with HIV from someone who already has a drug-resistant strain may also mean that you might quickly develop resistance to the drugs – a compelling reason for having safer sex. Anyone considering taking anti-HIV drugs needs to think carefully about the advantages and disadvantages. Before you decide to take the drugs, you should talk to your doctor, and contact one of the organisations listed at the end of this chapter. Ask questions and find stuff out for yourself.

Non-Specific Urethritis (NSU)

NSU is a bacterial infection that you get from unprotected fucking, fingering, rimming, deep kissing and oral sex. The pain and burning sensation when pissing is sometimes referred to as 'pissing razorblades' or 'pissing glass'. Untreated, NSU can spread to the balls which can become inflamed and can be very painful during sex. Sometimes there are no symptoms and NSU will only be picked up by a routine test at a sexual health clinic. However, symptoms are very similar to gonorrhoea and only a test will tell them apart. A course of antibiotics will treat most NSU infections.

Scabies

Scabies is caused by a common mite, invisible to the eye, that burrows into the surface of the skin to lay its eggs. This causes severe irritation and small rashes and/or reddish tracks. You can find them almost anywhere on the body but you will often find them in the groin area, between the fingers, chest and stomach and feet. Like crabs, they can easily be passed on though close physical contact and shared bedding, towels and clothing, but this is less likely. The treatment is the same as for crabs – get hold of the appropriate lotion from the chemist, and follow the instructions. You must also wash all used clothes and bedding at no less than 60°c wherever possible to kill the mites and their eggs.

Syphilis

Syphilis is caused by a tiny corkscrew shaped bacterium which is invisible to the naked eye. You get it through fucking, oral sex, fisting and most other physical contact with the sores or rash which are highly infectious. A blood test through a sexual health clinic will tell you if you haves syphilis. Over a period of years, symptoms develop through three stages as it spreads through the body and, if left untreated, will cause madness, heart disease and death. During stage one, a small sore appears on the cock, around the arsehole or the throat, no more than 1cm across; this heals in a couple of months. During stage two, about three months later, there is a skin rash which can be severe and is accompanied by headaches, nausea, flu-like symptoms, and loss of appetite. In some instances people lose their hair in clumps. During stage three, which usually starts within ten years of infection several things happen: the nervous system breaks down, heart failure, large ulcerous sores, madness and death. Syphilis is one a range of STIs which are tested for routinely at sexual health clinics and is rare in the UK although it is becoming more common in gay men.

Treatment

If detected early, syphilis is treated with penicillin or and antibiotics for those who are allergic. However, As you progress through the stages, it becomes increasingly difficult to treat effectively.

Warts

Genital warts are caused by the *papillomavirus* which you get from fucking, oral sex and most skin contact with them including touching, rubbing and scratching. They appear as small fleshy whitish cauliflower-shaped lumps on the cock, balls or the anus. They can also appear in the mouth, on the face and inside the rectal passage. While they are not known to cause harm to men, they can be unsightly and can be itchy or uncomfortable. Warts can be single or group tightly together. If you already have warts, shaving them or scratching them and them touching other parts of the body will cause them to spread. Sometimes warts disappear by themselves although you will still have the virus and they may appear months or years later. They are usually treated with a wart-removing liquid that is painted onto the warts until they go. They can also be frozen off with liquid nitrogen, o, in some cases surgery or laser treatment is used.

Protection against STIs

Condoms

The most effective way to protect yourself and your partner(s) from the risk of infection from STIs is the use of condoms and water-based lubricant – every time when you get fucked or fuck. In the past, condoms have been made out of all sorts of materials: horn or tortoise shell for that extra sensitive gentle touch, oiled paper, linen or animal gut. Up until the 1930s rubber condoms were thick, washable and re-usable. However, the development of latex in the later 1930s meant that thinner, disposable condoms could be produced. More recently we have seen the arrival of a polyurethane condom which is said to be twice as strong as latex and it's bloody expensive! However, being thinner, sensitivity should be greater and it is the only condom which can be used with oil-based lubricants.

Different shaped condoms are designed for different shaped cocks, so experiment. Although you can get extra large condoms, most come in two widths, 49mm and 52mm, and in a variety of shapes: ribbed, straight, plain-ended, flared and contoured. Most condoms are lubricated with sensitol, nonoxynol 9 or a spermicide. There are also flavoured condoms which usually taste revolting, but you can be pleasantly surprised. Used more often for sucking they are not recommended for fucking.

Stronger condoms

These include brands like Durex Ultra Strong, Mates Superstrong, HT Specials and Safeguard Special. Obviously thicker condoms will lessen sensitivity of the cock. If this is a problem for you, try using one of the thinner brands of condoms along with plenty of water-based lubricant but check it while you're fucking as there may be a greater chance of the condom tearing. Also, a drop of water-based lubricant in the condom (or placed on the end of you cock) before rolling it on may increase sensitivity. Although thicker condoms offer better protection under ideal circumstances, the benefits are probably outweighed if your dick is so de-sensitised that you have to shunt about for hours on end like an inter-city 125 before you can cum. (If you do tend to cum too quickly – a thicker condom may help delay your orgasm.)

Standards and condom failure

You should ensure that the 'CE' or 'British Standard Kitemark' is displayed on the packet, and although no condom is guaranteed not to break they will have been rigorously tested. There are two reasons why condoms fail: product failure (something was wrong with the condom when it was made) and user failure (when people haven't followed the instructions properly). Trials (involving vaginal intercourse) over several years have shown that condoms are very effective for regular users. It's unfamiliarity and poor technique which can cause problems.

Using condoms

- If you're going to fuck make sure you have a pack to hand and remove all pets and ex-boyfriends from the area!
- Place some lube on a finger or two and gently work it up his arsehole. He'll get more pleasure if he's relaxed and the rubber is less likely to tear. Checking the use-by date first, take the rubber out of its wrapper avoiding sharp/jagged finger nails, teeth and cheap jewellery.
- With a thumb and forefinger pinch the end of the rubber as this will get rid of the air and make room for the cum. Make sure it's not upside down or you won't be going anywhere! Then, roll it all the way down your dick. A hard dick makes this easier to do but it may go soft at this point. Simply work up some steam and – using a new rubber – try again later.
- Rubbers do make a difference: you can't feel as much and they can be awkward to use. But every six hours there is a new HIV infection between gay men in the UK. Using rubber and lube every time you get fucked or fuck greatly reduces the risk HIV infection. Rubbers help protect against other sexually transmitted infections including gonorrhoea, syphilis, herpes, hepatitis, and NSU. Wanking with rubbers can also improve your technique and get you into the idea of using them.
- Smother your dick with lube and ask him if he's ready before putting it up his arse. Enter slowly, if you go in quickly you could hurt him. Once inside, off you go… checking occasionally to see that the rubber is still in place and intact. When you've finished, hold the rubber at the base of your dick before pulling out. You don't want to lose it up his arse do you? Don't leave the rubber lying around for children to find as there is a risk of suffocation! Knot it, wrap it in a tissue or loo roll and bin it. (Not down the toilet, it will bob back up).
- Now, take a break… put on the kettle… leave… start again… or fall asleep in his arms.

Lubricants

Traditionally there have been two main types of lubricant: oil-based and water-based. More recently through synthetic lubricants have appeared on the market; these are condom compatible, but have the consistency of oil-based lubricants. Depending on what you want to do, you need to know which lubricant to use, and whether it contains a spermicide, eg nonoxynol. Although useful against HIV and other STIs, spermicides can irritate the inside of your arse and cause allergic reactions.

In one way, oil-based and water-based lubricants behave similarly in that they reduce the friction between whatever is going into your arse and the arse lining. However, you need the right amount of lubricant to do the job. Too much – and the practicalities of what you're trying to do can become difficult. Too little – and you cause discomfort and pain (to both partners) and run the risk of damaging the condom, the arse, or both.

Water-based (condom-compatible) lubricants

Water-based lubricants dry up because your intestine absorbs the lubricant's water content back into the body leaving a useless sticky residue. Insufficient lubricant increases friction and is a major factor in condoms tearing or damage to the lining of your arse. In fisting particularly, it's essential but not necessarily easy to come out for more lubricant.

Oil-based (non-condom-compatible) lubricants

Oil-based lubricants don't dry up because your intestine is not capable of absorbing any of its components back into your body. It therefore stays there, goes further and lasts longer but this in itself can cause problems. Your lower intestine down to your arsehole is now a bobsleigh run and any shit left can shoot out at a moment's notice! If you're into dildos or fisting then oil-based lubes are generally a better option. If you have a fist up a mate's arse, a comment like 'excuse me I've just got to pop out for some more lube', doesn't go down well. However, oil-based lubricants damage condoms (some would argue render them virtually useless) and so increase the risk of HIV/STI transmission. If you're going to fuck, using a water-based or condom-compatible lubricant is essential.

Nonoxynol 9

In test tube conditions, nonoxynol 9 has been shown to inactivate HIV. However, laboratory conditions don't exist in your arse and we don't know how effective it is there. Most usually, it is added to condoms and lubricants. Some guys find that it causes irritation. So, while it may offer additional protection against HIV, an arse lining irritated by nonoxynol 9 could make you more susceptible to infection and there seems to anecdotal evidence to support this.

Gloves

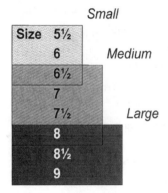

Not everyone who fists uses gloves. Some guys find that wearing them defeats the object, that it's physical closeness of 'naked' hand against arse – mixed with the intensity of the scene – which turns both partners on and plays a major part in completing the experience. It is generally accepted that if your hands are in good condition the risk of HIV is very low. However, you will reduce the risk further by wearing gloves and if you feel safer wearing them – use them. Wearing gloves creates a barrier between infections (present in blood, cum, piss and shit) and routes into your bloodstream (like cuts, sores, abrasions, broken skin and wounds). It also means that a shitty glove can be pulled off, turned inside out and disposed of easily.

Where to get them and what to look for

Some clinics give away free gloves but you will probably have to ask for them. You can buy them in shops; unfortunately you will find that some retailers have bought them in bulk, split them into pairs and are knocking them out at vastly inflated prices. Whether gloves come individually, in pairs or in bulk (boxes of 50 or 100), the standards to which they have been made should be clearly visible. Gloves should meet the International ISO 9002 or British Standard BS4005. 1995 saw the arrival of the CE European Standard. If you don't see these standards you should ask if they are medical grade A examination gloves, not to be confused with grade B gloves which are for non-clinical use. You should remove all rings, jewellery or sharp objects before putting on gloves which should fit snugly. You may find the guide (above) helpful in deciding which size of glove would best suit you. Some gloves come pre-powdered which can make them easier to put on but the powder can irritate the arse if it gets inside. Veterinary (calving) gloves can be used for fisting although this is probably excessive and you may find that they restrict your hand and finger movements, and sense of touch.

Further information and contacts

- **AIDS Treatment Phoneline** Run by HIV positive people, many of whom are on treatments themselves. Answers questions and concerns. 0845 947 0047 Mon/Wed 3pm – 9pm and Tue 3pm – 6pm / www.tht.org.uk

- **National AIDS Helpline** Help, advice and information and details of UK sexual health services 0800 567123 / www.healthwise.org.uk

- **National AIDS Manual** Probably the best and most comprehensive guide to HIV treatments in the world 020 7267 3200 / www.aidsmap.com / 16a Clapham Common Southside, London SW4 7AB

- **Terrence Higgins Trust National Help Line** Helpline volunteers offer confidential support and up-to-date information 020 7242 1010 / Daily 12noon-10pm / www.tht.org.uk

- **Avert** Clearly presented and accessible on-line HIV information www.avert.org.uk

- **BIGUP for Black Men** Delivers culturally specific HIV and AIDS information to black men who have sex with men. 020 7501 9264 / Eurolink Centre, 49 Effra Road, London SW2 1BZ

- **Black Lesbian and Gay Centre** Advice, information, health, social and cultural events 020 7620 3885 / 5 Westminster Bridge Road, London, SE1 7AX

- **Blackliners** HIV/AIDS advice, support, information, and referral for men from African, Caribbean or Asian descent. 020 7738 5274 (Mon-Fri 10am-6.30pm) / Unit 46, Eurolink Centre, 49 Effra Road, London SW2 1BZ

- **Gay Men Fighting AIDS (GMFA)** Community based HIV prevention, sexual health. 020 7738 6872 / www.demon.co.uk/gmfa/gmfa/ Eurolink Centre, 49 Effra Road, London SW2 1BZ

- **Naz Project** HIV/AIDS education, prevention and support servises for Asian, Turkish, Arab and Irani Men 020 8741 1879 / nazlon@dircon.co.uk / 241 King Street, London W 9LP

- **Positive Nation Magazine** Comprehensive monthly publication covering all aspects of HIV www.positivenation.co.uk

- **Terrence Higgins Trust** National HIV/AIDS organisation providing a comprehensive range of HIV prevention, care and treatment services. 020 7242 1010 (12noon-12pm) / www.tht.org.uk / 52-54 Gray's Inn Road, London WC1X 8JU

- **Jewish AIDS Trust** Education counselling and support 020 8200 0369 / www.jat.ort.org / Colindale Hospital, Colindale Avenue, London NW9 5HG

- **Red Admiral** Counselling – a safe and confidential place where you can talk about your life and the ways in which it has been affected by HIV. 020 7835 1485 / www.tht.org.uk

- **Group B Hepatitis** 020 7244 6514 / 7a Fielding Road, London W14 0LL
- **Herpes Viruses Association** 020 7609 9061 / 41 North Road, London N7 9DP
- **Impotence Information Centre** P.O.Box 1130, London W3 0BB
- **Aegis** The largest HIV/AIDS website in the world, providing daily updates, new service, links, reference library, and information for the newly diagnosed. www.aegis.com
- **Iavi** International developments towards a vaccine for HIV www.iavi.org
- **Crusaid** Crusaid, the leading fundraiser for AIDS relief in Britain, 020 7833 3939 / www.crusaid.org.uk / 73 Collier Street London N1 9BE
- **UnAIDS** Global overview of the HIV epidemic with facts, articles, and comment www.unaids.org

sexual health clinics and check-ups

Sexual health clinics are also known as clap clinics, VD clinics, special clinics and genito-urinary medicine (GUM) clinics. The term 'sexually transmitted diseases' (STDs) has under gone a bit of a re-vamp in recent years and clinics are increasingly referring to 'sexually transmitted infections' (STIs) instead.

Clinics provide treatment for STIs and practical help to reduce the risk of getting them in the future. For many years, clap clinics were hidden away in hospital basements but, since the HIV epidemic, many of them have improved enormously and developed a more positive understanding of gay men's health. For those who want them, there are clinics specifically for gay men with evening opening times. Support groups and sexual heath counsellors have been introduced and many services have expertise in HIV – offering pre- and post-HIV test counselling, treatment options and a co-ordinated approach to care. Even the waiting rooms have been brightened up with drinks machines, some half-decent magazines and positive poster images of gay men. Having said that, these improvements are not universal and the quality of service can still vary enormously between clinics. In some cases, we are still patronised and mistreated by homophobic and judgmental staff but they do seem to be on the way out.

Choosing a clinic

Unless a clinic has been recommended to you by a friend, it can difficult to know where to go whether you're looking for your first clinic or moving to a different one. Most cities and larger towns have clinics which are usually part of a hospital. Check your local phone book or phone the National AIDS Helpline free on 0800 567123 which has listings of all clinics in the UK. With few exceptions, most of us use clinics run by the National Health Service – they're free (including treatment prescriptions) and generally very good. Alternatively, you can go to a private clinic and pay for it. Depending on where you live and work, it can be worth thinking about the clinic location although this should be secondary consideration after the quality of the service you receive. Even if there's just the one'locally, some gay men do go elsewhere to reduce the likelihood of recognition or because the service is crap. So shop around to find a clinic which best suits your needs. Phone up the clinic and find out if you need an appointment, or whether it is a 'walk-in' service. 'Walk-in' clinics can be very busy and it's almost impossible to gauge how long you'll be there. It is advisable to put aside a morning or afternoon until you have a clearer idea of how the clinic works. You might want to ask if they have a special clinic for gay men.

Confidentiality

STI clinics are bound by law to ensure the confidentiality of your records and it's usually okay to give your real name and address. If you're going to have an HIV antibody test you may decide to give a false name and this is not against the law. However, you should remember it and any other false information you provide. Unfortunately, the same standard of confidentiality cannot be assured outside your clinic if you're referred to another hospital department or service.

The check-up

When you arrive, you should report to reception where you will be booked in and given a numbered ticket depending on the system. You then wait until your ticket number or name is called. If it's your first time, you may need to answer a few questions or complete a short questionnaire. Some guys feel the need to give a different name which is okay as long as you remember it and respond when it's called out. At some point you will be given a reference number. Don't lose it as it links you with your clinic file which sits amongst tens of thousands of other records. Although they can be found by your name and/or date of birth, looking for records in this way causes delays and extra waiting time for you.

Visits take up to two hours, sometimes longer, but don't be afraid to ask how long it is expected to take. Longer waits usually occur in clinics that provide a 'walk-in' service where it can be difficult to match demand with staff. If the waiting room is packed and the clinic is short staffed, you could be there for several hours – it's unavoidable. Pre-arranged appointments are more likely to keep to time but are not always available for routine check-ups. Everyone is there for the same reasons and nobody is likely to feel any less awkward than you. Just get on with it and take a book to pass away the time.

The consultation

Practice varies between clinics but you can usually expect the following during a routine check-up:

- You will be called by name or number and shown to a consulting room by the doctor; while the consultation is taking place the door should be closed.
- The doctor should introduce him/herself. (Sometimes there is a student present and you should asked whether this is okay. If you'd rather see the doctor alone – say so, particularly if it's your first time at the clinic or if you are feeling in any way nervous).
- The doctor will ask you about any problems or concerns you might have.
- Explain in your own words what seems to be the matter and describe any symptoms.
- The doctor is also likely to ask you the following questions:

  - How many people you've had sex with recently and their sex.
  - Whether your partners were casual or regular.
  - The kind of sex you've had and whether you protected yourself.
  - Whether you've had STIs before and if you have any general health problems or allergies, including recreational drug use.

Difficult and embarrassing though they might be, try to answer them as specifically as possible. If you hide anything (eg say you always use condoms when in fact you don't) or are economical with truth you may be not be tested for something you have.

- The doctor will need to examine you and this is likely to include the cock and balls, the throat, the arsehole, the glands in your throat and the skin.
- The doctor or a nurse will need to take samples to find out whether you have a sexually

transmitted infection. Using swabs , samples are taken from the rectum, throat and the end of the cock. These are used to test for chlamydia, gonorrhoea and NSU which are routine tests. The presence of chlamydia can also be tested using a urine sample.

- The smear from the rectum is taken using a proctoscope (a finger sized plastic tube). To do this, you will be asked to lie on your side with your knees pulled towards your chest. If you have a big arse, you may be asked to hold your arse cheeks apart. The arsehole is lubricated with some jelly and the proctoscope is gently slid into the entrance of the arsehole where the sample is taken. If you've never had anything up your arse then this will be a new sensation for you. Above all: relax. It doesn't take long and is rarely unpleasant.

- A blood sample is taken from the arm to test for syphilis; again this is routine. After discussion with your doctor you may also be tested for hepatitis B to find out whether you need vaccination or, if you've been vaccinated for a few years, a booster.

- You will not be tested for HIV unless you have discussed it with the doctor, consented to having the test and received counselling.

- If the doctor suspects that you may have other STIs you will be tested for these too.

- The doctor may suggest you see a health advisor

- Some of the test results will be available during your visit, others will take a week or so and you will have to go back to get them. However, you can usually phone up to find about routine tests but you will always have to see a doctor or health advisor if you're getting an HIV test result.

- After you have been examined and provided the necessary samples you are likely to be returned to the waiting area for a short time before seeing the doctor again. Depending on the diagnosis and whether you have to wait for further results you may be given a course of treatment (usually antibiotics) and a follow-up appointment. A thoughtful doctor will close the session by checking that everything's okay and give you an opportunity to ask any other questions.

The service you can expect

Good clinic practice is about staff respecting your dignity and treating you with the least possible discomfort. When you're there you should be able to:

- Understand and be kept fully informed about what's going on.
- Have questions asked with sensitivity and in plain language.
- Have time and attention to express concerns and ask questions.
- Have your questions answered honestly and in plain language.
- Be given time to understand the answers.
- Be asked for your consent to any tests or treatments.

Sometimes doctors and staff assume that you are heterosexual or if they know you're gay, pigeonhole sexual activities by simply asking whether you had 'active' or 'passive' sex. Some of us accept that doctors rarely have an accurate understanding of gay lifestyles and resign ourselves to this clumsy line of questioning. Even if staff are making assumptions, saying so can be awkward and embarrassing and besides, why should you take on the education needs of clinic staff? It's only when we start saying what we want and how we expect to be treated that services will improve.

Questionnaires, surveys, studies and trials

You may be asked to take part in a survey or, if you are receiving HIV treatments/therapies, a clinical trial. Before you make any decision you need to understand the purpose of the survey/trial etc; what is involved; your rights and whether there are any dangers or risks. If you have difficulty in understanding what is being asked of you, ask that the questions)or information are rephrased or re-explained. You should also be given time to think about what has been said before you make any decision.

Treatment

If you have an STI then you'll be prescribed a course of treatment. If you're given antibiotics then it is very important that you complete the whole course even if you think the symptoms have gone away. The infection may not have been fully cured and if it comes back then it can be more difficult to treat second time round. You will be asked to come back to check the infection has gone away. If you don't understand what the treatment is and you want to know, don't be afraid to ask, or if you are unhappy with what you've been given then ask if there's an alternative. All treatment and prescriptions are free.

Telling your partner(s)

If you have or have had a recent infection you should tell all your partners (if you can) so that they can also go for check-ups. This may not be easy – but think about it if the roles were reversed. Health advisers will want to make sure that all your recent partners are traced so that they can be warned that they need a check-up too. You don't have to give any details of who you've had sex with, just assure the health adviser that you will personally tell all your partners. Then do it! Remember, you can have most sexually transmitted infections without there being any external or recognisable symptoms. The situation is more complex if you test HIV antibody positive but the health adviser will help you tackle the issues.

Saying thank you and making complaints

Acknowledging when and where clinics get it right is just as important as complaining. Many dedicated staff work very hard to ensure that clinic services meet our needs with the least discomfort and embarrassment. Quite simply, if you're pleased with the service say so and spread the word.

Making a complaint can be difficult and embarrassing particularly if it involves coming face to face (again) with the member of staff you're complaining about. Think carefully about why you are complaining, what you want to say, and what you want to get out of the situation. Maybe it's an apology you want, or an improvement in the service you've received. Being clear and calm will not just help you but also the clinic in understanding why you've made the complaint in the first place. You may want to deal with the situation then and there. Alternatively, when you get home make a note of the incident before contacting the clinic again. (An irate call to the clinic may make you feel better – but unless you provide your name, who was involved, and what happened, it's unlikely that the clinic can carry the complaint further.) It may be useful to talk it through with a friend – preferably one who'll be supportive but objective. If you don't wish to contact the member of staff concerned directly, try the clinic's business manager, the senior health advisor, or the senior consultant. Some clinics have a system for complaints and suggestions and this may be a useful place to start.

Further information and contacts

- **National AIDS Helpline** Help, advice and information and details of UK sexual health services 0800 567123 / www.healthwise.org.uk
- **Terrence Higgins Trust National Help Line** Helpline volunteers offer confidential support and up-to-date information 020 7242 1010 Daily 12noon-10pm / www.tht.org.uk
- **Terrence Higgins Trust** National HIV/AIDS organisation providing a comprehensive range of HIV prevention, care and treatment services 020 7242 1010 (12noon-12pm) / www.tht.org.uk / 52-54 Gray's Inn Road, London WC1X 8JU

stressanxiety **&**depression

Stress, anxiety and depression are closely related; sometimes they're just different manifestations of the same problem. All of them arise to some extent from a difficulty in dealing with the pressures and demands that we face in everyday life – and although they're hard work at the time, it's important to remember that nearly everyone has suffered from some form of stress-related incident in their lives..

Stress is your response to the reality of a situation when demands outstrip you supply of physical and mental resources and – very often – time.
'My boyfriend and I seem to be drifting apart, but there's never time to sit down and talk about it… I just don't know what to do.'

Anxiety is the fear or apprehension you feel when you think something unpleasant is going to happen.
'I'm worried my boyfriend's seeing someone else and is going to leave…
I have sleepless nights thinking about what would happen if he did.'

Depression is an overwhelming sense of negative thoughts about the past, present and future.
'My boyfriend left me last week and he's taken most the stuff. I feel lonely and can't stop crying. Life's just not worth living anymore.'

Stress and anxiety

If you're always struggling to meet deadlines or coping with pressure, either at work or in your personal life, you may start suffering from stress. Here are a few things to look out for.

- You work too hard and for too long.
- You have little or no time for rest and relaxation.
- You don't get enough sleep.
- You don't eat enough.
- You don't exercise enough.
- Your your friendships and relationships are suffering.

Anxiety is caused by events, circumstances or situations which are threats, dangers or generate strong emotions. The body's response is to release hormones such as adrenalin which bring about physical changes preparing us to work at maximum efficiency and which enabled our ancestors to attack wooly mammoths or run like hell. Today, this is known as the 'fight or flight' response. The body reacts in the following ways:

- Blood sugar levels rise to provide energy.
- Our heart beats more rapidly and we breathe more deeply to increase oxygen supply to the muscles.
- We sweat to prevent overheating
- Our pupils dilate to enable us to see better.
- Our stomachs churn and we need to shit to reduce body weight for running.
- Our balls pull themselves up into the body for safety.

While the need to fight mammoths and marauding invaders no longer exists, the response to stress still exists and the threats and have evolved. Our worries about where we're going in life, our feelings of insecurity and low self-esteem also fuel stress. Furthermore these threats rarely require us to 'flee or fight' and so anxiety tends to build up rather than get burned off running like hell or knocking the shit out of the enemy. The symptoms of anxiety are varied. Some happen immediately, others develop over time – weeks, months, even years.

Mental and emotional signs and symptoms
- Inability to cope.
- Feeling of helplessness
- Fear of failure (and success).

- Fear of rejection.
- Poor memory.
- Inability to concentrate.
- Being easily distracted.
- Irritability.
- A build-up of emotions such as anger, jealousy and guilt.
- Cumming pre-maturely or not being able to cum at all.
- Dependence on alcohol, smoking, and recreational drugs.
- A feeling of impending doom.

Physical signs and symptoms

- Racing pulse and palpitations (unusually forceful heat beat).
- Trembling and shaking.
- Sweating and flushing.
- Dry mouth.
- Lump in the throat.
- 'Pit' in the stomach.
- Stomach pain and peptic ulcers (raw area in the stomach eroded by excess acid).
- Loose shit / diarrhoea.
- Headaches, nausea, dizziness and faintness.
- Numbness, pins and needles.
- Aching muscles, eg: shoulders and neck.
- Eczema and skin conditions.
- Insomnia, tiredness and bad dreams.
- Depressed immunity with increased susceptibility to infections
- High blood pressure
- Angina (chest pain), stroke and heart attack.
- Compulsive or obsessive behaviour, eg: eating
- Loss of appetite.
- Loss of interest in sex.
- Needing to piss often.

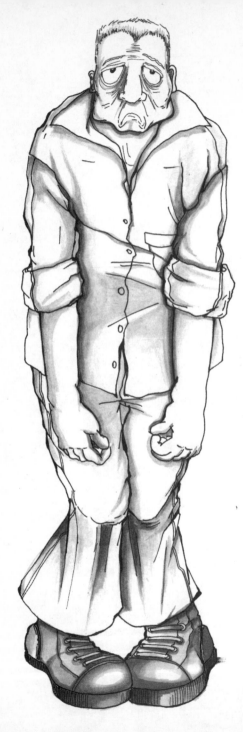

Anxiety is a perfectly normal reaction to a problem or a fear which cannot be resolved or doesn't have an immediate solution. For example you may feel mildly anxious starting a new job or very anxious if someone you care about has just received a positive HIV diagnosis. But no one would think they were extreme or out of proportion in the circumstances. While it might be distressing for your friends to see you so worried over the diagnosis of your friend or puzzling to see you worrying about the job, your reactions in both situations would be normal. Both these scenarios involve feelings about something which you think might happen: not getting on with your new work colleagues, for example, or fearing the death or illness of your friend. We use words and phrases like 'I'm feeling apprehensive…', 'dreading the worst…', or 'feeling nervous…'. A certain amount of anxiety is all part and parcel of life whether it's the financial difficulties, interviews, illnesses or losing your mobile phone.

When anxiety works

Anxiety uses up energy and feeds on strong emotions, and that is not necessarily a bad thing. When a problem presents itself we can be motivated to make decisions, engage in practical activities and find a solution to deal with the problem. Anxiety can be a good thing insofar as, without it, lots of things would be left undone, and so a degree of stress in our lives is a motivator. Difficulties arise when we dwell incessantly on the result of a threat or problem, feel unable to prioritise the key components of a response or cannot find a solution. Eventually, the anxiety is out of proportion to the circumstances. In severe cases we can cease to function at all. Work and home lives are neglected either because we're too anxious to start anything or we're easily distracted by some other more worrying job. The fear of anxiety can attach itself to specific areas like agoraphobia or claustrophobia. Some people get panic attacks which trigger overwhelming anxiety, fear and dread. Before we know it we're pacing up and down (or rooted to the spot), stomach knotted, and feeling as if the world is about to close in on us. An over-active thyroid gland and depression can mimic anxiety in younger persons and heart, lung and digestive problems may produce similar symptoms. However, the more symptoms you have – the more likely anxiety is to blame.

Managing and reducing stress and anxiety

Stress

The best way to deal with stress is to be positive and constructive, see situations in perspective, analyse problems logically and find realistic solutions. Easier said than done? Here are some suggestions:

- Work out which situations and people cause stress and why; you may be able to make changes in a positive manner. Talk honestly – but sensitively – to those you see as being at the root cause of your troubles.
- Change those things that can be changed, learn to accept those that cannot.
- Find solutions and make decisions as calmly as circumstances allow and not under the pressure of deadlines.
- Break problems or tasks into bite-sized chunks and tackle them one step at the time.
- Set realistic targets and goals.
- Expect to make mistakes and don't give up when the going gets tough. It's all experience, learn from it and use it to your advantage.
- Talk more slowly and listen without interrupting.
- Learn to be patient and lose your great sense of urgency.
- Don't say something will take two hours when it will take four, just to please someone. If it takes four, say so.
- Learn to value your strengths and acknowledge areas that need support – both are part of you.
- Don't compare yourself to others; but if you feel there is a need – don't be unfair to yourself.
- Don't expect others to change before you are prepared to change yourself.
- If things are getting on top of you: say so. Express your emotions.

Anxiety

- Accept that your anxiety is a reality.
- Talk to a trusted friend who is a good listener and whose judgment you trust.
- Talk to someone who has been through a similar experience through a self help group, for example.
- Regular exercise, relaxation techniques and mediation can all help – not just when the crisis is on top of you but by making it a part of your everyday life.
- Keep a note of situations which cause anxiety, and look for patterns. Is your anxiety precipitated by events, circumstances, and/or people? Prioritise the level of stress they cause.
- Identify what helps to relieve and manage your stress.
- Examine what measures you can take to reduce anxiety at work and at home. Here are a few suggestions:
  - Decide on a range of relaxation techniques, eg a massage, meditation, swimming, a walk.
  - Re-schedule duties or tasks to reduce anxious situations blurring into each other.
  - Buffer anxious situations with 'relaxation slots', eg a ten-minute break, a full lunch hour or a massage.
  - Re-allocate priorities, make a list and stick to it.
  - A realistic 'hit list' of things to do for the day/week, tackling tasks and problems one at time – allocating each of them a action plan and ticking them off as you achieve them.
  - Delegate more.
  - Be more assertive.
  - Be more realistic about deadlines and being more assertive when negotiating them.
  - Improve your most frequently used environments, eg flowers, incense, a ticking clock, soothing music, a more comfortable chair.
  - Switch on the ansaphone during breaks whether you're doing the housework or between meetings.

If symptoms of anxiety persist despite or if you feel there is no noticeable improvement, it's important to seek professional help. It's certainly better to receive treatment early. Just talking through the issues with your GP may be enough. Alternatively therapy may be suggested to help you better understand and manage your anxiety. Admittedly it's heavier stuff but it's about helping you to help yourself and not about carting you off to a hospital against your will! In some case, tranquillizers are prescribed as a short time measure to provide some 'head space' – they don't deal with the root cause of your anxiety.

Exercise and diet

Regular exercise such as swimming, cycling, going to the gym or other non-competitive sport is essential in managing and reducing stress and anxiety effectively. Look at it as a modern day equivalent to the 'fight or flight' response: the body has primed you for activity – exercising will help you use this energy and reset your stress responses at a manageable level. A balanced and healthy diet will help you combat the effects of stress and anxiety. However, caffeine and nicotine mimic the body's anxiety response and are best avoided when you're under real pressure.

Tips

- Eat high-fibre whole foods
- Lower your intake of sugar, salt and saturated fats.
- Eat little and often to prevent hypoglycaemia (low blood sugar levels) which also trigger the release of adrenalin and heighten the symptoms of stress.
- If you smoke, try to stop. In the short term, smoking may seem to quell your stress, but in the longer term it will magnify the harmful effects of stress on your health.
- Keep alcohol intake to within the safe maximum.

Rest and relaxation

One of the most successful ways of dealing with stress is to make time for yourself, learn to relax and enjoy yourself.

- Consider turning off your mobile phone once in a while or switching on the ansaphone.
- Set some time aside for you at home at least twice a week. Cook yourself a favourite meal or experiment with a new recipe. Look forward to a particular TV programme or watch a video. Settle down with a book. Write a chatty letter or send a few e-mails. Relax in a candlelit bath.
- Consider going to the cinema, theatre, exhibition, art gallery, market or local park. Doing at least one of these each week provides a varied programme of social activities.
- Go out for a meal or invite friends round for a simple meal and fun company.
- Go for a walk to a part of town you've not been to before, perhaps visiting a landmark or tourist attraction.
- If you have a computer, spend some time exploring the internet (having checked out the costs – you don't want to get stressed over a massive phone bill).
- Make sure you give yourself a holiday at least once a year and a weekend break at least twice a year. They don't have to be expensive.

Depression

All of us have times when we're unhappy, miserable, fed-up, pessimistic and feeling low, which usually comes about due to disappointment, frustration and loss. We sometimes rationalise it and call it 'exhaustion', 'overdoing' it or 'nothing a club night won't put right'. They're reasonable things to say because we do get tired, we can overdo it and a night out might be just what we need to relax and let our hair down. Problems start when you start to feel this way more often than not. Little interest or enjoyment in life, feeling helpless and/or inadequate, feelings of loneliness and isolation and lack of motivation and drive are all examples of this. You may also have difficulty in making decisions, may no longer feel able to cope at work and personal relationships are difficult and strained. You begin to feel that life isn't worth living. Sometimes the cause is obvious: the end of a relationship, chronic money worries, a bereavement, unemployment or physical illness. However, depression can seem to 'just happen' which makes it difficult to comprehend. Depression becomes an illness and requires medical attention or professional treatment when it won't go away.

Persistent warning signs and symptoms of depression include:

- Lack of enjoyment of activities that are usually fun or enjoyable.
- Poor concentration.
- Inability to sleep properly, lying awake or waking up in the early hours.
- Frequent feelings of gloom and sense of despair.
- Emotional outbursts and crying for no apparent reason.
- Extreme apathy.
- Difficulty concentrating.
- Noticeable increase or decrease in appetite.
- Reducedsex drive.
- Loss of self-confidence or self-esteem.
- Heavy drinking or drug abuse.

Self help

If the following steps don't help you then seek professional help:

- Talk problems and worries through with a trusted friend.
- Don't bottle up your emotions. If you need to cry: cry.
- Take some regular exercise.
- Eat a balanced diet and avoid binge eating.
- Don't drink alcohol to feel better – the immediate relief will only be followed by a deeper depression.
- Take up a relaxation exercise.
- Don't cut yourself off from close friends. If you can tell them the truth.

Not everybody can accept that they are depressed. It may not sit comfortably with how you see yourself or how you like others to see you: strong, masculine, in control. It's a very male thing stemming from all the macho stuff we pick up in childhood, from family and on TV and film. Attitudes are starting to change for the better although many of us find it very difficult to show our feelings and emotions. Ironically, coming to terms with depression and acknowledging the need for treatment will probably be one of the truly brave things you will do in your life.

Professional help

Depression doesn't usually just go away – its there for a reason although you may not know what the reasons are. You should seek professional help, and in the first instance, this is likely to be your GP. However, if you think or know that your depression is related to sex or your sexual health, speak to your sexual health clinic who may be able to provide support, counselling or a referral service. If these steps are too much, phone one of the helplines listed below which may give you the confidence to see someone in person. Professional help is usually based on the idea of helping you to help yourself, and the appropriate counsellor or psychotherapist will encourage you to talk about your feelings and explore and confront the possible reasons for them which can take weeks, sometimes months, occasionally years.

Anti-depressants

One of the problems with depression is knowing where to start particularly if you're feeling de-motivated and apathetic. Anti-depressants can kick-start the recovery process and let a little light in. This allows you see that you can feel better, be more responsive to help and support and that further treatment will be beneficial. Unfortunately some anti-depressants have had a bad reputation because some of the older drugs have worked but have had side-effects such as drowsiness, blurred vision, heart irregularities, constipation and a dry mouth. However, a new generation of anti-depressants called selective serotonin reuptake inhibitors (SSRIs) have fewer side-effects. It is increasingly accepted that depression can be caused by disordered biochemistry within the brain. Nerve cells (neurons) – which take information across the brain – communicate with each other using electrical signals. These signals have to jump tiny gaps between the cells called synapses but can only do so with the help of chemical neurotransmitters such as serotonin and noradrenaline which are thought to affect mood. Like ferries carry passengers across a river, neurotransmitters carry electrical signals across synapses. Fewer neurotransmitters mean fewer signals can take information across the brain and, in this instance, we can become depressed. SSRIs boost levels of neurotransmitters. Familiar brand names include Seroxat and Prozac.

Further information and contacts

- **Friend Counselling, helplines and support groups for lesbians and gay men**
  BM National Friend, London, WC1N 3XX.
- **London Lesbian and Gay Switchboard** with details of Regional Switchboards 020 7837 7324 / www.gayswitchboard.org.uk
- **PACE** Counselling, advice, advocacy and workshops 020 7700 1323 / 34 Hartham Road, London N7 9JL
- **Terrence Higgins Trust** National HIV/AIDS organisation providing a comprehensive range of HIV prevention, care and treatment services 020 7831 0330 / www.tht.org.uk / 52-54 Gray's Inn Road, London WC1X 8JU
- **CRUSE** 020 8940 4818 / 126 Sheen Road, London TW9 1UR
- **CRY-SIS** 020 7404 5011 / BM CRY-SIS, London WC1N 3XX
- **Depression Alliance** 020 7633 9929 / www.gn.apc.org/da/ 35 Westminster Bridge Road, London SE1 7JB
- **Depressive Anonymous** 01482 860619 / www.ribblewebdesign.co.uk/fda / 36 Chesnut Avenue, Beverley, East Yorkshire HU17 9QU Essex SS17 8EX
- **International Stress Management Association** 020 8876 8261 / The Priory Hospital, Priory Lane, London SW15 5JJ
- **Manic Depression Fellowship** 020 8974 6550 / 8-10 High Street, Kingston -upon-Thames, Surrey KT1 1EY
- **MIND (National Association for Mental Health)** 0345 660163 / contact@mind.org.uk / Granta House, 15-19 Broadway, Stratford, London E15 4BQ

- **MIND Association**   01375 642 466 / P.O.Box 8, Stanford-le-Hope
- **National Back Pain Association**   020 8977 5474 /
  31/33 Park Road, Teddington, Middlesex TW11 0AB
- **Seasonal Affective Disorder (SAD)**   01903 814 942 / P.O.Box 989, Steyning BN44 3HG

alternativeand **complementary** therapies

Alternative and complementary therapies can help to overcome stress and encourage relaxation. These include massage, acupuncture, herbal medicine, homeopathy, yoga, reflexology, aromatherapy. Alternative therapies (eg herbal medicine and homeopathy) work in place of a conventional diagnosis and treatment from your GP, whereas a complimentary therapy (eg reflexology and tai chi hu'an) works alongside this.

Alternative and complementary therapies have grown immensely in recent decades both in popularity and use. Complementary therapies aim to treat the individual as a whole person (holistically) to mobilise the body's own defences. Many therapies use the idea of a 'lifeforce' and that health and contentment depend on achieving a harmonious balance of our physical, mental, emotional and spiritual natures.

Points to consider:

- Personal recommendation or word of mouth is a good way to find a practitioner.
- Check the practitioner is a member of the appropriate regulatory body or a professional association where no regulation exists.
- Therapists should be willing to provide a scale of fees.
- Therapists are unlikely to begin treatment without first building up a picture of you as an individual. Amongst other things, you are likely to be asked about your health, lifestyle and existing medications.
- Therapists should be able to let you know how long it will be before you will see an improvement to your condition or problem.
- Session lengths will vary so give yourself plenty of time.
- Medicines will often originate from a natural plant, herb, oil or mineral many of which will be available from pharmacies and health stores.

- Orthodox (traditional) drugs and complementary therapies can interact or interfere with each other. Make sure you keep your doctor and complementary therapy practitioner informed.
- If you have any questions, eg you're uncertain which remedy to take, talk to a qualified practitioner.
- If you have an adverse reaction to your treatment, stop taking it immediately and seek advice.
- If in doubt: don't.

Aromatherapy

The use of essential oils started as long ago as 2000 BC, but it wasn't until the 1920s that the scientific study of their therapeutic properties and the term 'aromatherapy' came into being. Aromatherapy works primarily through the sense of smell that's closely linked with mood, memory and emotions. It is recognised for its ability to lift the spirits and relieve stress and can also be used to ease pain and tension caused by tight and overworked muscles. In addition to the therapeutic effect of the fragrance, some essential oils are also believed to have healing properties.

Acupuncture and acupressure

Acupuncture revitalises the body by rebalancing the body's flow of energy by stimulating the body's 'acu-points' with fine needles. Factors believed to disturb the flow include poor diet, hereditary factors, infections, injuries, stress, emotional upset and the weather. Health problems that can respond well to acupuncture include painful arthritis, headaches, migraines, and neuralgia. Acupuncture can also help healing after fractures and sports injuries, and can alleviate depression and anxiety, drug addiction, allergies, sinusitis and conditions aggravated by stress. It can also assist people who feel run down but do not have any apparent physical illness or disease.

Working on the same principle as acupuncture, acupressure provides an alternative for people who don't like needles. The other advantage of acupressure is that you can learn to use it on yourself to treat minor ailments such as tiredness, constipation, headaches and colds. However, it is less precise than acupuncture and therefore results are usually slower.

Herbal medicine

Healing with herbs is one of the oldest therapies in the world and aims to restore the body to a state in which it is better able to heal itself. Herbal medicine can promote health by correcting imbalances within the body and encouraging your body to work as efficiently as possible. Treatments are likely to include recommendations about changing diet and lifestyle and reducing the amount of stress in your life.

Homeopathy

The principle of homeopathy is that 'like cures like' and that if a substance triggers symptoms similar to those from which a patient is suffering, then a small dose of that same substance will encourage the patient's body to fight the illness or disease. Homeopathic remedies are derived from plants, minerals, metals, insects and recognised poisons many of which have been used medicinally for generations. Homeopathy is believed to be suitable for many health complaints including depression and chronic conditions such as arthritis and post-viral fatigue syndrome.

Meditation

The aim of meditation is to revitalise the mind by resting it from continuously processing information and responding to the world around us. Meditation can improve your well-being, encourage more positive thoughts and feelings, lift self-esteem and help you to develop a more tolerant and stable attitude towards life. Research shows that people with stress related conditions can derive great benefits from practising meditation. There are many ways to meditate; most involve sitting comfortably in a peaceful place and breathing rhythmically while focusing on a single thought or object. There are many groups where you can learn these skills; some are associated with religion others are secular.

Massage

Massage is probably the best known alternative therapy, possibly evolving out of our instinctive response to soothe aches and pains by rubbing the affected area. Massage is a highly enjoyable and it can be very helpful in dealing with the physical and mental stress that life imposes on you. Massage can relax and tone the muscles, improve the flow of blood through the body and encourage the removal of waste products and toxins. It can also reduce stress and increase your body awareness so that you begin to notice areas where you store tension.

Osteopathy

Osteopathy is recognised by many conventional doctors and is one of the more accepted complimentary therapies. Osteopaths work on the muscles, joints and bones using massage and manipulation to improve the health of the whole body. By using manipulation to balance the tensions in the body structure and improving the functioning of the framework, it is thought to boost the health of the whole body. Conditions such as back disorders, slipped discs, neck pain and chronic muscular tension can benefit.

Reflexology

Reflexology works on the theory that health depends on the flow of energy within the body that begins and ends in the hands and feet. Medical conditions upset this flow. Reflexologists interpret the health and condition of the body and – by massaging certain reflex points – believe that it is possible to improve the health of body organs. Stress is thought to respond well to reflexology relieving tension, improving circulation, ridding the body of wastes, and re-balancing the body.

Shiatsu

Shiatsu literally means finger pressure although therapists also use the palms and heels of their hands, their elbows and knees. Although Shiatsu cannot cure diseases, the symptoms of stress and stress-related conditions seem to respond to this therapy. People with asthma, muscular aches and pains, tension headaches, migraine, depression, insomnia and digestive problems can benefit. Shiatsu is believed to help in tuning a person's general health and keeping the immune system at its best which makes it a largely preventive therapy.

Tai chi hu'an

Tai chi (as it's usually referred to in the West) is an ancient Chinese exercise system. It involves sequences of slow movements made up of individual movements, each with a symbolic meaning and name, which seek the natural harmony that surrounds and is in each person. As well as helping you to remain physically strong and supple, it can also centre the mind, putting it in touch with the body and encouraging a state of calm. Ideally you should learn from a teacher but it is important to practise regularly, setting aside a specific time and place, preferably outside.

Yoga

Combining physical postures, breath control and relaxation, yoga provides a comprehensive work-out for the mind and body. While some practise yoga as a way of working towards the ultimate goal of spiritual realisation, it is perfectly possible to do it simply as a means for relieving stress or improving overall health, with no special knowledge of the philosophy that lies behind it. The enormous advantage of yoga is that it can be safely undertaken by almost anyone, even those who are unfit or overweight. Yoga postures move all the major joints through a full range of motion, reducing stiffness and stretching and toning almost every muscle and tendon in the body. In the first instance, it is much better to go to a yoga class run by a properly qualified teacher than to attempt to learn yoga out of books.

Further information and contacts

- **Aromatherapy Organisations Council** 01858 434242 /
  3 Latymer Close, Braybrooke, Market Harborough, Leicestershire LE16 8LN
- **British Acupuncture Council** 020 8964 0222 /
  Park House, 206-208 Latimer Road, London W10 6RE
- **British Chiropractic Association** 0118 950 5950 /
  Blagrave House Street, 17 Blagrave Street, Reading RG1 1QB
- **British Holistic Medical Association** 01273 725951 /
  Royal Shrewsbury Hospital, South Shrewsbury, Shropshire SY3 8XF
- **British Homeopathic Association** 020 7935 2163 /
  27a Devonshire Street, London W1N 1RJ
- **British Reflexology Association** 01886 821207 /
  Monks Orchard, Whitbourne, Worcester WR6 5RB
- **British Wheel of Yoga** wheelyoga@aol.com /
  1 Hamilton Place, Boston Road, Sleaford, Lincolnshire NG34 7ES
- **Council for Complimentary and Alternative Medicine** 020 8968 3862 /
  179 Gloucester Place, London NE1 6DX
- **Federation of Holistic Therapies** 01703 488900 / gr34@dial.piper.com /
  Eastleigh House, 3rd Floor, Upper Market Street, Eastleigh, Hampshire SO50 9FD
- **Natural Medicines Society** 01773 710002 /
  Market Chambers, 13a Market Place, Heanor, Derbyshire DE75 7AA
- **Osteopathic Information Service** 020 7235 5231 /
  Premier House, 10 Graycoat Place, London SW1P 1SB
- **Society of Teachers of the Alexander Technique** 020 7351 0828 /
  20 London House, 266 Fulham Road, London SW10 9EL
- **The Shiatsu Society** 01773 758341 /
  Barber House, Sedgate, Peterborough PE1 5YS
- **Yoga for Health Foundation** 01767 627271 /
  Ickwell Bury, Biggleswade, Bedfordshire SG18 9EF

index

Unlike weekly and monthly gay publications, Together has a much longer shelf-life and so it is likely that that some of the information listed here will become out of date. You are therefore asked to phone with care and take it as read that Mrs Jones is telling you the truth when she says that she doesn't hold a Fetish Night on the 3rd Saturday of each month! If your desired listing doesn't work, check-out a recent copy of Gay Times or try the Internet.

LONDON

London dialling code (020)
LONDON LESBIAN AND GAY SWITCHBOARD
7837 7324 24 hours

LONDON CLUBS

ATELIER The End, 18 West Central St, WC1. Thu 7419 9199 Stylish crowd. House, Garage.

BICHA Voodoo Lounge, Cranbourne Street. 7287 7773 Latin. Funk. Last Thu

CLUB KALI Dome, 1 Dartmouth Park Hill, N19. 1st / 3rd Fri. South Asian music.

COCO LATTE Velvet Room 143, Charing Cross Road WC2 Funky Fri nighter.

CRASH Arch 66, Goding Street SE11. 7278 0995. Big South London cruisy hard dance club.

DTPM Fabric, 77A Charterhouse Street, EC1. Sun 8pm-late. 7439 9009 Hard House. Serious dancing.

DUCKIE Vauxhall Tavern 372 Kennington Lane, SE11. 7737 4043. Sat 9-2. Alternative, trashy arty night. Fun.

EVOL Upstairs at The Garage, Highbury Corner, N1. 7607 1818. Monthly, Sat, 9pm-3am. Live bands.

FACTOR 25 Rock, Hungerford House, Victoria Embankment WC2. Sun, 7pm-2am.

FICTION The Cross, Bagleys Yard, Kings Cross N1. Fri. Mixed, House. 7251 8778.

G.A.Y Astoria, 157 Charing Cross Rd, WC2. 7734 6963. Mon, Thur, Fri & Sat 10.30-4. Big, busy, young crowd.

GLP Gay London Professionals meet Mon evenings, Ormonds, Ormond Yard, SW1. 7352 8228.

HEAVEN Under the Arches, off Villiers St, WC2. 7930 2020 Mon: Popcorn! (Indie, Pop), Wed: Fruit Machine (Glam, Disco), Fri; There (Mixed), Sat: HEAVEN

LOUNGE 3 Green St, W1. 7355 2300. Members club for professionals. 6pm-1.30am, Mon- Sat.

LOVE MUSCLE The Fridge, 1 Town Hall Parade,Brixton. 7326 5100. Occasional Sats. Sth London's big night out.

MORE SCIENCE Upstairs at The Garage, Highbury Corner, N1. 7607 1818. Monthly, Sat, 9pm-3am. Underground beats. Live bands.

OFF THE HOOK Velvet Underground, 143 Charing Cross Road, W1. 0973-628585. Mon. Garage, soul.

ONE NATION UNDER A GROOVE Turnmills 63b Clerkenwell Rd. EC1 07931 424 905 Big, gay black music night. 10pm-4am Every Su.

PHOENIX 37 Cavendish Square, W1. Club with cabaret. Fr & Sa 10.30-3.

POPSTARZ The Scala, 278 Pentonville Road, King's Cross, N1. 7738 9988. Fri 10-5am. Britpop, Indie.

QUEER NATION 9 Substation South, Brighton Terrace, SW9. 7737 2095. Popular Black music night. Sat.

SALVATION Cafe de Paris, 3 Coventry Street, Leicester Square. 2nd Sundays.Musclebound tea dance.

SHINKY SHONKY West Central, 29-30 Lisle Stree, WC2. 7479 7981. Frids. Alt fun, trashy night.

SOUND ON SUNDAY The Sound Bar, Leicester Square. Gay tea dance, Sun 6-11pm. Young, pop, retro, chart.

SUBSTATION SOUNDSHAFT Hungerford Lane (behind Heaven) WC2. 7278 0995. Tue: Twisted. Thu: Medikation. Fri: Spunk. Cruisy, dance bar.

SUBSTATION SOUTH 9 Brighton Terrace, SW9 7737 2095 Late night cruisy club Mon: Y Fronts, Tue: Massive, Wed: Boot Camp, Thu: Blackout, Fri: Dirty Dishes, Sat: Queer Nation, Sun: Marvellous (Indie).

THE TUBE Falconberg Ct, off Charing Cross Rd, W1. 7287 3726. Tue: Babe. Wed: Mamma Mia! Fri: Babe.

Sat: Wig Out! (Trash)

TRADE Turnmills, 63b Clerkenwell Rd, EC1. 7250 3409. Sun morn. 4am-1pm. Very busy, long, hard dance night.

UNDERGROUND Central Station 37 Wharfdale Rd, N1. 7278 3294. Cruise club.

UP The Rhythm Factory, 16-18 Whitechapel Road, E1. Alt Sats. 7375 3774

DRESS CODE/FETISH CLUBS

A 82 Great Suffolk Street SE1. 7928 3223. Mon-Sun.

BACKSTREET Wentworth Mews, Burdett Rd, E3. 8980 8557. Thu-Sat 10-3 Su 9-1

BLOCK 28 Hancock Rd, E3. 0909 464 6804 Wed-Sun 10pm-late.

CLUB SUBMISSION Monthly mixed fetish parties. 7916 0180 for details.

FIST 299 Imperial Gardens, Camberwell New Road SE5. 7252 6000. Strict fetish dress code. 2nd Sat.

GUMMI Central Station (Islington & Hackney). 7278 3294. 2nd Sun, 6-12. Mems £4, guests £5. Rubber club.

HOIST Railway Arch 47, S Lambeth Rd, SW8. 7735 9972. Fri, Sat 10-3, Sun 8-12, 3rd Wed S/M Gays.

DRAG/SPECIALITY CLUBS

EXILIO 229 Great Portland St, W1. Alt Sats Dates: 0956-983230. Salsa.

JUANCHITO The Phoenix, Cavendish Square, Oxford Street (behind BHS). 2272 3465. Alt Fri. Latin, Salsa.

LOUGHBOROUGH HOTEL Loughborough Rd, SW9. Latin classes & clubs Info: 7771 3134 or 7642 5806. Thu: Go Bananas 8-2am. Fri: La Salsa 9.30-2am Sat: Hotel Tropical 10-2.30am

PINK JUKEBOX Warren Bar, Grafton Hotel, 130 Tottenham Ct Rd. 0374-443627. 2nd & 4th Sun. Latin, Ballroom classes.

RUBY'S TEA DANCE 49 Carnaby St W1 83026651. Sun. 5.30. Ballroom /latin/sequence.

WAY OUT CLUB Tiffanies, 28 Monories EC3. 8363 0948. Sat 9-4. Drag.

CENTRAL LONDON

BARS/PUBS

ADMIRAL DUNCAN 55 Old Compton St W1. 7437 5300.

THE BAR 36 Hanway St, W1. 7580 9811

BAR CODE 3 Archer St, W1. 7734 3342.

BOX 32-34 Monmouth St, WC2. 7240 5828.

BRIEF ENCOUNTER 41 St Martin's Lane, WC2. 7240 2221.

CITY OF QUEBEC 12 Old Quebec St, W1. 7629 6159. Older crowd.

COMPTONS 53 Old Compton St, W1. 7479 7961. Popular. Skins, etc.

HALFWAY TO HEAVEN 7 Duncannon St, W1. 7321 2791.

JACOMOS 8-9 Cowcross Street EC1. City bar.

JONATHANS 16 Irving Street, WC2. 7930 4770. Members' bar.

KING'S ARMS 23 Poland St, W1 7734 5907.

KU BAR 75 Charing Cross Rd. W1 7437 4303 Food 12-6. Young crowd.

KUDOS 10 Adelaide St, WC2. 7379 4573. † Cafe-bar

RETRO BAR 2 George Court, Strand, WC1. 7321 2811. Indie.

SAUNA BAR 29 Endell Street, WC2 7836 2236.

VILLAGE SOHO 81 Wardour St, W1. 7434 2124. Younger crowd.

YARD 57 Rupert St., W1. 7437 2652. Open air bar.

CAFÉS

BALANS 60 Old Compton St, W1. 7437 5212. 8am-5am.

BAR AQUDA 13-14 Maiden Lane, Covent Garden, WC2. 7557 9891. Cafe-bar.

FIRST OUT 52 St Giles High St, WC2. 7240 8042. Mon-Sat 10-11. Sun 12-10.30.

OLD COMPTON CAFE 34 Old Compton Street, W1.

LATE BARS

EDGE 11 Soho Sq, W1. 7439 1313. Mon-Sat 12-1. Sun 12noon-10.30pm.

ESCAPE 8-10 Brewer St, W1. 7734 2626. 4pm til 3am.

FREEDOM 60 Wardour St, W1 7734 0071. Stylish bar, til 3am.

MANTO SOHO Old Compton Street W1. 7494 2756. Huge bar, 3 floors, DJs. Til midnight.

LIQUID LOUNGE 257 Pentonville Rd N1. 7837 3218. Fri, Sat. 5.30pm-2am. 7738 2336. Indie.

RUPERT ST 50 Rupert St, W1. 7734 5614.

79CXR 79 Charing Cross Rd, W1. 7734 0769. Mon-Sat 1pm-2am, Su 1-10.30pm

WEST CENTRAL 29-30 Lisle Stree, WC2. 7479 7981

UNDERGROUND CLUB in basement, til 3am. Wed: Pick-Up. Thu: 70s. Alt Fri: Shinky Shonky. Sat: Camp.

NORTH LONDON

BLACK CAP 171 Camden High St, NW1 7428 2721. 12-2 except Sun 12-12. Late bar upstairs, famous drag bar downstairs.

THE FLAG 29 Crouch Hill, Crouch End N4. 7272 4748.

KING WILLIAM IV 75 Hampstead High Street, NW3. 7435 5747.

ISLINGTON & HACKNEY

ARTFUL DODGER 139 Southgate Rd, N1. 7226 0841. Popular, late cruise bar.

CENTRAL STATION 37 Wharfdale Rd, N1. 7278 3294. Open til very late. Busy bar, cruisy club.

DUKE OF WELLINGTON 119 Balls Pond Road N1. 7254 4338.

JOINERS ARMS 116-118 Hackney Rd, E2.

KING EDWARD VI, 25 Bromfield St, N1. 7704 0745. Daily 12-12.

OAK CAFE BAR 79 Green Lanes, N16. 7354 2791. 5pm-late. Big, mixed.

RAM CLUB BAR 39 Queen's Head St, N1. 7354 0576.

ROUTE 73 36 Barbauld Road, N16. 7254 5865.

EAST LONDON

ANGELS 21 Church Street, E15. 8555 1148. Cabaret bar.

BENJYS 2000 562a Mile End Rd, E3. 8980 6427. Young, club night. Sunday 9pm-1am.

BLACK HORSE 168 Mile End Rd. 7790 1684. 7pm-late.

BLOCK (see Dress Code)

BRITISH PRINCE 49 Bromley Street, E1. 7790 1753.

CENTRAL STATION WALTHAMSTOW 80 Brunner Rd, Walthamstow, E17. 8520 4836. L

CHARIOTS I Fairchild St, EC1. 7247 5333. UK's biggest sauna.

CHARIOTS III VIP 57 Cowcross St EC1. 7251 5333. Sauna.

COCK & COMFORT 359 Bethnal Green Rd, E2. 7729 1476. Fri-Sat til 2am. Big pub

CORONET 119 The Grove E15. 8522 0811

OLD SHIP 17 Barnes St, Stepney E14. 7790 4082.

RAILWAY TAVERN 576 Commercial Road, E14. 7790 2360. Mixed.

REFLECTIONS 8 Bridge Rd E15. 8519 1296. Club.

ROYAL OAK 73 Columbia Rd, E2 7739 8204.

SPIRAL 138 Shoreditch High St, E1. 7613 1351. Popular, late bar.

WHITE SWAN BJs 556 Commercial Rd, E1. 7780 9870. Busy, large pub, open late.

SOUTHEAST LONDON

DEW DROP INN 17 Clifton Rise, New Cross, SE14. 8694 9132.

DUKE OF CLARENCE 57 Portland Rd, South Norwood, SE25. 8655 4184.

FORT 131 Grange Rd, SE1. 7237 7742. Very cruisy pub. Dress code nights.

GEORGE & DRAGON 2 Blackheath Hill, Greenwich SE10. 8691 3764.Cabaret.

GLOUCESTER King William Walk, Greenwich, SE10. 8858 2666

JUBILEE TAVERN 79 York Rd, Waterloo. 7928 7596. Mixed.

LITTLE APPLE 98 Kennington Lane SE11. 7735 2039.

NAVY ARMS 60 New Kings St, SE8. 8694 1224.

QUEEN'S ARMS 63 Court Hill Rd, Lewisham, SE13. 8318 7305.

ROEBUCK 25 Rennell St, Lewisham, SE13. 8852 1705

SKINNERS ARMS 60 Camberwell New Road SE5. 8582 3397.

SOUTHERN PRIDE 82 Norwood High St, West Norwood, SE27. 8761 5200 Mo-Fr 6-2, Sat 12-2, Sun 12-12.

WOOLWICH INFANT 9 Plumstead Rd, SE18 8854 3712.

ROSE & CROWN Crooms Hill, Greenwich, SE10. 8293 1898.

STEAMING@309 309 New Cross Road SE14. 8694 0316. M-Th 11-11pm. Fr-Sun open 24 hrs. Sauna.

VAUXHALL & OVAL

COCK 340 Kennington Rd SE11. 7735 1013. Big pub.

CRASH Arch 66 Goding Street, SE 11. 7278 0995. Club.

CRASHBAR Arch 66, Goding Street, SE 11. Late cruise bar/club. Mon-Thur.

DUKES 349 Kennington Lane, SE11. 7793 0903. M-Tu 8-1, W-Sa 9-2, Su 2-10.30.

HOIST (see Dress Code)

LITTLE APPLE 98 Kennington Lane, SE11. 7735 2039. Mo-Sat 12-12, Su 12-10.30

RED STILETTO 108 Wandsworth Road, SW8 7207 4944.

VAUXHALL TAVERN 372 Kennington La SE11. 7582 0833 Eves. Sun 12-12. Various alt club nights. Sat DUCK-IE 9-2am.

WEST & SOUTHWEST

BUZZ BAR 136 Battersea High Street. SW11. 7787 0105.

CHAMPION 1 Wellington Terr, Bayswater Rd, W2. 7229 5056.

GATE 68 Notting Hill Gate, W11. 7243 0123.

GEORGE 114 Twickenham Rd, Isleworth. 8560 1456. Cabaret.

PENNY FARTHING 135 King St, Hammersmith, W6. 8600 0941 Busy, big bar, til 12am t

QUEEN'S ARMS 223 Hanworth Rd. Hounslow. 8570 9724.

QUEEN'S HEAD 27 Tryon St, Chelsea, SW3. 7589 0262.

REFLEX 184 London Rd, Kingston. 8393 4343. Bar til 3am.

RICHMOND ARMS 20 The Square, Richmond. 8940 2118.

ROCKET 10-13 Churchfield Rd, Acton, W3. 8992 1545.

WEST FIVE Popes Lane, Ealing W5. 8579 3266. Big pub, til 1am Fri, Sat.

CLAPHAM & BRIXTON

BREWERY TAP 78 Lingham Street, SW9. 7738 6683.

BUZZ BAR 136 Battersea High Street SW11. 7787 0105.

KAZBAR 50 Clapham High St. SW4. 7622 0070. Café-bar. 5pm-12.

SUBSTATION SOUTH 9 Brighton Terrace, SW9. 7737 2095. Late night cruise club. See London Clubs.

SW9 11 Dorrell Place, SW9. 7738 3116. Mixed cafe/bar.

TWO BREWERS 114 Clapham High St, SW4 7498 4971. Big cabaret bar & club.

CHARIOTS II Rear of 292 Streatham High Road SW18. 8696 0929. Sauna.

EARLS COURT

BALANS WEST 239 Old Brompton Rd SW5. 8478 6530. Brasserie

BROMPTONS, 294 Old Brompton Rd, SW5. 7370 1344. Warwick bar M-Sa 4-2, Su 2-12. Bromptons club M-Th 10.30-2, F & Sa 10-2, Su 2-7, 9-12. Tu leather, Sun C&W 2-7. Popular, leather.

COLEHERNE 261 Old Brompton Rd, SW5. 7244 5951. Established leather pub

CLONE ZONE Old Brompton Road, SW5.

SHOPS

CENTAURUS 100 Old St, EC1. 7251 3535. Mo-Sa 10.30-6.30, vids, books, cards, gallery.

CLONE ZONE 266 Old Brompton Rd 7373 0598. Mags, videos, toys etc.

CLONE ZONE 64 Old Compton St, W1. 7287 3530. Gay shop, grooming centre above: 7287 3334.

COMPENDIUM, 234 Camden High St, NW1. 7485 8944. Bookshop.

EXPECTATIONS 75 Gt Eastern St, EC2. 7739 0292. Leather/rubber/toys. Mo-Fr: 11-7, Sa: 11-8, Su: 12-5.

GAY'S THE WORD 66 Marchmont St, WC1. 7278 7654. Mon-Sat 10-6.30; Su 2-6. Bkshop.

HOUSMAN'S 5 Caledonian Rd, N1. 7837 4473. M-Sa 10-6.30. Radical books.

PROWLER CAMDEN 283 Camden High St, NW1. 7284 0537. Sex emporium for men.Large range of sex toys, books, mags, videos, cards, rubber and leather. Mail order catalogue avail free. M-Sa 10-6.30.

PROWLER SOHO 3-7 Brewer St, W1. Big gay department store. 7734 4031. 11am-10pm.

RECOIL 557 1The Railway Arch, Redcross Way, SE1. 7378 0557. Rubber wear, fetish gear.

REGULATION 17a St Albans Place, Islington Green, N1 7226 0665. M-Sa 10.30am-6.30pm. Fetish gear, toys, made-to-measure

ROB LONDON 24 Wells St, W1. 7735 7893. Rubber/leather/fetish. Mon-Sat 10.30-6.30

LONDON LOCAL GROUPS

BARNET GAY SOCIAL GROUP 8367 2930, Jez /Robert 8366 6632

BATTERSEA & WANDSWORTH AREA GAY SOCIETY 0793 948 5646

BROMLEY G&B MENS GROUP David 8289 6698

CANARY WHARF L&G SOCIAL GROUP canary2869@aol.com

CROYDON GAY SOCIETY David 8656 9802, CAGS, PO Box 464, SE25 4AT.

CROYDON LESBIAN & GAY FORUM Monthly meetings at Old Town Hall, 8 684 3862

CROYDON LESBIAN AND GAY YOUTH GROUP Under25s, meets Sun 07071 225577

EALING GAY GROUP John 8870 4549 Neil 8998 6708 PO Box 130, London W5 1DQ. GLP (Gay London Professionals) Mondays, call for venue. 7352 8228.

GAY EAST LONDON (GEL) East London social group. 1st & 3rd Fri, 8597 5835.

HARROW&BRENT G&L GROUP Mon 8.30 Tenterden Sports Club, Preston Rd, Wembley. Lisa: 07769 686182. Peter 8908 1795

KINGSTON&RICHMOND AREA GAY SOC POBox158a SurbitonKT6 6RS. 83974903

LEWISHAM GAY ALLIANCE Meets Tu 8694 2246 Seeking new members

MAGNET SELond/N Kent L&G social Dave 8851 6106. PO Box10036, London SE14 5WZ

MARYPAD Gay mens group, Meets Tuesdays in members house. Non-scene group for all gay men seeking friendship and support in the London area. 7607 4755.

METRONET LGB, Womens Drop-ins, Black & Asian support, Greenwich. 8265 3311.

MFG LGB Social Group. PO Box 102 Shepperton TW17 8UP. 01932-243388.

NETWORK BCM Box 2272, WC1N 3XX. GLB social grp. Meets Weds 7.30-11pm Queens Arms (London West). Lizzie 07957-739735.

OCTOPUS E Lon/Essex. Socials. 8270 2006, 8-10pm M-F. BM Box 8485, London WC1N 3XX.

OUT EAST Social/supprt for E London Gay & Bi men. 8558 0551.

PALACE PINKS group for lgb based in Crystal Palace, Contact Ruby: 8670 9559.

PINK CANARIES Canary Wharf LG Social Group, Meets 2nd Thurs, Via Fossa, 1st Floor Bay, West India Quay.

QUEST GLB Catholic group. Fri 7-10pm 0808 808 0234

SIGNIFICANT OTHERS Gay singles, introduction night. Thursday at The Lounge. 7499 5939.

SLAGO Surrey & London Association of Gay Organisations. 01737 766651

SOUTH LONDON GAYS PO Box 243, SW19 1XW. 8674 5191

SUNDAY AT TWO NE London multicultural social group

8985 3324

SUTTON G&L SOCIAL GROUP PO Box 623, Sutton SM2 5ZF. Meet 3rd Fri

WRAGS (Waltham Forest gay & bi men's group). Meets Tu Ilford. 8527 9547

CAMPAIGNING GROUPS

DELGA (Liberal Democrats for L&G Action) c/o Liberal Democrats, 4 Cowley Street, London SW1P. info@delga.libdems.org

GALHA (G&L Humanist Assoc) 7.30 2nd Fri, Conway Hall, Red Lion Sq WC1 Derek 0207 704 1612

GALLON (G&L London) lobbying candidates for Mayor. info@gallon.org.uk

HOMAN defending Iranian LGBS. BCM Box 7826, London WC1N 3XX. www.homan.cwc.net

HYDE PARK GAYS & SAPPHICS Sun noon-2pm Speakers Corner. Public speaking, followed by social.

LESBIAN&GAY IRISH SOLIDARITY CAMPAIGN BMBox7970 LondonWC1N 3XX

L&G ARA (Anti-Racist Alliance) meets regularly. 7278 6869. PO Box 150, WC1X 9AT

LONDON MONDAY GROUP Social/campaigning Mon 8.30 Central Stn (Islington & Hackney) 7229 8272

OUTRAGE! PO Box 17816, SW14 8WT. 8240 0222. Th 8pm Central Station. http://www.OutRage.cygnet.co.uk

SCHOOL'S OUT! LONDON LGBs in education.Geoff 7582 2325 7pm 1st Fri (term time) Institute of Education, 20 Bedford Way, WC1.

SEXUAL FREEDOM COALITION PO Box 4ZB, W1A 4ZB. info@sfc.org.uk. Campaigning for the sexual freedom of all consenting adults.

ETHNIC & CULTURAL

AHBAB GL Arab soc. http://www.glas.org/ahbab

AMACH LINN! Irish L & G in London Hammersmith

Irish Ctr, Black's Rd, W6. 8450 4022 First Th.

BAGELS UK Jewish LGB Students Group. bagelsuk@email.com

BEIT KLAL YISRAEL Alternative Jewish community. Jews, partners/friends. PO Box 1828, W10 5RT. 8960 5750

BIG UP Sexual health organisation for and led by Black gay men. Office hours 0207 501 9264. Helpline Thursday 6pm-9pm 020 7501 9315

BLACK L&G CENTRE Helpline: 7620 3885.Rm 113, 5/5a Westminster Bridge Rd, SE1. Tu & Th 11.30-5.30pm.

CYMDEITHAS GYMRAEG LESBIAID A HOYWON LLUNDAIN 7607 8214

CYPRIOT L&G GROUP meets 1st Sun, 6pm, Central Station (Islington & Hackney)

DOST for South Asian, Turkish, Arab and Irani gay men meets 7-9 first Weds. 8741 1879.

GAON Orthodox or formerly Orthodox Jews 07957 485365

GAEILGEOIRÍ I LONDAIN Grúpa Aerach, neamh-pholaitiúil, neamh-sheicteach. Ach scairt ar Bhreandán 7564 3738

GAY LONDON ARMENIANS e-mail: zvartlondon@hotmail.com

JEWISH L&G HELPLINE 7706 3123 M&Th7-10 BM Jewish Helpline, London WC1N 3XX

JEWISH G&L GROUP Social & services. 8922 5214.

BM/JGLG, LONG YANG CLUB Orient/West 8311 5835 Sat 8pm Kings Arms, 68 Great Titchfield St, W1. Sun: The Gaia Bar, 9 Hanover St, W1.

HINEINU Jewish young adult L&G group under 28. 8905 3531.

KOEKSUSTERS LGBs from Sthn Africa. Martin 0788-436 3564. Meets Central Station, Th 8pm.

MASALA Gay youth of South Asian origin, 8741 1879.

NORTHERN LESBIAN & GAY JEWISH GROUP

c/o Box 71 Frontline Books, 255 Wilmslow Road, Manchester M14 5LW.

ORIENTATIONS South East/East Asian LGBs, Social & Meetings 0956-535 871 or jsun@ic.ac.uk

TRANSGENDER

TRANSGENDER LONDON Central Station (Islington & Hackney) 3rd Sa, 6-8pm

LONDON SUPPORT GROUP for trannies & friends. Lst Fr, In-Time Studio, 5 Tenter Ground, off Whites Row, EC3. 7247 3848

SPECIAL INTEREST

ALLEGRO MUSIC GROUP classical/opera lovers 01895-234 573, Tom 8778 4394

BIG & TALL INTERNATIONAL for taller and bigger lgb. bigandtall@talk21.com

BRIDGE North London Tu 7.30, Central Station (Islington & Hackney), 7229 1680

BRIDGE South London. Social Group We & Su 8898 4403 or 8671 3489.

BRIDGE West London Mo 7.30pm. Andy: 8903 9893

BRIDGE UK Events. 0160- 865 1680.. Fax 2059.

DIGITAL DIVERSITY cyber queers: http://www.diversity.org.uk/diversity/ Email info@diversity.org.uk.

GALIA (G&L in Accountancy) Meets last Thu Richard 8503 3929.

GAY ARTISTS GROUP Life drawing. Artists & models. George: 7624 6181

GAY GRADUATES in Greater London (GGIGL) Meet monthly. Robert 7262 6308.

GAY LONDON WRITERS Peter 7733 4047.

GAY CREATIVE WRITING WORKSHOP 7241 6450.

HALL CARPENTER ARCHIVES research/ gay history. BM Archives, London WC1N 3XX.

HISTORIC HOUSES, GARDENS & WALKS GAY GROUP G020-8989 5295 Mondays.

L&G REAL ALE DRINKERS first We at Kings Arms (Central baras/pubs) 7pm.

LONDON GAY MEN'S CHORUS Mo 7-10 Steve: 8981 5200, PO Box 21039, N1 0WQ.

LONDON GAY NATURIST Events. 51A Vernon Rd, Leytonstone, E11 4QT

LONDON GAY SYMPHONY ORCHESTRA Meet Sun eve Richard 8809 5518

NATURIST Social & swimming 8988 0152. BM Box 5147, London WC1N 3XX.

PINK SINGERS GL choir rehearse wkly central London. Info: 07020-934 916. PO Box LB 738, London W1A 9LB.

PRIDE ARTS FESTIVAL June 20 - July 12. BM PAF London WC1N 3XX. 7737 5763.

SISTERHOOD OF KARN (Dr Who & SF fans) 2nd & 4th We 8pm, 1st floor, Central Station (Islington) 07092 185781

TRANSPORT ENTHUSIASTS Ken7402 8053 Alan 8657 2569.

VEGETARIAN & VEGAN GAY GROUP Sun: 8690 4792 mts Lst Sun.

VOCAL MINORITY Gay choir Tu 7pm Steve/ Marco 8743 7609

STUDENT LGB SOCS

BRUNEL UNI LGB SOC UBS, Brunel Uni, Cleveland Rd, Uxbridge 01895-462200.

CITY UNI LGB GROUP CUSU, Northampton Sq, EC1V OHB. lgb@city.ac.uk

INSTITUTE OF EDUCATION LGB SOC 20 Bedford Way. Meet F 5.30. LGB@ioe.ac.uk.

KINGSTON UNI LGB SOC We 7.30-9pm. 8255 0032. E-mail: lgbsoc@kingston.ac.uk.

OPEN UNIVERSITY LGS BCM OULAGS London WC1N 3XX

ROYAL HOLLOWAY LGB SOC
www.freedom@sonow.com. 0467-796 101

SOUTHBANK UNI LGB SOC Thu 6pm SU, Keyworth St, Elephant & Castle

ULU G&L SOC ULU bldg, Malet St W1 8-10.30pm Thu 7580 9551

FETISH

BEARS CLUB Fri 8pm, Kings Arms (Central).

LONDON BLUES. Uniform club. Meet Central Station (Islington), Wed 9.30pm. 7607 8064

MSC Motor Sports Club, mt Jubilee Tavern, York Rd SE1, 3rd Fri 9pm.

RUBBER MEN'S CLUB last Fr, Central Station.(Islington & Hackney) Del: 7624 0305

SM BISEXUALS meet 2nd Sun monthly, 7.30 at Central Station (Islington & Hackney).

SM GAYS. BM SM Gays, London WC1N 3XX

SUIT & TIE SOCIETY Mts 7.30 Lst Fri. Robin: 8374 8190

TORTURE GARDEN BMTG, WC1N 3XX. 7401 3811. fetish club, strict dress code.

OLDER GROUPS

LIBERTINES Men 50+ in SE Lond Dave: 01689-859806 (eves); Box 55, 12 Brownhill Rd, SE6

WILLING SUBMISSION for mature men into bondage and control. Ivan 01438 728509.

SPORTS & SWIMMING

BLOOMSBURY SWIMMING CLUB Sa/Su, Russell St, WC1 1to1 lessons for aquaphobic adults. 8349 1844

EAST LONDON TENNIS CLUB 020-8539 1680

GRACE'S CRICKET GROUP G & L players & supporters: Duncan 7278 3294

4PLAY SQUASH CLUB Players of all levels.

We, Sa & Su. Information: Hugh on 020 8993 6471.

FRONTRUNNERS Sa 10am We 7pm Achilles Statue HydePk,Sue 7820 1907.

GAY FOOTBALL SUPPORTERS SAE: Box GFSN, Central Station, 37 Wharfdale Rd, N1

G&L KAYAK CLUB 07779 852099.

GLWC (G&L Windsurfing) 8568 5021 1st Mon, Queens Head, (South & Southwest)

GAY MEN'S RUGBY Central Station (Islington Wed 8pm. Milton 7928 0668

GAY OUTDOOR CLUB PO Box 16124, Glasgow G12 9YT. Walking, mountaineering, climbing, caving, cycling, swimming etc. 0141-342 4088.

GAY SAILING GROUP 2nd Tue 9pm The Edge, Soho. Tony 01273-721933.

GAY SKI GROUP Richard 8572 0623

GAY SUNDAY WALKING GROUP GSWG, PO Box 130, W5 1DQ. John: 7701 1013.

GOC Walks: Bob 8674 8367.Climbing: Colum 7603 6779 or David 7976 6052.

GOSLINGS BADMINTON Ian: 8802 9639 .

GOSLINGS CYCLING Peter: 8747 4640.

GOSLINGS SWIMMING Dave: 8521 7567. Meets at Oasis WC1.

FUDOSHINKAI KARATE ENGLAND Kevin 8804 3844

HARROW GAY BADMINTON CLUB Su 7.30-9.30 John 8952 8293.

ILGLU Gymnastics union. Alex 07966 510 297.

IRONS Gay golf group. Martin 020 8780 9409.

ISHIGAKI JUJITSU CLUB GLBT martial arts. Simon 7739 8442.

KINGS CROSS STEELERS RUGBY FOOTBALL CLUB E London rugby union team. Info: 7476 6647 Email: London@ compuserve.com

LEFTFOOTERS Football club "for those with no talent who still want to play". Brian 07931-534155.

LONDON CRUISERS Basketball. Jordi 7582 7009

LONDON FRONT RUNNERS meets Saturday for morning run in SW7. Also Mon, Weds eve. Antonio 07808 475 195.

LONDON GAY TENNIS CLUB (Islington) Derick-8445 3641 or Peter 8368 7504

MSC Motor Sports Club, mt Jubilee Tavern, York Rd SE1, 3rd Fri 9pm.

NUDE MALE SWIMMING Meets London E5. Gymnos 8988 0152.

OUT TO SWIM Competitive-5 sessions wkly, Phil Collins 7639 9875.

OUTRIGGERS ROWING 8450 4214

SCUBA DIVING Underwater Group Rupert 7625 5789.

SOFTBALL Rainbow Raiders. Mixed LG softball. Peter: 07970 237705.

STONEWALL FOOTBALL CLUB Wkly training 5-a-side & league. All standards 7565 4254

TENNIS CLUB Sun 11am Islington Tennis Ctr, Market Rd, N1 8368 7504 or 8445 3641

TENNIS GROUP S London/Croydon. Anthony: 07957 231 897.

VOLLEYBALL for gay men, Ths & Suns, Richard 7237 4578.

WATERBABIES 1st Sun Latchmere Leisure Ctr, Latchmere Rd, Clapham

YOUTH GROUPS

ANYTHING BUT Str8 (Romford Youth Group) LGB&T group 11-25yrs. Youth Zone, 10 Hedley Close, Romford, Essex RM1 1AH 01708 768512 (Mob 07719 325166) anythingbutstr8@hotmail.com

BOY BLUE Sexual health info and support for G&B men under 25. We 5-7.30pm. Block G, Barnsbury Complex, Offord Road, Islington N1. 7525 5627.

BRENT MOSAIC for young G & B men U-25. Neil 8838 0527 email mosaicyp@hotmail.com meets

CHILLIN' OUT Drop in Su 2-5pm, Soc & Advice under 26s. 8265 3311

CROYDON LGB GROUP Under 25s. 7725 577.

DIASPORA Under 25 G&L of colour Meet Th 8533 2174

DROP IN Sexual health for young lgb. Tu Hackney 8533 2174.

FANTASY YOUTH meet last Sun. Promote safe SM practices, under 26s 7460 0464.

FIRST MOVE Colindale based YGB under 25 call Mon 4-6pm 8205 0006 firstmove @baeu.demon .co.uk.

FIRST STEP Under 21s meet Mon 7.30-10. 8461 4112. PO Box 1992, WC1N 3XX

FORBIDDEN FRUIT under 25. Hackney. Graham/Gareth 8533 2174

FREEDOM Phone line Tu 2-4 Young LGB 8533 2324 Based at Staying Out in Hackney

FREEDOM YOUTH Basingstoke, 01256-376486.

FREEPHONE HELPLINE Young, looking for info. GLB Helpline, Fris 5-8pm 0800-073 0233.

GAY YOUNG LONDON gay men 18-30 Mon 7.30-9pm. Central Station (Islington & Hackney)

GREENWICH FREEDOM YOUTH LGB under 26. Phone Loraine or James 8316 4397

GB HARLOW Yg&bi men. Harlow Tu 7-9.30pm. Alex 0973-541974 24 hrs

HARROW LGB YOUTH 16-25s. Info Ewan or Emma 8424 7536. Also social, support, drop in.

HILLINGDON LGB YOUTH GROUP u21 Su 6.30-9.30 Paul/Sam 01895-235777. www.geocities.com/-WestHollywood/Heights/2314

IDENTITY g&b men u-26. W/chair. Chiswick Sun 6.30-8.30. 08000 854 036

LGB TEENAGE GROUP 7263 5932, Su 4-7, Wed 7-10., 6-9 Manor Gdns, N7 6LA.

LONDON CONNECTION LESBIAN & GAY GROUP Homeless and/or unemployed L&G 16-25yo.Th 6-9pm.

12 Adelaide St, WC2N.

MALE OUT Camden male youth We. 6.30pm nr Kentish Town 7267 8595 grp times.

THE MIX LGB & TG under 25 in Kentish Town. Tu 6.30-9.30pm. Info: 7267 8595 group times. Minicom: 7387 2404.

MYNORS (Merton Youth Not of Rigid Sexuality) We 6.30-9.30pm, 8646 3033

NORTH LONDON LINE YOUTH PROJECT Under 25yo. Mo: Mixed 6-9pm, Tu: L&B Women 6-9pm, We: Mixed 2-5pm. Info: 7607 8346.

NORTH SEVEN SOCIAL G&Bi men 16-25, Tu7-10 Old Fire Stn, 84 Mayton St N7 7700 4658

NOTTING HILL L&G YOUTH GROUP 7229 3266. Thu 7-10

NRG YOUTH GROUP LGBTG U-25, Th 6.30-10 Nr Waterloo 7620 1819.

OUT ON THURSDAY Hammersmith young gay, bisexual men u-25 Th 6-10. 0800- 169 4318.

OUTLINKS LGB youth u-26. 7378 8732 Drop-in Tu 4-7-for one to one.

OUTZONE Support & social for G/bi m U-25 in N London. Meets Fris 6.30-9.30pm Andy 8348 1785

PHASE TOWER HAMLETS YOUTH PROJECT Under 25s. We: Mixed drop in 3-5pm, L&B Women 6-9pm, Th: G&B Men 6-9pm, Sa & Su LGB Drop-in. Info: 7515 4617 group times.

SHOUT SW London LGB youth grp. Fri 7-10. Charlotte 8675 0306.

STAYING OUT Hackney. U-25s Tu 7-10. U-17 1st Sat 2-5 8533 2174

STEPPING OUT Social for under 26. Fri 8-10, Central Station (Islington & Hackney).

SURVIVAL GUIDE 0For young men under 26, coming out or new to the scene. Meets in the West End. Details: Liam 0207- 734 1794.

TRIBE U16s in Greenwich. 8265 3355.

WOW - WE'RE OUT WEST for gay men U-26, meets in Kingston-Richmond Fri 7-9.30pm. Details 8549 7654 at this time.

YOUNG PEOPLE'S STEERING GROUP Support for isolated & vulnerable LG youth. 8533 2174.

YOUTH OUT g&b men u-26. Mo 7-10pm. Pastures Youth Centre, Davies Lane, London E11. Info: 8532 8008 group times.

LONDON HIV & AIDS RESOURCES

ACE PROJECT Eagle Court, 224 London Rd, Mitcham CR4 3HD. 8646 0646 M-F 9.30-5.30

AIDS GUIDE http://aids.miningco.com

AIDS TREATMENT PHONELINE 0845 947 0047 Mo & We 3-9pm, Tue 3-6pm

AXIS Sexual health clinic for u-26 G&B men.Th 7-9pm. Mortimer Market Centre, off Capper St, WC1. 7530 5061.

BIG UP Sexual health organisation for and led by Black gay men. Eurolink Centre, 49 Effra Rd, SW2. 7501 9264, Helpline: 7501 9315

BLACKLINERS Helpline for Blacks/Asians. 7738 5274. Monday-Friday 9.30-6. bp@bodypositive.demon.co.uk

CARA CENTRE Emotional & spiritual support 178 Lancaster Rd, W11 1QU. 7792 8299.

CATHOLIC AIDS LINK, PO Box 646, London E9 6QP. 7485 7298. & Positively Catholic

CHALK FARM OASIS AIDS SUPPORT CENTRE Salvation Army Hall, Haverstock Hill, NW3. 7485 2466 Mon 4pm

CHINESE HIV/AIDS SUPPORT Queens House, 1 Leicester Pl, WC2H 7BP. 7287 0904

CRUSAID 73 Collier St, N1 9BE. 7833 3939.

EALING HIV/AIDS SERVICE (TURNING POINT) 8840 3313 Support

EDDIE SURMAN TRUST 359 Southwyck House, Clarewood Walk, SW9 8TT. SW9 7DJ. 7738 6893. Counselling, housing advice.

FACTS 23/25 Weston Park, Crouch End, N8 9SY. 8348 9195.

FOOD CHAIN 25 Bertram St, N19 5DQ. 7272 2272 Delivering meals to people with Aids

GAY MEN FIGHTING AIDS (GMFA) Unit 42, Eurolink Centre, 49 Effra Rd, SW2 1BZ. 7738 6872

GLOBE CENTRE 159 Mile End Rd, E1 4AQ 7791 2855 Support centre HIV/Aids. Isle Of Dogs Outreach Simon 7538 1601 Youth.

HEALTHY GAY LIVING CENTRE outreach, training, counselling. 40 Borough High St, SE1. 7407 3550.

HEALTH INTIATIVES FOR YOUTH Support, info for U-27s. 0800-298 3099.

HILLINGDON AIDS RESPONSE TRUST Beasleys Yard, 126 High St, Uxbridge 01895 813874

THE HOUSE - ENFIELD'S HIV CENTRE 33 Eaton Rd. 8363 2141. M-F 9.30-5

IMMUNE DEVELOPMENT TRUST 7 704 1777. Free Complementary Therapies

IMMUNITY LEGAL SERVICES 7388 6776, 1st fl, 32-38 Osnaburgh St, NW1 3ND.

JEWISH AIDS TRUST 8200 0369. HIV Education Unit, Colindale Hospital, Colindale Avenue, NW9

JEWISH AIDS TRUST HELPLINE 7.30-10pm Mo- Th, 10am-1pm Su. 8206 1696.

LANDMARK 47 Tulse Hill, SW2. Help & support. 8678 6686. Gay men's eve Mon 5-9

LEAN (London East Aids Network). Stratford: 8 519 9545. Ilford: 8478 7619.

LONDON LIGHTHOUSE 111-117 Lancaster Rd, W11. 7792 1200; 7792 2979 (minicom).

MILDMAY MISSION HOSPITAL Hackney Rd, E2 7NA, 7739 2331

NAZ LATINA Latin American group, 8741 1879 ext 208 (Guillermo)

NAZ PROJECT 241 King St, W6. 8563 0191. Nazfounduk@compuserve.com South Asian, Turkish, Arab, Irani.

OASIS AIDS CARE CENTRE, 9 Ram St, Wandsworth SW18. 8874 3230 (4-9 Tu-Fr).

POSITIVE PLACE 52 Deptford Broadway, SE8 M-Tu 1-4; W 4-9, F 10-1. 8694 9988.

POSITIVELY EAST Self-help group in E London. PO Box 2224, London E15 4SL.

THT COUNSELLING 51a Philbeach Gdns, Earls Court SW5 9EB. 7835 1495. Free HIV/Aids counselling, inc for partners and friends

WALTHAM FOREST HIV & AIDS SUPPORT GROUP 8521 7441

ZONE 15 St Anns Sexual Health Centre, St Anns Hospital N15. Sexual health check-ups and advice. 8442 6536.

ADVICE & SUPPORT

ACAPS 34 Electric Lane, Brixton 7737 3579 Counselling L&G's & ptnrs with drink probs.

ALBANY TRUST Psychosexual counselling, 28G Balham High Rd, SW17 8767 1827

ALBERT KENNEDY TRUST Homeless teenagers. Manchester: 23 New Mount St, M4 4DE. 0161-953 4059. London: Unit 305A, 16/16A Baldwins Gardens, EC1N 7RJ. 7831 6562.

ALCOHOLICS ANONYMOUS L&G group details 7833 0022

ALCOHOL EAST lg support group, & youth service. 8257 3068.

AFLAGA Armed forces LG Association (Rank Outsiders) National advice and support line. 0870 740 7755

ALZHEIMERS SOCIETY For carers and sufferers. Bruce 01865 847 471.

AT EASE Armed forces support 28 Commercial St, London E1 6LS. 7247 5164 Su 5-7

BEAUMONT TRUST TV/TSs 7287 878.

BM Box 3084, London WC1N 3XX.

BISEXUAL GROUP Helpline 8569 7500/ 0131-557 3620 meets London Friend see below

BROTHERS & SISTERS CLUB For deaf L&G. 25 Cruickshank St, London WC1X 9HF. Minicom 7837 5561

CHUBBS 'N' TEDS Info and advice for men interested in big, hairy men. 020-7253 0309

CROYDON FRIEND 8683 4239.M&F 7.30-9.30pm. Events/helpline. PO Box 454, London SE25 4AT

DLAGGS deaf groups 7 Victoria Ave, South Croydon, Surrey CR2 8660 2208minicom eves

EAST LONDON FRIEND (PO Box 551 Dagenham, Essex RM8 3BZ. 020-8593 8030

ELOP (East London Out Project) 8558 0551. Counselling, advice & support

FFLAG (Families & Friends of Lesbians & Gays). Eileen 7791 2854

FRENZ Support Grp for recently out or isolated. We 7-9pm New Cross. 8691 3381.

GAY & BISEXUAL MEN'S DRINK SUPPORT GROUP Tu 6.30-8.30pm, Soho. 7737 3579 (LGB Alcohol Project)

GAYS & LESBIANS SHARING SOBRIETY for those living with drink problems. Craig 01142-880350.

GAYSCAN men's cancer support network , 50 Avenue Rd, N12 8PY Help: 8446 3896

GALOP Assistance to LGB in dealing with homophobic violence & the Police.,2G Leroy House, 436 Essex Rd N1 3QP 7704 6767 Helpline 704 2040 Mo 5-8, Tu 1-3, We 3-6, Fr 12-2.

GAY ME Box 3210, Action for ME, PO Box 1302, Wells, Somerset BA5 1YE.

GENDER IDENTITY COUNSELLING BM 5434, London WC1N 3XX. 7828 9575.

GLAMS MS Support c/o London Friend 86 Caledonian Road, London N1 9DN.

HAPPY FAMILES For partners of lesbians, gay men. 01302-738776.

KAIROS Counselling & Psychotherapy referral service. Appointments: 7437 6063.

KLINEFELTER ORGANISATION
In-house group for gay men with Klinefelter Syndrome (47 XXY) KO PO Box 60, Orpington, Kent BRA 8PR

L&G BEREAVEMENT PROJECT Helpline & face-to-face 8455 8894 7pm-12. c/o Vaughan Williams Ctr, Colindale Hospital NW9 5HG

L&G FOSTER & ADOPTIVE PARENTS NETWORK 7336 8860

LESBIAN, GAY & BISEXUAL ALCOHOL PROJECT counselling, info & complimentary therapies. 7737 3579.

L&G CARERS 3rdWed7.30-9 Netherwood Ctre, 5 Netherwood St, NW6. 7372 0750;

LESBIAN & GAY HELPLINE 7.30-10pm 7837 3337

LESBIAN HELPLINE Su-Th, 7.30-10pm 7837 2782

LESBIAN LINE 7251 6911. M & F 2-10; Tu-Th 7-10pm Minicom 7253 0924.

LAGPA L&G Police Assocation: BM LAGPA, London WC1N 3XX. 07020 911 922 (24hr); info@ lagpa.org.uk

LEWISHAM FRIEND 8690 619 5 Tu &Thu 7.30-9.30pm. Advice & info helpline

LONDON FRIEND 86 Caledonian Rd, Kings Cross, N1. Coming out groups, counselling. 7833 1674

METRONET LGB MENTAL HEALTH DROP-IN Greewich Th 1-4pm support, advice Clive or Natalie: 8265 3311.

NARCOTICS ANONYMOUS L&G 7351 6794 helpline daily 10-10, 7730 0009, & g&l meetings.

NATIONAL AIDSLINE 0800-567123

NATIONAL BISEXUAL HELPLINE 8 569 7500 Tue-Fri; 0131-557 3620 Thu.

NEW BEGINNINGS Friendly discussion group for people unsure of their sexuality - all ages. Meet Sat 7.45pm, 2nd floor Central Station, Kings Cross. 7265 9655.

THAMES REACH HOUSING PROJECT Parker House, 144 Evelyn St, SE8 5DD, 8692 7557. SE London Housing

Association Accomodation for homol;ess & vulnerable LGBs.

N.O.R.M UK support for men affected by circumcision. Call 8372 1936

NORTH LONDON LINE L&G Youth Groups, one-to-one, res w/ends 7607 8346

OUTCOME N London lgb mental health drop-in. 7272 5038.

OUT-TAKE support for L&G with mental health problems. Derek 7613 5326/Lynne 613 3616

OUT-SIDE-IN Volunteer Support for G in Prison. PO Box 119, Orpington, Kent, BR6 9ZZ.

PACE 34 Hartham Rd, N7 6DL. Counselling: 7697 0014 Advocacy: 7697 0017

PARENTS TOGETHER 8650 5268. or PO Box 464, London SE25 4AT

PARTNERS GROUP Families of TSs. 01323-641100. BM 6093, London WC1N 3XX

PINK THERAPY ACAPS, 34 Electric Lane, SW9 Network for g&l counsellors

POSITIVELINE 0800 1696806 Nationwide HIV and Aids support and advice. Support for newly diagnosed. Mo-Fr 11am-10pm, Sa-Su 4pm-10pm.

POST-ADOPTION LGB GROUP Aroldus Coppens, Post-Adoption Centre, 5 Torriano Mews, NW5 2RZ or ring: 7284 0555.

QUEST LINKLINE L&G Catholics 0808 808 0234 Fr 7-10 (24hr answerphone)

RANK OUTSIDERS ex & serving LGB armed forces 7652 6464 BCM Box 8431, WC1N 3XX

REGARD National Organisation of Disbaled Lesbians, Gay Men and Bisexuals. Unit 2J Leroy House, 436 Essex Road, London N1 3QP. Helpline 020-738 6191. Admin: 020-7688 4111. regard@dircon.co.uk BM Regard London WC1N 3XX. 7738 6191. Tu 7-9pm

SOUTHWARK HELPLINE Support & advice in homophobic violence & abuse. Freephone: 0800-731 4716.

STONEWALL HOUSING ADVICE LINE 7359 5767 M,F 10-1pm, Tu, Th 2-5pm. Minicom 7359 8188.

STREETWISE YOUTH advice to men 25 & under , selling sex. 7370 0406

SURVIVORS of male rape 7833 3737. Tu 7-10pm. PO Box 2470, London SW9 9ZP

TALKING SHOP health & welfare advice for men in S.London. Mo&Th. LADS: 7717 1655.

TURNING POINT Men's coming out grp. We 8-9.30pm London Friend, 86 Caledonian Rd N1

RELIGIOUS/SPIRITUAL

AFFIRMATION UK G&L Mormons. Michael or Cheryl 7221 4846

AGLO Action for g&l ordination (CofE) PO Box 318, London WC1H 9NZ. 7278 1204.

BRIXTON UNITARIAN CHURCH Effra Rd, SW2 11am Sun. Gay positive. 7737 7576.

CALLED TO BE ONE support for Catholic parents of lgbs. PO Box 24632 E9 6XF. 01642-465020.

CHANGING ATTITUDE Action, support for Anglicans. 8788 1384.

CHRISTIAN SCIENCE LGB GROUP Bi-monthly. Scott Bryanston: 7515 6427

EVANGELICAL FELLOWSHIP for L&G Christians John 01245-252214. Brenda 01276-24893

GAY SPIRITUAL GROUP,BCM ZEAL WC1 8846 8593.

HARROW SPIRITUALIST CHURCH 1 Vaughan Road, HA1 4DP. Serv: We8 & Su7.30

INDEPENDENT FREE CHRISTIAN CHURCH Offering all Christian services, blessings, funerals etc. Contact National Office 01305-260675.

KAIROS IN SOHO 56 Old Compton St W1. 7437 6189 Social & spiritual project.

LGCM Central Drew 8968 4317, East: Michael 8980 2074

L&G CHRISTIAN HELPLINE 7739 8134. Wed & Sun 7-10pm. Ansaphone 24 hrs.

L&G CLERGY CONSULTATION Support and newsletter. clergy.consultation@virgin.net

MCC BM/MCC, London WC1N 3XX. 7485 6756

MCC LONDON Brixton 8678 0200. Mile End 0171 538 8376. Camden Trinty URC Buck St, Kentish Town Rd, NW1. Su 7pm. 8304 2374.

NICHIREN BUDDHISM OF HONMON BUTSURYUSHU (HBS) Tony 0789-9904747.

PAGAN WICCA GROUP 01761-433372.

QUAKER L&G FELLOWSHIP 46 The Avenue, Harrogate HG1 4QD

QUEST GLB Catholics BM Box 2585, London WC1N 3XX

ST BOTOLPHS CHURCH Aldgate EC3. 7283 1670.

THREE F L&G Christians meet 3rd Fri, 7.30, Grosvenor Chapel, Mayfair. 8968 4317.

UNITARIAN GAY FELLOWSHIP Mansford St Church, 117 Mansford St, London E2. 8548 0754 Sun 11am (3rd Su 6.30, Last Su 7)

NATIONAL ORGANISATIONS

Also: Advice & Support, Special Interests, Professional Groups

AFLAGA Armed forces LG Association (Rank Outsiders) National advice and support line. 0870 740 7755

AVERT Aids Education & Research Trust, 4 Brighton Rd, Horsham, W Sussex, RH13 5BA. 01403-210202

BRITISH G&L SPORTS FEDERATION c/o Central Station, 37 Wharfdale Rd, N1 9SE.

CHE Campaign for Homosexual Equality PO Box 342, London WC1X 0DU. 0402 326151.

DELGA, (Liberal Democrats) 4 Cowley St, London SW1P 3NG. Call Chris 020-8673 3157.

DEAF FLAG (Federation of Deaf L&G Groups) 7 Victoria Ave. Sth Croydon, Surrey. CR2 0QP.

EDWARD CARPENTER COMMUNITY Personal growth,Gay Men's weeks 0870-3215121.

FFLAG Support for young gays and their families. 0161-628 7621. PO Box 153, Manchester.

FORD GLOBE Ford Motor Co LGB employees group. PO Box 4206, Brentwood, CM13 3EF or internal mail to GB-12/600.

GAY TIMES ON TAPE Free to visually impaired. GTOT, 66 Marchmont Street, London WC1N 1AB. 01273-729663.

G&L MENTAL HEALTH SERVICE 10 Harley St, W1 020-7467 8330.

GBA Gay Business Association BCM-GBA London WC1N 3XX. Tel: 0700-2255 422 (CALLGBA). Fax: 0700-2329 422 (2FAX GBA). E-mail: hello@GBA.org.uk

G&L HUMANIST ASSOCIATION 34 Spring Lane, Kenilworth, Warks CV8 2HB. Phone/fax: 01926-858 450.

GAY OSTOMY ASSOCIATION Support & Friendship. Total discretion. 0151-726 9019.

GAY OUTDOOR CLUB PO Box 16124, Glasgow G12 9YT. Walking, mountaineering, climbing, caving, cycling, swimming etc. 0141-342 4088.

HAPPY FAMILIES GLB & TG parents. c/o Community House, 7 Netherhall Road, Doncaster, DN1 2PH. tel/fax: 01302-361319

INTERNATIONAL G&L ASSOCIATION 81 Rue du Marche au Charbon, B-1000 Brussels. LABOUR CAMPAIGN FOR L&G RIGHTS PO Box 306, London N5 2SY

LAGER L&G Employment Rights, Unit 1G, Leroy House, 436 Essex Rd, N1. Women 7704 8066; men & mcom 020-704 6066

L&G CHRISTIAN MOVEMENT Oxford House, Derbyshire St, London E2 6HG. 020-7739 1249

LGB NATIONAL PEN PALS Free E mail service: http://www.angelfire. com/in/horwich/index.html

LAGPAN (L&G Postal Action)24 Briggs St, Queensbury, Bradford BD13. 01274-883845

LIBERTY 21 Tabard St, SE1. 020-7403 3888 (office hrs). National Campaign for Civil Liberties

LIBERAL PARTY G&L Campaign. 41 Sutton St, Liverpool L13 7EG. 0151-259 5935

LONG YANG CLUB Orientals & friends. BCM/Wisdom, WC1N 3XX. 020-8311 5835

NATIONAL AIDS MANUAL (NAM PUBLICATIONS) 16a Clapham Common, Southside, London, SW4 7AB. 020-7627 3200.

NATIONAL AIDS TRUST (NAT) New City Cloisters, 188/196 Old St, London EC1V 9FR. 020-7814 6767.

NATIONAL FREEDOM YOUTH for LGBT under 26. SAE: PO Box 72, London, HA5 2UJ

NATIONAL FRIEND UK network of LGB helplines. 0121-684 1261

NATIONAL L&G FEDERATION OF IRELAND PO Box931, Dublin 4. 710939.

N IRELAND GAY RIGHTS ASSOC PO Box 44, Belfast, BT1 1SH. 01232-664111.

NUS L&G CAMPAIGN Nelson Mandela Hse, 461 Holloway Rd, N7. 020- 7272 8900.

OPEN UNI L&G SOC BCM OULAGS London WC1N 3XX

PARENTS FRIEND/PFLAG support for parents/ families of LGB c/o Voluntary Action Leeds, Stringer House, 34 Lupton St, LS10 0113-267 4627

POSITIVE PARENTING Support & campaigning for LGB foster & adoptive families. Dep 7, 1 Newton St, Manchester M1 1HW.

QUAKER L&G FELLOWSHIP National network with local groups. Contact: Ruth (GT), 3 Hallsfield, Swindon, SN6 6LR

QUEST GLB Catholics. Nationwide support with local groups BM Box 2585, London WC1N 3XX. 0808 808 0234 Fri 7-10pm (24hr ansaphone)

REGARD Nat org of disabled L & G.Helpline 020-7738 6191/7698 4111. BM Regard, London, WC1N 3XX. Email: regard@dircon.co.uk

SCHOOLS OUT LGBT equality in Education. Tony 01582 451424, Sue: 020-7635 0476.

STONEWALL 46-48 Grosevor Gardens London SW1W 0EB. 7881 9440

PARENTING GROUP 0207-336 8860.

STONEWALL IMMIGRATION support/campaign c/o Central Station 020-7713 0620

TERRENCE HIGGINS TRUST 52-54 Grays Inn Rd, London WC1X 8JU. 020-7831 0330. Hepline: 7242 1016.

TORCHE Tory campaign for gay equality. BM Torche, London WC1N 3XX.

UK COALITION HIV/Aids 250 Kennington Lane, SE11 5RD. 020-7564 2180.

PROFESSIONAL GROUPS

AFLAGA Armed Forces Lesbian and Gay Association c/o Rank Outsiders. 0870-740 7755.

ALGBP-UK L&G psychologists. PO Box 7534, London NW1 0ZA

BIFU L&G NETWORK 020-8944 5417.

BLAGG L&G barristers and students. 020-7 353 1315.

BURNING ISSUES Librarians & information workers. Email bissues@yahoo.com

CPSA LGRG PO Box 122, Burgess Hill, West Sussex RH15 8FB

CWU LG&B MEMBERS Al 020-8971 7205

FIRE BRIGADES UNION G&L SUPPORT GROUP PO Box 10555 London N1 8XT. flag.ship@lineone.net

GAY & LESBIAN TEACHERS Online group http://egroups.com/group/gayandlesbianteachers

GALIA (G&L in Accountancy). See London Local Groups.

GLADD (medics, dentists & students) PO Box 5606, London W4 1WY. gladd@dircon.co.uk.

GLOVES G & L Veterinary Surgeons. Darren: 0131-662 4565.

GLSA G&L in science. www.glsa.co.uk

LAGIM Members of MSF. Reg London & national meetings. 020-7738 5469.

LEGII l&g in IPMS BM 6771 London WC1N 3XX. 020- 86775380 eves; 020-73237547 day

LAGLA L&G Lawyers Association. PO Box 71 Beckenham, Kent. Sarah: 020-8450 9883, Martin: 01273-625625.

LAGPA L&G Police Assoc. BM LAGPA, WC1N 3XX. 070-2091 1922; info@lagpa.org.uk

NACAB L&G workers in Citizens Advice Bureaux. 020-7833 7138

PD3Q for theatre, entertainment industry. 01274-631078.

TEACHERS IN NATFHE 27 Britannia St, WC1X 9JP. 020-7837 3636

UNIFI L&G NETWORK 020-8944 5417.

UNISON L&G GROUP 020-7551 1241

SPECIAL INTERESTS

ABLE TOGETHER Mag for G&B disabled. PO Box 460053, San Francisco CA 94146.

AUTHORS WORKSHOP SAE: Gemma, BM Box 5700, London WC1N 3XX

BEARS CLUB UK PO Box 89, Hoylake D.O. Wirral L48 4LD

BIG & TALL ASSOCIATION for taller than average lgb. PO Box 1 Prestatyn, LL19 8ZL.

BLUE HAZE Gay Smokers. BM Blue Haze, London, WC1N 3XX

BOOT CLUB SAE: TBC, PO Box 662, Harrow HA3 8HF

BRIDGE UK info line: 0160-865 1680

CLASSIC CAR GROUP BM Box 5901, London WC1N 3XX.

FREEDOM GAY CARAVANING & CAMPING CLUB 01242-526826.

GARDENERS' CONTACT GROUP SAE to PO Box 284, York YO10 3ZX

GAY BIKERS MOTORCYCLE CLUB PO Box 33, Long Eaton, Notts, NG10 2BF

GAY BIRDERS CLUB Birdwatchers. Stamp to GBC, Deneside, Foulden, TD15 1UL

GAY CARAVAN & CAMPING GROUP Robert 01772-461104.

GAY & DISABLED COMPUTER BULLETIN BOARD 01638-743 655.

GAY NUDIST GROUP UK-wide. BM Box 372, London WC1N 3XX for local contact

GAY SKINHEAD GROUP (GSG) Non-political. PO Box 234 Witham, Essex CM8 2JZ.

GRAPEVINE Wrestling contacts. PO Box 107, Stockport SK4 4FH

GREY HANKY CLUB For rubber/leather men into bondage. Send SAE to EBC PO Box 9945, London W6 8WW.

INTER-ACTION UK activity & action sports group for gay men. 0956-550616

KILT APPRECIATION SOC Mervyn Tacy, 20 Ordsall Pk Rd, Retford, Notts DN22 7PA.

KONTROLE CP/BD/Control for GM PO Box 662 Harrow MIDDX HA3 8HF.

LEATHER HANDS Deaf Leather group. DLAGGS, 7 Victoria Ave, Croydon, Surrey CR2

MORRIS DANCING Pete 020-8684 0020

PINK TRIANGLE Computer bulletin board for gay men. 020-8963 1411

PHOENIX Men into mature men 18-85 POBox 103 Wallington Surrey SM6

QUEER SPIRIT Pagan group, magazine, e-mail discussions. Box QS, Out Books, 4-7 Dorset Street, Brighton BN2 1WA. queerspirit@excite.co.uk

RED WARRIORS Fisting newsletter, SAE: Red Warriors,
BM Spike, PO Box 12, London WC1N 3XX

RUGBY LEAGUE SUPPORTERS NETWORK
PO Box 267 Bradford BD1 5XT

SOLEMATES Foot fetish & footwear group . John 0208
519 6587

STATELY HOMES APPRECIATION GROUP
Peter 0162-372 1879.

SUIT & TIE SOCIETY smart/formally dressed men.
PO Box 12453 London N10.

VEGETARIAN/VEGAN, lgb, all ages. SAE: GV, BM Box
5700 London WC1N 3XX

UNSURE ABOUT YOUR SEXUALITY?

NEED SOME SUPPORT OR A CHAT?

We offer a number of services, including:

- Free and confidential information and advice about HIV/AIDS and sexual health
- Free condoms and lube
- Support and social groups run weekly and fortnightly
- Support and advice about coming out and being gay
- Face to face meetings available
- Counselling by appointment
- Advocacy (working with others on your behalf)
- Offering a GU Clinic accompaniment service.

The services that we offer are free, confidential and can be anonymous. For more information on how we might be able to help you, call us on one of the numbers below, email us, or visit our web site.

Gay Men's Health
WILTSHIRE AND SWINDON

SALISBURY
Telephone/fax: 01722 421951
Greencroft House, 42 – 46 Salt Lane,
Salisbury, Wiltshire. SP1 1EG

SWINDON
Telephone/fax: 01793 695300
139 Victoria Road, Swindon,
Wiltshire, SN1 3BU

INTERNET Email: info@gmhp.demon.co.uk Web: http://www.gmhp.demon.co.uk

heart of the matter

free condoms
free counselling
free events
free info
free advice
free support

gay men's health

gay men's health
10a union st
edinburgh

0131 558 9444
www.gmh.org.uk

the best things in life are free

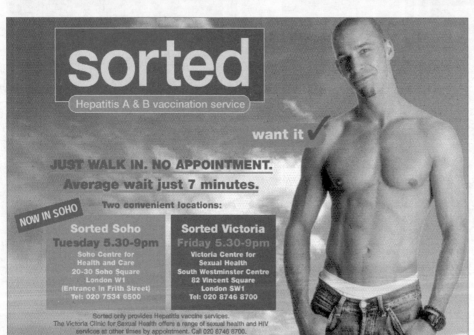

Chelsea and Westminster Healthcare

NHS Trust

Enjoy your sex
Safeguard your health
and be informed

Chelsea & Westminster Hospital Healthcare offers totally confidential, totally free and accessible service for either walk-in or appointments basis.

St Stephen's Centre
Kobler Daycare - 020 8846 6151
Kobler Outpatients - 020 8846 6161
Provides specialist HIV patient care
369 Fulham Road, London SW10 (next to Chelsea and Westminster Hospital)

The John Hunter Clinic - Sexual Health Services
Provides same day HIV testing and specialist services for women
369 Fulham Road, London SW10 (next to Chelsea and Westminster Hospital) 020 8846 6172/6154

West London Centre for Sexual Health (formerly known as Charing Cross Hospital GUM Department)
Fulham Palace Road, W6 020 8846 1567
Includes HIV/AIDS daycare and specialist services for lesbians

Victoria Clinic for Sexual Health
Provides male only services and same day testing, SORTED which is a Hepatitis A & B vaccination clinic
South Westminster Centre, 82 Vincent Square 020 8746 8700

A service for people whose lives are effected in any way by HIV/AIDS • HIV/AIDS outpatients, daycare and inpatient services • Same Day HIV tes and counselling • Psychosexual counselling • Advice on condom use, lube, dental dams etc • Advice and testing for STIs and other genitourir infections • Health advice and counselling • Sexual health check ups • Cervical smears • Family planning and contraception • Safer sex informati

TOGETHER WE CAN CHALLENGE
THE WAY OUR COMMUNITIES ARE POLICED

GALOP is London's lesbian, gay and bisexual anti-violence and police monitoring charity.

GALOP offers assistance to lesbians, gay men and bisexual people who experience homophobic violence, abuse or harassment and we can assist when dealing with the police. GALOP also provides dedicated services for Black and young members of our communities.

If you have experienced any form of homophobic and/or racist violence contact the

GALOP SHOUTLINE (020)7704-2040

GALOP PO box 32810, London N1 3ZD Minicom (020) 7704-3111 Fax (020) 7704-6707 or e-mail galop@onetel.net.uk

Registered charity (1077384)

the AFTER ⑤ Clinic

We provide

- HIV TESTING SERVICE WITH RESULTS IN 24 HRS • HEPATITIS A and B SCREENING AND VACCINATION
- PSYCHOSEXUAL COUNSELLING AND ADVICE • SHORT TERM COUNSELLING AND CRISIS HELP • GENERAL HEALTH SCREENING, INFORMATION AND ADVICE • FULL SCREENING FOR SEXUALLY TRANSMITTED DISEASES • FREE CONDOMS AND LUBRICANT • A SAFE SPACE IN WHICH TO DISCUSS YOUR HEALTH, RELATIONSHIPS ETC

The After 5 Clinic, Lloyd Clinic, 2nd Floor, Thomas Guy House, Guy's Hospital, Guy's and St. Thomas' Hospital Trust, St. Thomas Street, London SE1 9RT
Phone: Appointments (020) 7955 2108 Health Advisor (020) 7955 4940
Opening Times Mon 9am-5pm Tues 9am-5pm (The After 5 Clinic 5pm-7:30pm) Weds 1pm-8pm Thurs 9am-5pm
Buses 17, 21, 22A, 35, 40, 43, X43, 47, 48, 133, 344, 501, 505, 521, D1, D11, P3, P11
British Rail and London Underground Northern Line — London Bridge Station

Hounslow Young Gay & Bisexual Men's Project   presents i-DENTITY, a place to i-DENTIFY with young gay and bisexual men in West London

08000 854 036

i-dentity@bigfoot.com

A Hounslow Youth Service Project

• • • • • **Project LSD** • • • • •

we provide information, advice, support and education on drugs to the lesbian, gay & bisexual communities

Ear Acupuncture

This is a branch of Chinese medicine –
it helps to reduce stress, pain and
withdrawal symptoms and toxins in the body.

Free, drop - in session 5.45 - 8pm

Clients can also go on the waiting lists
for our range of one-2-one therapies.

Support Group

Would you like a safe place to talk
about issues concerning your drug use?

Have you questions you'd like to ask?

Would you like the support of people
in a similar situation to you?

**If the answer is yes to any of these then why not come along.
It an informal and relaxed environment.**

Drop - in 6.30 -8.30pm

Helpline

...if you would to talk with someone about your drug use, get information or advice or
simply have someone who will listen, then call 020 7439 0717 between 6.30- 8.30pm

Project LSD at The Hungerford Project, 32a Wardour St. W1, on the corner
of Wardour St. and Gerrard St, nearest tube Piccadilly Circus or Leicester Sq.

EAST ONE CLINIC

at the Ambrose King Centre, Royal London Hospital

Whitechapel High Road, E1 1BB. **Nearest tube** Whitechapel
(District, Hammersmith & City and East London Line) **Buses** 106, 253 and 25.

Appointment only clinic for gay men on Thursday evenings
Telephone **020 7377 7313** for an appointment.

One-Stop-Shop for all your sexual health concerns
Sexual health screening, treatments and vaccinations.
Assessment and referral for sexual health counselling.
H.I.V. testing. Free condoms, lube, dams and gloves.

Ambrose King Centre walk-in routine clinic:
Mon.,Thurs. and Fri. 09:15 to 16:30 Tues.11:45 to 18:30 Wed. 11:45 to 16:30
It is advisable to telephone **020 7377 7306** before attending the routine
clinc as times of opening may change in future.

Barts and The London

NHS Trust